Ship

Suitcase

Home

Living and Working in
Australia

If you want to know how...

Getting a Job in Australia
A step-by-step guide to finding work in Oz

Getting into Australia
The complete immigration guide to gaining your visa

Getting a Job Abroad
The international jobseeker's directory

Living & Working in New Zealand
How to build a new life in New Zealand

Going to Live in New Zealand

For full details, please send for a free copy
of the latest catalogue:

howtobooks
Spring Hill House, Spring Hill Road,
Oxford OX5 1RX, United Kingdom
info@howtobooks.co.uk
www.howtobooks.co.uk

Living and Working in

Australia

NINTH EDITION · REVISED AND UPDATED · **9**TH

All you need to know for starting
a new life 'down under'

LAURA VELTMAN

howtobooks

AUTHOR'S ACKNOWLEDGEMENTS

The author would like to acknowledge the help and support of many friends and 'all the family'. Thanks also to the Public Affairs Officers at Australian federal, state and territory government departments for advice and assistance with research.

Published by How To Books Ltd,
Spring Hill House, Spring Hill Road,
Oxford OX5 1RX. United Kingdom.
Tel: (01865) 375794. Fax: (01865) 379162.
email: info@howtobooks.co.uk
http://www.howtobooks.co.uk

Seventh edition 2000
Reprinted 2001
Reprinted 2002
Reprinted with amendments 2003
Eighth edition 2005
Reprinted 2005
Ninth edition 2007
Reprinted with amendments 2008

British Library Cataloguing in Publication Data
A catalogue record for this book is available from the British Library

ISBN: 978 1 84528 183 0

Cover design by Baseline Arts Ltd, Oxford
Produced for How To Books by Deer Park Productions, Tavistock
Typeset by PDQ Typesetting, Staffordshire
Printed and bound by Cromwell Press, Trowbridge, Wiltshire

Contents

Preface

to the Ninth Edition

Welcome to the ninth edition of *Living and Working in Australia*.
Since we first went to press in 1987 things have certainly changed
– and this volume tracks some key changes and how they may
affect people like you, who are keen to consider the benefits and
drawbacks of the move to Australia. Whether your time in
Australia is permanent, or as a holidaymaker, or as a temporary
resident, there are plenty of facts and foibles about your intended
destination that I hope make this book worthwhile.

By 2008 Australia achieved its highest migrant intake for 20 years
– and immigration targets look like continuing at around 150,000
newcomers annually. As this book seeks to explain, today's
newcomers will have quite different profiles to the largely
penniless generations who drifted to Australia in the aftermath of
World War II or to escape the various regional conflicts that
followed. Not much was known about Australia by the majority
of these people who came as a result of war and political
upheaval.

These days, by contrast, Australia has become something of a
playground and career move for many more affluent settlers. It
has a strong reputation as a sports-made, culturally diverse and
visitor-friendly nation. With the exception of around 12,000
refugees who are settled in Australia each year, today's migrants
tend to come for the climate and as a career move. They speak
English, have education, money and arrive full of expectations,
not desperation.

Politics and economics are important if you want to understand what makes Australia tick. The federal government's frank encouragement of newcomers who can bring financial and employment benefits to the nation has been, at times, controversial. Many Australians debate decisions to grant or deny entry to 'refugees'. This is a young country still trying to accommodate the applications of would-be migrants in a way that makes economic and political, as well as humanitarian and ecological, sense.

Whether you are here for a short stay or hoping to settle permanently, I hope you enjoy the Australian experience as much as I do. All the best in your plans to make the most of your time Down Under.

Laura Veltman

First: The Good News

There are so many tall tales about Australia – including the myth that it's difficult to get in. Yet doors are positively flung open to the 'right' kind of people, with an awareness of how to present their case. For Australia seeks to skim off the cream of applicants from other countries. With changes in the economy and pressure on migration policy, the number of people allowed to settle permanently has increased in recent years, and now stands at about 150,000 annually. It is usually necessary to have skills that have been specified as 'in demand' in Australia, or to have a definite job, business opportunity and/or a very close family member waiting for you Down Under if you seek to live there permanently. There is some flexibility for those who want to live and work or study in Australia on a temporary basis, as long as they can pay their own way.

- Perhaps you are thinking of leaving the uncertainties and rigidities of your home behind, and restarting a career or business in a better place?

- Maybe the notion of almost year-long warmth and sunshine appeals to you? Do you hope to live and work in an environment like Australia's on a temporary basis – either for the adventure or as a test run?

- Do you have close family living in Australia whom you'd like to join when you retire, or are you simply considering Australia as a chance to change your lifestyle, while investing your financial assets so that you can afford to live well without having a regular job?

- Is there a course of study you'd like to take in one of the many universities or tertiary colleges? Are you planning to travel the country in your holidays? Do you have friends and relatives you'd like to see on an extended working holiday?

- Are you seeking a peaceful, beautiful and successful 'home' nation? Eruptions of violence around the world in the first years of this millennium demonstrate that Australia is a relatively safe haven for travellers and long-term residents.

The world sees Australia in an ever more positive light, as a highly desirable place to live or visit. For their part, Australians are more open to newcomers than ever before, if they fulfil local immigration requirements.

> **The tough screening of migrants means that successful applicants are widely recognised as a boon, both socially and economically.**

The hurdles that face asylum seekers, 'boat people' and other illegal immigrants who often end up in Australia's detention centres are designed by the Australian government as a warning that backdoor methods of entry don't work. Hundreds more are deported each year or are in jails constructed especially for illegal immigrants, where they can be held for years while their applications for refugee status are investigated. Furthermore, Australia has new face-recognition identity systems at major airports. The automated border technology is a new way to verify the identity of travellers without the need for human intervention (and error) and Australian Customs Service experts say each passenger can be face-scanned in a mere 10 seconds. Front-door entry involves red tape and application fees. Neither your time nor your money will be refunded if you are rejected.

It is vital to be prepared for the form-filling and interviews before you go, as well as to know what to expect on arrival. This book provides a general guide to gaining residency and work permits. It also seeks to dispel some post-arrival fairytales – and portray the lifestyle, social, education and business conditions you might reasonably expect on making a move to Australia. So, before Australia makes up its mind about you, consider carefully whether your expectations of the place, people and lifestyle are realistic.

FAIRYTALES FROM THE LAND OF OZ

Question: How can you tell that a planeload of moygrants is on the landing strip at Sydney Airport? *Answer*: After the engines switch off, the whining goes on . . .

Australians have a veritable library of jokes about 'whining' immigrants. New arrivals have some dreams which come true and others which are swept away when they are confronted with real life Down Under.

Homesickness or culture shock are common reasons for complaint and rejection of life in Australia. After coping successfully with the hassles of migrating, a small number of people find themselves so traumatised they feel obliged to leave. Yet the inability to make 'a go of it' in Australia – or in any unfamiliar environment – is often due to insufficient planning of the move in advance.

From a distance, Australia may, superficially, seem to be the land of the *Neighbours* TV series, full of Ockers and Sheilas, Paul Hogans and Dame Ednas. So people who seriously consider living in Australia are often misled by myths. If you have never lived there, or simply visited as a tourist, it might seem a land of sunny opportunities which – like the endless backyard swimming pools you see as your plane comes in to land in any Australian city – go on and on as far as the imagination may stretch. Can you smell prawns sizzling on the barbecue, taste the cold beer and feel a fatter pay packet in your pocket? Many dream of a country where lucky citizens occasionally take a break from sunshine, beaches and outdoor sporting events with sprees in luxurious air-conditioned shopping centres, to tuck into shellfish at a seafront restaurant, or to spend time in the local pub, club, disco or theatre. Terrorism and street violence are almost unthinkable and hard work is unheard of, or so it seems, from a distance. Get ready to wrestle with the Aussie 'slanguage', to adopt the local drawl, embrace the notion of a classless society, and revel in the Great Outdoors (humidity, flies and mosquitoes notwithstanding), because Australia sounds like paradise...a permanent holiday on earth, a land for adventurers convinced their 'old world' is running out of steam.

However, if you are seriously thinking about moving to somewhere that is a better place to live, put the myths aside (no need to forget them entirely – since there's more than a grain of truth in most Aussie fairytales) and consider the facts of Australian life – warts 'n' all.

IT'S NOT FOR EVERYONE

Though a host of international celebrities love to visit Down Under for work or pleasure and declare it an ideal place to live, it's worth noting that about 120,000 people are *leaving* Australia each year. A million Australians are estimated to be living and working around the world though nearly 90,000 return to Australia each year to make it their home once more – showing that absence often makes the Aussie heart grow fonder.

Since Australia's post-Second World War migration programme began in 1945, some six million people arrived to make their lives Down Under. Of these one-time immigrants, many have departed Australia permanently, preferring to live and work elsewhere. The most likely newcomers to return permanently to their countries of origin are New Zealanders, Britons, Hong Kong-Chinese and United States citizens, according to recent statistics. The number of departures by both Australian-born and immigrants to Australia is higher than ever. These people plan to stay away permanently or for the foreseeable future. Many are not just backpackers, but young professionals seeking higher wages and the chance to enhance their career while experiencing other cultures and environments.

Concerns that this brain-drain may damage the nation's culture, industry and technology are countered by an immigration policy that increasingly targets highly skilled and talented newcomers. Consider how many famous Australians have moved away and find the thought of actually living in their birthplace uninspiring and inconvenient. Why have people like media magnate Rupert Murdoch, actors Nicole Kidman, Russell Crowe, entertainer Barry Humphries, and broadcaster Clive James spent much of their lives elsewhere – or relinquished their citizenship rights entirely?

BLUE SKIES

In many ways, the wife of cricket star Ian Botham summed up the drawbacks of living in a land which so many former residents see as a nice place to visit – but irritating in the long term. Botham was keen to take up a lucrative cricketing contract (temporarily) in Queensland. His wife Kathy said: 'I spent four months (in Australia) once, and I was sick of all that blue sky and sunshine. I couldn't wait to get home'.

Sunshine is certainly an attraction for many would-be settlers, though once again outsiders have unrealistic expectations of the weather. In fact, it is a land of extremes. Much of Australia is desert, so most people live on the coast. But more than a quarter of the coastline is in the tropics. It can be sweaty, searingly hot and stormy. In the temperate zones where Sydney, Melbourne,

Perth and Adelaide are located, it can rain heavily for days on end or linger in drought for years, with tough water restrictions. People are killed and properties ruined by flash floods that occasionally strike in the south and east of Australia, while cyclones are a menace in the north. Bushfires regularly decimate the suburbs of the towns and cities where the danger is magnified because these areas are often densely populated.

IMMIGRATION TARGETS

Historically, Australia's migration philosophy was motivated by a 'populate or perish' paranoia. Until the 1950s, the idea was to gain quantity rather than quality through mass arrivals of what polite Australian society still calls the 'New Australian' – who are also referred to by irreverent or downright rude locals as wops, wogs, poms and worse.

Although Australia's land mass accounts for a quarter of the entire Asian Pacific region, it is home to just 21 million people. Population growth is slow, the birth rate is flat (1.75 children per adult Australian woman) and by 2050 it is estimated Australia's population may be under 30 million. Since most people want to live around a few big cities by the coast, urban infrastructure is often stretched and the crowded hubs can be a surprise if you are assuming Australia is all about wide open spaces. As in the beginning of mass-migration, many settlers still come from Britain, though these days newcomers from the Asian and African regions are increasingly important. There are large numbers of people of Middle Eastern, Southern European, Central and South American origins, adding to the cultural mix. About half of Australia's immigrant population is British by birth, with the next largest ethnic groups being Italian, Greek and Yugoslav. Of the six million immigrants post-Second World War, many came to Australia in the first few years after 1945. Intake declined sharply in the early 1950s due to the Cold War and Australia's isolated position as a largely white, Christian outpost in the Asian-Pacific region.

Confronting racism

Supporters of what became known as the White Australia Policy displayed all the racist attitudes of other isolated and, therefore, xenophobic societies.

More reasonable opponents of wholesale migration – many trade unionists among them – still argue that the influx of 'cheap' workers undermines their jobs through their acceptance of low wages and living conditions repellent to 'real dinky-di' Aussies. With most people living in coastal cities, they say Australia already has too many people. Overpopulation will lower the quality of life, deplete the stock of natural resources and retard economic growth. Migrants will be housed and then kept by the welfare state, according to the anti-migration lobby of the old school.

Yet Australia developed a pluralistic approach to immigration in the 1970s and 1980s. This multicultural policy has led to Australia's reputation as a friendly, tolerant climate for newcomers. However, there is also a strong backlash against the ugly side of having so many different cultures trying to make their ways, and sometimes struggling to co-exist side by side. Living in Australia's social melting pot can mean that a local community experiences, at one extreme, inter-ethnic gang wars on the neighbourhood beach and, on the other hand, a flourishing market for exotic new restaurants. There is plenty of support for politicians who seek to protect Australia's comfortable lifestyle by limiting numbers of the millions of penniless refugees from around the world to the merest trickle. Not surprising that these days most new immigrants are skilled or business migrants.

Australia's long-serving conservative Liberal Federal government focused in the past decade on remaking immigration rules and quotas to attract well-heeled, appropriately educated people of working age. By 2007 Australia was chided by refugee groups for being the only Western country to have mandatory detention for illegal immigrants either caught inside the country or trying to enter as 'refugees'. Australia's rules allow men and women and children to be held under the terms of detention for indefinite periods, frequently for years. The detention centres themselves are starkly prison-like and located on nearby islands or in remote, arid parts of Australia. Many Australians are embarrassed by regular reports of detainees' mental health problems, self-harm while in detention, hunger strikes and anti-social behaviour. Supporters of a strict code that keeps refugee intakes to a minimum, point out that these very behaviours may have been pre-existing and indicate that such people are not suitable citizens. However, in late 2007 a Labor Government under Kevin Rudd – who himself speaks fluent Mandarin and has an Asian son-in-law – signals a more progressive era. Political thinkers are starting to push for a larger humanitarian element within Australia's immigration programme. Some economists argue that this should be accompanied by less generous minimum wage levels in Australia, so it could make financial sense to allow entry to lower skilled newcomers who would not cost so much to hire.

Realistically, with the slowdown in the world economy, the ability for many low-skilled workers to find jobs in Australia appears limited.

The new multiculturalism

The current policy of encouraging the 'right' kind of settler is based on an economically defined profile of the Australian Ideal Migrant. If a person gains acceptance because they have made a case that they are going to enhance the local economy and help raise the level of employment and commercial activity – or even if they are one of the tiny number of refugees and asylum seekers accepted under the current policy – they won't be expected to 'blend in' and become part of a uniform social wallpaper, nor is there the tendency of governments to ignore ethnic interest groups in the hope that they'll assimilate, as in the United States with its 'melting pot' philosophy of ethnicity.

In Australia, the buzzword is 'multiculturalism' – whereby Australia's new citizens are given financial and social incentives to retain the lifestyles, languages and artistic traditions of 'the old country'. Since the White Australia Policy was scrapped in the early 1970s by a new Labour Party national government under Prime Minister Gough Whitlam, the idea of allowing immigrants to nourish a young nation with the best of their respective skills and cultures appears to have been a success. Though some Australians object to multiculturalism, claiming that it leads to communication problems and social divisions, it has been adopted by progressive state and local administrations around the country as the best solution for a country with only 220 or so years of modern history and in continuous demand as a tourist and migration destination.

THE NEW MIGRANT

Clearly, new Australians are an investment in human capital, and as such each is expected to provide good returns over the years.

In just over a decade immigration policy has been restructured so that applicants must fall into one of a clear set of categories in order to succeed. Successive Australian governments have continually revised the migration policy with two aims:

◆ To show the government to be remedying the skilled population shortage by selecting people with education, experience, English language fluency and money so they can actively contribute to Australia's prosperity;

◆ To select newcomers who are unlikely to be a burden on the welfare system because they are well-funded and able to support themselves and their dependents with ease while they settle in.

In common with most Western nations needing domestic consumption and export revenue to keep the wheels of capitalism turning, Australia continues to suffer from an uncomfortable degree of unemployment and inflation, and favoured migrants are those most likely to generate jobs immediately and reverse national economic troubles.

2

Great Expectations

People have great expectations of life in Australia – and can be very badly informed as well. Outsiders often imagine that kangaroos hop down the main streets and that there's a cuddly koala in every tree. In Britain, for example, a monthly newspaper which specialises in preparing would-be migrants and visitors for Australia regularly provides answers to readers' weird and wonderful questions, such as: 'Are there flush toilets in Australia?' 'Is it possible to have a gas stove rather than an electric range?' 'Where can you buy fish 'n' chips?'

This book won't list the thousands of fish 'n' chip shops Down Under, but it is designed to save you time and money by providing a realistic guide to the lifestyle, history and culture, as well as the ins and outs of a complicated migration policy.

UNDERSTANDING YOUR MOTIVATION

Immigration experts talk of 'push and pull factors' when they analyse why people like you may be attracted to the idea of changing your lifestyle by going to Australia. A typical push factor for Britons or others from the Northern Hemisphere is eagerness to escape gloomy winters and cold, wet summers. Another important push is lack of economic opportunity in your present environment, due to so many people competing for a small piece of available action. High cost of housing, food, heating, and relatively low wages are strong push factors from the more depressed regions of Britain or Europe.

Immigrants from warm, relatively cheap places like South-East Asia are also pushed by the overcrowding of their current environment – and pulled by the notion of wide open spaces and a more egalitarian society Down Under.

Pull factors are all the optimistic notions of what you imagine daily life is like in 'ideal' countries like Australia, Canada or the United States. But the whole world has heard of the violence of American cities, and is aware that frozen winters are a feature of life in Canada and Northern Europe.

> **The grass-is-greener-on-the-other-side syndrome is particularly prevalent among people considering Australia.**

Australia has a much lower crime rate than many other urban societies, while the majority of its population lives in relatively warm seaside suburbs.

NON-NUCLEAR BUT NOT ALWAYS UNPOLLUTED

One important 'pull' factor encouraging a move to Australia is a concern to minimise the threat of nuclear pollution or nuclear war. Despite being a major source of the world's uranium, other sources of energy are so abundant in Australia that there's no need for nuclear power stations, and none are planned. The environmental lobby is vocal but not yet as politically powerful as in Europe or North America. This has been demonstrated by Australia's refusal to support international efforts to cut carbon dioxide emission targets to a uniform level for developed countries. Despite its high emission of greenhouse gases, Australia raised the ire of international environmentalists – and caused red faces among Aussie greens – by making representations that it should be considered a 'special case'. The government argued that greenhouse targets be tailored to Australia's circumstances as an economy dependent on primary industry and mining, although some environmentalists argue that it produces more greenhouse gases per capita than any nation on the planet.

As for water pollution and environmental problems, it may come as a shock to learn that many of the famous beaches are often closed to swimmers because sewerage and stormwater have been pumped into the oceans for decades and the waste disposal and storm water problem has risen with Australia's coastal population. Water supply as well as sewerage are at last burning political issues and are more fully explained in Chapter 9 on Playing Down Under.

FAMILY AND FRIENDS

Another attraction of life in Australia may be that your friends and relatives have moved Down Under already. A family to advise you, help with the application for temporary or permanent residence, and ease the transition to a totally different culture, should be a wonderful advantage in terms of making the transition.

Since nearly half the people in Australia came as immigrants or are children of immigrants, the government's policy remains somewhat biased towards 'family reunion' on humanitarian grounds. In fact, 'Family' is a specific category for people with relatives in Australia. The urge to join close family members accounts for over half the people who go to live there, under rules which may allow them to join their immediate or extended family.

TOLERANCE OF IMMIGRANTS

Most migrants have to cope with a degree of disrespect – from the mild and usually jocular 'Pommy bashing' of British newcomers, to cracks about 'wogs' from Southern Europe and the Middle East and, most recently, an outbreak of discrimination against people of Oriental Asian appearance and even attacks against Muslims.

Immigrants' experiences

Prominent Chinese-Australian Irene Moss – who conducted an inquiry into racist violence for the federal government – declared: 'I experienced specific incidents. When I was younger I had people calling me unusual names'. She also tells of walking into a restaurant, causing a woman to walk out complaining of a 'bad smell'. Moss's punchline is not without wry humour: 'That put me off my food!'

Ms Moss conducted the inquiry into racist violence as Race Discrimination Commissioner of the Human Rights Commission, presiding over discrimination complaints and disputes, as well as research and educational projects. 'I wonder how you can ever know the extent and cost of indirect racism.' She argues that many people never say openly that they don't want you just because of your race.

Specific incidents investigated by Ms Moss included systematic attacks on Sydney shop windows, which were smashed and stickers with the word 'Jew' plastered on the walls; a Thai woman who was beaten up in a country town and a Turkish family which found its pet killed and left on the doorstep as a warning.

Franca Arena, retired politician and a leader of Australia's ethnic community, speaks from her own experience about the general problems of coming to live and work in Australia. She arrived in 1959 from Genoa in Italy: 'Moving from one country to another is a great trauma – even if you are not a refugee and have a job to go to, relatives to help you, a place to stay and are able to speak the language,' she says. 'Australia today is a tolerant, sophisticated society with some of the best back-up facilities for immigrants and minority groups in the world. There is an ethnic affairs commission and equal opportunity employment office set up by the governments of most states. Australia leads the world in ethnic television and radio. Governments are responsible for English classes for adults and children, assessment of overseas qualifications, translation services and general advice for migrants.'

Emanuel Klein, a Sydney management consultant with extensive government contacts, states that he is something of a 'professional migrant'. Born in Romania, Klein emigrated to Israel, studied for his medical degree in Italy, and settled in Australia with his Australian wife, Wanda, in 1972. 'We have facilities for newcomers like translator and telephone interpreter services simply unheard of elsewhere, even in countries like Israel, which is also a nation of migrants.'

However, he agrees that there is a degree of discrimination against people for whom English is not the mother tongue. Klein recalls arriving for work at Parliament House in Canberra, where he spent years as an adviser on migration and ethnic affairs. 'The security guards said I should go to the tradesmen's entrance as soon as they heard my accent. "The door for domestics is out the back," they told me.'

CULTURE SHOCK

Like many migrants of British or European origin, Emanuel Klein at first found some aspects of life Down Under very strange indeed.

'I arrived in Darwin, and was shocked to see all these men in shorts and long socks and I did not know what the hell they were doing dressed like that,' he recalls. The answer, he now knows, is that Aussies dress for comfort whenever they can – which is why people at beach suburbs can be seen shopping in their swimsuits.

Some migrants adopt an 'if you can't beat 'em, join 'em'

approach; they don't lie down and take the inevitable culture shock, but do their best to develop a shocking culture. For instance Max Markson, from Bournemouth in England, managed to raise eyebrows even on Sydney's brash social scene with his efforts as a public relations consultant. A local gossip columnist nominated Markson as one of his 'top ten high flyers'. He explained his selection thus: 'Nicknamed Mad Max for his perpetually oddball line in promotions, there is no depth of bad taste that this immensely likeable 24 carat hustler has not plumbed to publicise his clients.' For instance, Markson's wet T-shirt contests for women so angered feminists that he ran wet underpants competitions for the blokes. They were a raging success.

Bill Shipton, from Dorking in Surrey, came to Australia in 1962. He was 23, and a carpenter by trade. Today he is a wealthy man and is associated with very up-market construction projects, specialising in buildings and renovations for clients who can afford to pay millions of dollars for a place to hang their (sun)hat.

'The thing that's different about Australia is they don't put the same emphasis on a business being old and established. So what if it was founded in 1704? Here it doesn't matter if you started up last year, as long as you do a good job.

But a lot of English migrants really earn a reputation as "whingeing poms". If you emigrate here, don't think it's going to be easy. You've got to be prepared to work.'

Shipton agrees that what Australia lacks, compared to his native England, is cultural diversity and choice of places to go visit. From his happy position as a millionaire, the solution is simple: 'It only takes a day to fly to London. Then you can spend a month going out to the theatre, if you like.'

REALISTIC EXPECTATIONS

Whatever the hopes and dreams which may persuade you to become a New Australian, the facts show that most can realistically expect a high standard of living.

Migrants typically live longer, are healthier, more educated and have fewer children than other Australians according to official government statistics. They are also significantly younger on average – 72% are under 35 compared with 48% of the wider Australian population.

A recent Australian Bureau of Statistics report entitled Overseas Born Australians says that 50% of the overseas-born had post-school qualifications, compared with 40% of other Australians. Migrant men, on average, can expect to live three to five years longer and migrant women two to three years longer than the Australian-born.

Of course, this good news is at least partly because of strict immigration screening processes, health checks and employability criteria applied to anyone wanting to enter as a permanent resident.

3

Australia – the Making of a Nation

CONVICT TRANSPORTATIONS

Australia's modern history began with an influx of people who did not want to go there. The first Europeans who came to live and work in Australia were convicts and their guardians. Australia, so alluring nowadays as a place to live and work, was a giant jail for the criminal elements of Georgian and Victorian England. Old-fashioned histories politely refer to its first decades as 'colourful'. At first, starvation was a threat when crops failed repeatedly, then the imbalance of convicts to free settlers and a gold rush in many colonies meant crime was rife and social conditions even rougher than for pioneers of America's wild west. More modern, X-rated versions demonstrate that from 1787 to 1868 the colony was little more than Britain's social sewer. According to the experts, between half and two-thirds of the convict transportees were violent criminals while four out of five were thieves. Australian historian Robert Hughes wrote: 'People used to suppress convict history in the nineteenth century because it was thought to be a disgusting stain and an inherent disgrace on the Australian genes.'

Today some Australians will tell you that they descend from convicts and are proud of it, because their ancestors were freethinkers sent from Mother England as political prisoners. In truth, the first transports of people deported for political reasons did not arrive in Australia until well into the nineteenth century.

NEW FRONTIERS

Eventually the lower and middle classes back in England got wind that Australia was not such a bad place. Newspaper and personal reports soon spread the word that adventurers as well as convicts who had finished their sentences were doing very nicely, thank you, on their own bits of bush or in fledgling townships. Though distant as the moon, and despite its rough social fabric, the colonial settlements around Australia gained a reputation as a fine place to make a fresh start and even a fortune. In 1851 gold was discovered in Victoria and New South Wales. Some 600,000 immigrants came to try their luck, bringing a blast of prosperity for a few and untold poverty for many more since most able-bodied men, including soldiers and shopkeepers left their jobs and families to try their luck. The gold rush over, a new breed of 'free' Australian settler was starting to dominate. An interest in improving the fabric of society resulted in 'anti-transportation' leagues, which sprang up with the aim of persuading Britain to dump its criminals elsewhere. The last convict transport ship arrived in 1868, at Fremantle in Western Australia.

Meanwhile, more free settlers came and joined Australian-born adventurers with the urge to explore and exploit the interior of this vast continent.

SINNERS AND CYNICS

Twenty-first century Australia retains some characteristics of the island jail. People tend to be on the cynical side about those who run their country. As in convict days, people take it for granted that the law, politics and organised crime still go hand in hand.

Politicians, judges, police chiefs, newspaper editors and other figures of authority often have trouble commanding respect and are generally low on the scale of professions in terms of public prestige. In fact a recent survey reported that, Australia-wide, people put more trust in a corner-storekeeper than in a judge. While judges command about as much respect as a travel agent in Australia, the most trusted of people in trades or professions include firefighters and nurses. Politicians and real estate agents tend to be almost universally disbelieved by the typical Aussie, says this survey. Regular revelations about unions, 'pollies', police and magistrates being on the take or otherwise caught with their pants down reinforce the impression that life in 'Godzown' country is far from politically, judicially or morally perfect.

Yet, while cynics suspect that crooked activities emerging publicly are the tip of the iceberg, others say that this proves the sound health of Australia's democracy, and are gratified that such scandals come to light at all.

AUSTRALIA'S POLITICAL SYSTEM

At first glance, Australia's political system is a complicated bastard, bewigged and gowned in vestiges of Britain's Westminster system. A closer inspection reveals that the nation has adapted some of the best features of systems for law, order and democracy from British, North American and Western European societies. In these places the wheels of justice and politics may clank and grind medieval-style, shackling the present to centuries of history. Australia, on the other hand, has barely 220 years of Western civilisation to draw on, no traditional 'ruling class', and certain advantages in geographic isolation; so it can afford to be selective about the bits of government it adopts, while free to fit other features to the circumstances. The influence of political convicts from Britain made Australia one of the first countries in the world with universal suffrage and gave rise to a strong union movement. Australia remains a most egalitarian democracy with progressive industrial and anti-discrimination laws.

Politically, Australia's history began with colonies on the eastern coast at Sydney Harbour, a few miles inland at Parramatta, then settlements established in the north at Brisbane and south at Melbourne and in Tasmania. Gradually, the British colony expanded westward and divided into various states which combined in Federation on the first day of the twentieth century –

1 January 1901. There is a Prime Minister at federal (national) level, and Premiers heading the cabinet of each state parliament, except for the Northern Territory and Australian Capital Territory which each have a Chief Minister.

THE PUSH FOR A REPUBLIC

'If you want your children to have a chance of being Australia's head of state, you could marry Prince Charles – or vote for the Australian Republican Movement.'

'Gidday. This Constitutional convention (to decide on the way forward for the proposed Australian republic) will be wonderful; a fantastic junket. I'll mingle with celebrity windbags and the golf course is nearby. As President of Australian Constitutional Monarchists, I've been intimate with the entire Royal family including the corgis.'

These extracts from the campaign literature for elections of representatives to Australia's Constitutional Convention way back in 1998 still say it all and probably indicate why, so far, Australians have not bothered to create a Republican mode of government. While scathing about Australia's historical ties to Britain, many Aussies proved unsure and even cynical about the real purpose and importance of a locally elected President to replace the Queen. Who needs another freeloading politician?

So, under the present constitution, the Monarch of Great Britain and Ireland is also King or Queen of Australia. The monarch's representative at national level is the Governor-General, and each

state has its own Governor with ceremonial duties as the
monarch's representative.

Republicanism was not a burning issue until 1975, when a
Governor-General decided to quit being an ornament on
Australia's political mantlepiece and exert political power. Sir
John Kerr used the monarch's undemocratic right to dissolve the
Federal Parliament against the wishes of the incumbent and
radical Labor Party Prime Minister, Gough Whitlam. Since then,
agitation for the severance of Australia from the monarchy of
Mother England culminated in a referendum in 1999. Australians
were asked to vote on whether and how Australia should become
a republic, and a clear majority wanted to retain the status quo.
Pro-monarchists led by forces within a conservative Federal
government fought and won a shrewd campaign based on
uncertainty about the precise form an Australian republic would
take. Although most Australians favour a republic, there are
many models for government under this system, including popular
election of Presidents along the lines of the United States or
France. It is unlikely another republican referendum will be held
despite the return of a Labor government in 2007 and even the
resignation of a recent Governor-General Peter Hollingworth over
a church-linked paedophilia scandal. Hollingworth, a former
Anglican archbishop, mishandled his own defence in choosing to
explain a tricky situation to the media. He was replaced with a
lower profile, less 'establishment' figure and it seems that the role
of a Governor-General in Australia will tend to be filled by bland
people who know how to keep quiet when the media spotlight
turns to them.

For now, Australia's republican element must continue to make do with the replacement of 'God Save the Queen' with 'Advance Australia Fair' as the National Anthem. On a legal level, appeals to the Privy Council in London ended after 1983. At least Australia's High Court has the final word within the nation's judicial system.

THREE TIERS OF GOVERNMENT

The federal government

The federal (or Commonwealth) government is based in Canberra, and like Washington DC, is designed as an administrative centre for the federation of states and territories. The parliament in Canberra has a House of Representatives and a States' house – known as the Senate. Members of both the House of Representatives and the Senate are chosen in general elections. Citizens and enfranchised residents over the age of 18 are obliged to keep the wheels of democracy turning by casting their votes at general elections held every three years. They are also required to vote for representatives in governments at other levels, as described below.

State governments

State governments are the second tier of Australia's democratic system, which may create confusion for newcomers used to one parliament per nation. Because the federal government has responsibility for making decisions on matters affecting the whole country, its elected representatives crop up continually in state affairs. Meanwhile, politicians in the states wrangle with Canberra over financial support via redistribution of federal taxes.

The Australian constitution gives the federal Parliament – through the administrative wing of its public service – responsibility for defence, migration, social services, overseas and interstate trade and national economic law as well as powers to legislate on banking, currency, the raising of loans abroad, income tax and other taxation. Much of the taxation revenue is siphoned back to the states, another reason why the politicians in Canberra have influence over education, health care, road building, and funds for the arts at state level.

Under the Australian constitution, if federal law clashes with that of a state government, federal legislation takes precedence. State governments, each with their own public service, have the constitutional right to make laws on matters not covered by the authorities in Canberra. The states are generally responsible for education, transport links, forests, healthcare, environment and conservation, water and mineral resources, community services, urban and industrial infrastructure. Though the federal government also has a fair grip on the purse strings for such services through its powers to raise and distribute to state governments income tax and the Goods and Services Tax (GST), the states finance their activities through other kinds of taxes and loans raised outside the country. Stamp duty on property purchases, insurance policies, leases and payroll taxes (on larger employers) are key devices used by state governments to keep themselves in business. The taxation system is discussed in greater detail in Chapter 14.

The state governments of New South Wales, Victoria, South Australia, Western Australia and Tasmania each have their own constitutions and parliaments comprising two houses – a legislative assembly (the lower house) and a legislative council (the upper house), except for Queensland, which has only the lower house, or legislative assembly. The Australian Capital Territory and the Northern Territory have legislative assemblies. By making policies on land, agriculture and the environment within their borders, the states and territories find themselves overseeing the establishment of new industry and business, and therefore wielding some influence on questions of immigration. A brief survey of economic conditions and migration incentives for each State and territory is provided in Chapter 13. State and territory governments advise Canberra of shortages in particular skills or professions, and the viability of proposed investments or businesses by foreigners or would-be immigrants.

Local government

This is the third tier of government in Australia. Shire, municipal or city councils run Australia's urban and rural regions. They are responsible for town planning, sewerage, garbage collection, maintaining roads, bridges and similar matters as well as local facilities such as public libraries. Local governments finance their activities through land and water rates or similar charges on households and businesses in their areas. Local councils are partly dependent on funding from the states.

THE ECONOMY: STILL THE LUCKY COUNTRY?

Swimming with the ebb and flow of global prosperity, the Australian economy tends to swing between rude health and the fear of a bust. The mining and farming sectors, once the most easily tradable commodities Australia could offer the world, have proved unreliable. In the past ten years the cost of imports compared to exports has dropped due partly to the rise in the value of the Australian dollar and booming trade with China and its neighbours. In the late 1990s markets suffered from financial jitters in the Asian region, where many of Australia's major trading partners are located. Then came an American-led recession due to the so-called 'tech-wreck'. This hit Australian employment and businesses after 2000 because so many fledgling technology and telecommunications investments failed to deliver with a promised boom in company profits.

Now in the first decade of the new millennium, Australia's economy slowed less than most of its trading partners in Europe, Japan, the US and Asia and is now jogging along at a comfortable annual growth rate of close to 4%. Its rather inward looking and politically conservative federal government joined the US in opposing measures like the Kyoto protocol to reduce greenhouse emissions in order to keep its economic engine ticking over during the downturn. This annoyed the environmental movement and Australia's small but vocal band of environmentalists. Then in 2007 the Federal government changed its political colours and the new Labor leadership was making a proactive attempt to tackle climate change and reduce environmental damage. Ironically, this strategy is to distinguish Australia as a travel 'experience' due to its unspoilt and beautiful landscape! Meanwhile, in Australia, tourism rivals agriculture and mining as the main source of the nation's export earnings. It is a massive employer, giving jobs directly and indirectly to some 500,000 Australians in hotels, resorts, airports and related services around the country.

Nevertheless, Australia's net export earnings are weak. Australia's foreign debt stands at about $A400 billion, or a scary $A18,000 for every Australian. The average Aussie household is in debt, spending on average 2.3% more than it earns each week. Yet local economists were confident that despite rising interest rates, the strength of its mineral exports to Asia and India will continue to drive Australia's economy forward. The breaking of the drought that has plagued many parts of the country for about eight years has boosted farm exports and is another factor to help Australians to service foreign debt.

At a personal level, and despite their loans and mortgages, Australians have never been wealthier – and this is what appears to be sustaining the local economy with relatively high consumer and business spending. Household wealth as a proportion of annual income has grown by about 2.4% annually for the past decade – three times the average for the world's richest countries. This is driven by the high level of home ownership in Australia, a country where most people aspire to own their own residence and enjoy substantial tax benefits on this investment. So home-owning Australians are less exposed to the fluctuations of the share market (where profits are taxed) than in other OECD countries. Success in real estate encourages Aussies to do it again – and profiting from investment property (which, unlike the profits from the sale of one's home, is taxable) has become a favourite strategy for building personal wealth and is likely to remain popular despite the inevitable peaks and troughs of the residential property market.

The property services and high-tech sector have weathered downturns in the past five years, many emerging leaner and more focused as a result of tough times. Many larger corporations have also been forced to lift their game after share prices, profits and reputations were battered by perceived and actual corporate excesses, weak underlying performance and poor prospects for business development.

Australia's economy remains relatively sound on a number of key measures. Inflation is low (around 3%), unemployment has been hovering at about 6% for a few years, and governments at state and national level focus on building strong export and domestic markets for value-added goods and services, since earnings from agriculture and mining are no longer the foolproof way to Australian economic success. Hence the adjustment to immigration policy, as would-be newcomers most likely to provide jobs or develop new or existing industries are given every encouragement to come to Australia.

COST OF LIVING

Australia is still a country where many believe they can get a 'fair go' when it comes to standard of living. As mentioned already, the wealth of individual households is rising steadily and remains high in Australia compared with many OECD countries.

The currency has been strengthening but as a nation there is great eagerness to attract newcomers with skills or talents to help generate more wealth. Fluctuations in the Australian dollar, a minor currency lately moving in the opposite direction to the US$, mean that many immigrants who sell up their homes, cars and other assets in their countries of origin may increase their spending power when they move to Australia.

However, Australia can be more expensive for food and petrol than the UK. In $A terms, research released in 2004 by the University of New South Wales suggested it cost about $A870 a week to maintain an acceptable standard of living for a family of four, with no frills in the budget. Some $A145 a week was the average required for food, far more if your family likes takeaway food, school lunches and dinners at casual restaurants. Surveys at the time of writing showed that housing expenses (based on an average home loan) accounted for at least a third of the family's income. The more you earn, the higher these basic food and shelter expenses seem to be in Australia especially given the zooming price of real estate in and around the highly population coastal cities. After paying off a mortgage and buying essentials such as food and transport, a high income earning person on, say, $A100,000 a year would have around $A29,000 a year left as 'spendable' income, according to the survey.

The cost of living naturally depends on where you live in Australia. Based on another recent survey of 200 goods and services across the major cities, costs are highest in Sydney and lowest in Canberra. Melbourne had the second-highest cost of living, followed by Brisbane, Adelaide and Darwin. A stronger A$ meant that by 2005 the price of imported consumer goods like electronic equipment, clothing, footwear and cars are falling though a buoyant economy has pushed up the prices of many essential goods and services – especially petrol, medical treatment, housing and property costs.

EMPLOYMENT PROSPECTS

Unemployment is at a historic low point in Australia, at around 5%. Job growth continues as business confidence grows, investment increased and consumer spending remains strong. However, real growth in jobs is countered by an increasing number of young people looking for full-time work. Sectors that were once major employers, like those related to farming and information technology, have suffered severe economic downturns due to drought since the late 1990s, though recovery is in sight.

The statistics suggest the chances of an immigrant being out of work in Australia are much higher than the average. In line with the long-term trend, people born outside Australia have a higher than average unemployment rate, as do Australian-born young adults aged under 25. As mentioned, unemployment benefits are *not* paid to long-term immigrants who lose their jobs in the first years in Australia. Immigration screening for employment skills and employability is focused on discouraging applications from people who want to live and work Down Under if they are even remotely likely to join the ranks of Australia's jobless at any stage of their career.

Would-be immigrants should consult the ever-changing official 'jobs in demand' list for entry to Australia. There are two useful publications – the *Australian Jobs Review* and the annual *Job Outlook* from the Department of Employment and Workplace Relations. The *Job Outlook* ranks the prospects for nearly 400 occupations and ranks the prospects for potential job vacancies in these occupations based on projected growth, vacancy rates, skills shortages, turnover, size of occupation and age profile. The

Australian Jobs Review is designed to help immigrants understand the local labour market and this will help you judge if you are likely to gain entry to Australia based on your particular skills.

Based on these publications, it seems likely that Australia will require many more high school teachers, medical technical officers, nurses, accountants and general medical practitioners in the next five to ten years, and these professionals have the very best job prospects. Jobs with the worst prospects, if you are considering coming to Australia as a working holiday or for a longer time, are registry and filing clerks, hand-packers, keyboard and data-entry operators, clothing workers and printing machinists. The widespread use of electronic communication in Australia has caused a drop in the number of clerical jobs available.

It seems house painters, building and architectural professionals, shop managers, secretaries, personal assistants, mechanical tradespersons, truck drivers and cleaners have 'average' job prospects. Meanwhile general managers, computing professionals, social workers, plumbers and primary school teachers are among those with 'good' job prospects at the time of writing.

There has been an exodus from nursing and teaching in recent decades because these are traditionally low-paid professions relative to the amount of professional training and dedication required. Nursing and teaching unions are showing success in recent years by achieving improved pay and conditions – but this success may be due also to shortages now that so many people have left these professions. This also applies to medical

Job	Projected demand 2009/10	Recent pay rates $A
Accountants Accounts clerk small/medium company 2–5 years Management accountant/business analyst large company 3–5 years	Very good	38,000 – 59,000 60,000–75,000
Registered nurses First-year enrolled public hospital Eight-year enrolled	Very good	34,000 55,000
School teachers Permanent teachers Public school principal Casual teacher	Very good to good	42,000–59,000 up to 95,000 180–250 per day
General managers Branch Divisions	Good	88,000–132,000 126,000–182,000
Sales and marketing Telemarketer Store manager Product/brand manager	Good	34,000–42,000 40,000–56,000 73,000–97,000
Medical practitioners (earnings after practice costs) General practitioners – non-rural obstetrics – general surgeon – anaesthesia – ophthalmology	Very good to good	103,000–115,000 270,000 150,000 235,000 150,000

Based on federal government and consulting data/newspaper reports

practitioners with strong professional associations to agitate on their behalf – but not strong enough to counter the high medical indemnity costs and a squeeze by the federal government on Medicare funding and bulk billing fees. Doctors in private practice in Australia have been obliged to absorb such costs in order to stay in business in recent years. The federal government has tried to attract young people back into the medical profession by providing more university places and GP training. It is trying to balance the need to keep doctors' insurance costs down while protecting the rights of patients for compensation if something goes wrong, for Australia is quite a litigious society with many eager legal practitioners devising new markets for their expertise – keenly priced to match the glut of lawyers in a competitive arena.

Meanwhile a projected demand for accountants in Australia is driven by more positive factors – tighter corporate governance requirements and complexity of the tax and financial systems that require greater specialisation by professionals working for both government and in private enterprise. With the proliferation of computer programs to crunch the numbers, accountancy can be seen as a more attractive profession than it once was in Australia – it is no longer mainly about balancing the books but more of a business science with many career possibilities in both government and private sectors. Workers in the hospitality and tourism-related industry are also in demand, with anecdotal evidence indicating that chefs and restaurant staff will continue to be keenly sought in Australia. Other skills shortages to be met by migrant workers are in trades such as welding, metal fitting, sheet metal working and motor mechanics.

On page 35 is a table summarising some jobs in Australia in terms of likely future demand and current pay rates.

Government has reacted to this general shortage in skilled tradespeople in metals, manufacturing and engineering fields. Extra skilled migrant places were created to meet industry demand in these fields and the trend continues.

PAY AND WORKING CONDITIONS

Working conditions are relatively kind to employees in Australia. However, if you reckon Australia is the land of the 'sickie' (unjustified sick day off work) or the long lunch, think again. Recent studies indicate that the average Aussie worker has nose-to-grindstone 1855 hours a year. Well ahead of any other worker in the developed world, including those famous workaholics, the Japanese. Australians are motivated by their employers to work more or – surprise! – by personal passion for their career and experts say too many are unhappy, unhealthy workaholics. Economic commentators debate the impact for business of generous workplace agreements and minimum wage laws (about $A440 a week for a full-time employee). Australia's industrial law is considered among the world's most progressive in protecting non-union employees as well as professionals and casuals from unfair dismissal. Critics say this is all too costly for business, especially given relatively high tax rates in Australia. However, the power of trade unions has been reduced, supposedly putting a smile on bosses' faces: in exchange for regular wage indexation which sent wages up whatever the capacity of the business to pay more, the unions have accepted a lesser role in representing workers in most industries. It is no longer mandatory to belong to a union and an estimated 25% of workers belonged to a trade union – lower than for the UK, Canada and most of Western Europe. Unions tend to make deals with employers about productivity, hours and other 'quality' of work factors while it is now guaranteed that employers will contribute at least 9% of each employee's pre-tax wage to superannuation (see next section and Chapter 14). There is still the occasional strike by drivers of trains and buses, and public school teachers over pay and conditions but these days most employees are covered by 'workplace agreements', which are individual tailored undertakings between employers and the people who work for them.

Workplace agreements
Workplace agreements are the cornerstone of Australia's so-called enterprise bargaining system. The system was invented under Labor governments in the late 1980s, ironically using Labor's close relationship with the union movement to persuade them to reduce the scale and scope of their agitation on behalf of workers. The range of issues that unions could go to court about was pared back to the over-arching industry 'award'. Then workplace agreements are negotiated with individual employers. Recent governments reduced the power of awards especially where they were seen to burden small businesses unduly, though this change could mean employees of small firms are disadvantaged.

Flexible hours
Employers can be more flexible in what they demand of their staff and these days many employees prefer to negotiate for part-time work, flexidays, maternity and paternity leave and other family-

friendly policies wherever possible. In Australia a 38-hour week is standard, though there are some alternative arrangements with working hours, particularly for shift workers and public servants. Holidays are for four weeks a year in most industries with long-service leave after ten years but this is also negotiable. For instance, some government employees may have valuable long-service leave commuted to a single pay packet in lieu of time off. A Queensland policeman reportedly had around 18 weeks of long-service entitlements commuted to a single pay packet because he showed a pay tribunal that this was the only way he could afford to put a deposit on a house. Government employees tend to lead the way on flexitime and other progressive deals on hours and leave, but pay rates are generally higher in private industry. A recent survey indicated that more than 80% of Australia's companies offered flexible hours and part-time work with their staff compared with the global average in similar economies where around 60% did the same, on average. Psychometric testing is also widely used in Australia to help judge if an employee and employer are likely to be a good fit. This is partly driven by tough dismissal laws, with an intricate system of warnings making it hard for employees to be fired without sound reasons. However, if an employee leaves a job voluntarily they are usually not entitled to unemployment benefits.

OLDER WORKERS

Life expectancy is improving and the Australian workforce is aging rapidly. Aussies often prefer to keep working and earning as long as they can. So the proportion of working people in their fifties is rising, and the trend is for people beyond retirement age

(55) to continue working at least part time for decades. Based on these demographics, there is a new approach to superannuation and pension rules that encourage people to continue in their jobs and make contributions to super for as long as they can.

SUPERANNUATION AND AGE PENSIONS

Compulsory employer-paid superannuation has been the norm in Australia since the 1980s, accepted as a bargaining tool to persuade unions to moderate their pay claims as part of the enterprise bargaining system previously outlined. Years of struggle between the federal government, private employers and employee representatives over superannuation have resulted in the compulsory Superannuation Guarantee Levy as its centrepiece, now at 9% of pre-tax wages, and rising. This must be paid by the employer into a complying superannuation fund – not the employee's bank account with no withdrawals by employees until they reach retirement age or meet other strict criteria.

Companies large and small with their own superannuation fund for employees are no longer allowed to access this investment, due to a gradual tightening up of the rules. So, to encourage people to save through super and top up the employers' contribution with contributions of their own, superannuation funds are more lightly taxed than most other entities, and there is no income tax to pay up to very generous limits from pensions drawn from complying superannuation savings. The aim is for people to protect and build their superannuation nest egg during their working lives so that on retirement a good income can be generated, thus taking the pressure off the public welfare system.

As well as the 9% compulsory employer contribution, employees can also add to their super either from pre-tax income up to certain limits (see Chapter 14) or from other savings, inheritances or windfalls. There are complex rules about access to the money under certain circumstances – if a person becomes jobless, for instance, and can show they need funds to live on prior to retirement. Most people in employment today can expect legal access to their money after 55, when they retire. Superannuation is a complex and ever-changing area of accountancy and tax law and you would be wise to seek professional advice should you make a permanent move to Australia. After all, superannuation savings are second to the family home in the list of most valuable investments owned by typical Australians approaching retirement age.

All these rules and regulations governing superannuation arise from government concern at the rising cost of publicly funded age pensions. Assets and income tests now ensure that only the genuinely needy receive the age pension on retirement, as the number of people retiring from paid work rises while the proportion of tax-paying younger people who can shoulder the burden of public welfare falls.

To encourage working people to save through super and top up their employers' contribution with 'salary sacrifices' and other (tax paid) savings of their own, superannuation funds are taxed at a flat 15%.

Yet it is estimated that most Australians approaching retirement age will not have enough income or capital invested in super to live on should they retire at 55. The reality is that many Australian tax-payers will be obliged to retire from paid work much later or sell the family home and live somewhere more modest in order to have enough money to live on. To encourage Australians to save for a self-funded retirement, age pension payments from the government have been kept unattractively low while tax incentives and discounts have increased over the last 30 years. Retirees' incomes are tax free up to about $25,000 a year for singles and $42,000 for couples, motivating people to work part time rather than to completely retire as soon as possible. As mentioned, having a large amount saved in super is also attractive once you are old enough to access this money after the age of 55, because income from a super fund does not count towards one's income and therefore attracts no tax at all. Depending on your age, there are tax breaks for people contributing lump sums to super, up to certain limits, which can also continue well into retirement.

SUPERANNUATION FUND CHOICES

There are hundreds of superannuation funds from which to choose, run by companies for their employers, industry funds for relevant unions, and independent unit trusts for the general public. You will pay fees to fund managers, perhaps a financial planner and a broker at either a wholesale and retail level, depending on the amount you have to invest. Returns by Australian funds vary and the fees can be a real bugbear in the inevitable lean years when the investments actually lose money.

Many rules apply to what super funds may invest in, to help ensure that they achieve their sole purpose in providing for each investor's financial needs when he or she reaches their retirement years. In particular, there are strict regulations that require separation of superannuation assets and savings from an individual's or company's other investments, to minimise the abuse of lenient tax rates or dishonest management by those in charge.

There has been a sharp rise in the number of self-managed super funds with a limited number of trustees and beneficiaries. Self-managed funds are often useful for small or family businesses seeking a tailored approach to their investment needs. The trustees (who are usually also the beneficiaries) must also be willing to take on a fairly heavy administrative and compliance burden. If you come to Australia as an economic migrant you might consider starting a self-managed super fund. Rather than pay fees to a professional fund manager, self-managed funds aim to keep running costs down because the trustees/beneficiaries make and implement investment decisions themselves. However, this entails a considerable commitment to researching investments and stock markets and some careful account keeping, since self-managed super funds are closely monitored by the Australian Taxation Office (ATO) and other relevant regulating authorities to ensure investments are appropriate and kept separate from the assets of businesses, trusts, partnerships or individuals.

4

Attitudes Down Under

Down Under, people have a way of looking at life which may not be easy for outsiders to comprehend. If, however, you plan to live and work in Australia, it is essential to know about a unique set of prejudices, stereotypes and social responses which affect the way locals see immigrant newcomers as well as each other.

LACK OF PRETENSIONS

One of the most refreshing things about Australians is their lack of pretensions. Lord Bradford, an English aristocrat, told the story of his time travelling around the country. Having been introduced as Earl Bradford, locals naturally greeted him with a cheery 'G'day, Earl!'

This is a nation where Prime Ministers appear on television news drawling, 'Owya going mate?' and everyone seems to be on first name terms. If you can't remember someone's first name, 'mate' will usually suffice – even if talking to a woman.

> **If it does not suit, the typical Australian will tell you straight – 'no bull', as they put it.**

Class and money

In Australia it is usual to sit in the passenger seat and chat to the taxi driver, in contrast to countries where a cabbie confronted with this behaviour might radio his base and report that he'd just picked up a weirdo. Like the script of some Aussie television soap operas, society is relatively classless. There's relatively little preoccupation with family history, royal titles or old school ties.

In fact, the authors of a Down Under edition of *Debrett's* – a publication which previously confined itself to the peers and titled classes of Britain – have been forced to play an entirely new ball game. Knights and Dames are thin on the ground in Australia, especially after state and federal Labor governments stopped nominating local luminaries for honours conferred by the Queen. As a local magazine columnist put it, the only thing that's hereditary among Aussie notables is a tendency to baldness. Therefore *Debrett's* in Australia is reduced to listing the spectacularly rich.

Naturally Australians consider 'old' money no better than new. New wealth will do fine, thank you, and no one gives a hoot if a bloke keeps his tinnies in the bath. What everyone *really* wants to know is: How many yachts do you own? Do your cars and refrigerators have internet access? Was a mountainside of marble imported to build your sixth en-suite bathroom? In other words, money buys class and if you've enough of it, most doors will eventually swing open.

But not *all* doors. To say that class consciousness does not exist at all Down Under is misleading. For example, rural Victoria's frightfully Anglicised 'squatocracy', as well as the more snooty residents of Melbourne's Toorak and of Sydney's North Shore and Eastern Suburbs, have similar social aspirations to their predominantly British ancestors. From Perth's Peppermint Grove to the rural estates of Warnambool in Victoria, from conservative boardrooms in Sydney city to millionaire pensioners in Melbourne's South Yarra – and in plenty of less well-heeled enclaves too – there are those who value the 'right' schools, the 'right' charity balls and the 'right' clubs. Catholics, Jews, Blacks and Asians still find it hard to get a foot in some doors, unless it's the tradesmen's entrance. Women are similarly excluded from the upper echelons of business and government, while if you are gay it is often best to stay low key.

DISCRIMINATION AND THE LAW

Certainly from a legal standpoint, Australia is an enlightened society, well-equipped to prevent and punish infringements of human rights on the basis of race, gender, sexual preference, marital status, colour, nationality or background. Legislation at both state and national levels enforces this official attitude in Australian society.

However, if you have the idea that governments are always in tune with the non-discriminatory, non-sexist, non-sectarian aspirations and jargon, think again.

Homosexuals and discrimination

Tasmania is the last state in Australia to maintain laws against sex between consenting male adults. In Victoria sex between male adults was decriminalised in 1980, and in New South Wales – home of the world-famous Sydney gay and lesbian Mardi Gras – decriminalisation came as late as 1984. At a federal level, Australia is signatory to international anti-discrimination codes, which overrule state law. Certain branches of government extend spouse entitlements to same-sex partners of gay and lesbian employees; for instance the Australian Federal Police and Department of Foreign Affairs. However, same-sex marriage, gay priests and child adoption rights for homosexuals remain highly controversial in most places. Even in Sydney, one of the gay capitals of the world, verbal abuse and physical attacks on this minority group are common. Recent reports also show gays from Asian and Middle Eastern migrant backgrounds were at risk from discrimination from both gay and their own ethnic communities.

Women and discrimination

It is illegal to offer women different rates of pay for doing the same job as a man, yet female workers still average about 20% lower pay. Although they often run their own businesses and are embarking on careers like mining, engineering, building trades and finance which were once all-male bastions, women are almost non-existent among the directors of major companies. In one survey, when the management of a major Australian company was asked if there were any women on its board, the unofficial answer was, 'God, no!'.

And when asked how many women were on its board, the head office of a large telephone company enquired, 'Do you mean the switchboard?' A census in 2003 by the optimistically titled 'Equal Opportunity for Women in the Workplace Agency' (EOWA) found that just five of Australia's top 200 companies have a female managing director, less than half the official tally for top United States companies. The census also found that only 9% of executive management positions were held by women in Australia, compared with around 16% in the United States.

Federal government policy is that 25% of all representatives on government boards and authorities should be women, rising to 50% in the longer term. However, less than 13% of board members appointed to government authorities and organisations are female.

Since the end of the 1990s real gains have been made in paid maternity leave and – among the most leading edge financial sector companies – even paternity leave was offered under some workplace agreements by 2003. There is also legislation in place protecting women's rights to return to permanent employment after they have a baby and take time off. Generally, after twelve months' continuous employment, a woman can expect twelve months' unpaid maternity leave and to return to a position at the same level of remuneration. But in 2008 it was reported that less than one third of women receive paid maternity leave from their employers.

In terms of women coming to prominence in traditionally male dominated spheres some headway has been made. Governments and unions in Australia have proved more progressive than business, when it comes to putting women in top jobs. In 2008

Julia Gillard (Deputy Prime Minister) became Australia's first woman PM when she acted in the top job while Kevin Rudd was overseas on official business. The move to appoint Dame Mary Gaudron to the High Court in 1987 – the first woman – was a milestone. Since then, a few women have been state premiers, leaders of political parties, national union leaders, head of the National Farmers Federation and the Australian Council of Trade Unions as well as becoming wharfies on Sydney's docks.

Migrants and discrimination

Migrants of non-English speaking backgrounds often work twice as hard to achieve half as much, especially if their English language skills remain poor.

Ken Edwards, a Queensland journalist whose articles on migration won the Media Peace Prize awarded by the United Nations, demonstrates the contradictory attitudes of the Australians with an anecdote about the old-timer who bemoans the supposed takeover by Italians. 'I can't abide 'em. Don't trust 'em,' he complains – then stops to say 'G'day' to a shopkeeper with an Italian accent. 'Nice little bloke,' he says, walking on.

In the major cities there are many migrant and interpreter services available, as well as a staggering variety of ethnic social clubs, restaurants, sporting groups and other means of making contact with those of a similar origin. There's even a kind of snobbery in reverse – people with 'natural suntans', foreign accents or backgrounds deemed 'exotic' attract the curious admiration of the indigenous White Anglo Saxon Protestant (WASP) majority.

Emanuel Klein, who could not speak a word of English when he arrived in 1972 – and became prominent in government and business as an ethnic community commentator – tells of the friendliness and sincerity of the locals. 'People I'd met once or twice invited me to dinner. What's more, Aussies actually meant it when they said, "We must get together some time". In Europe where this would be a mere politeness, with no genuine invitation intended.'

However, to presume that people who do not fit the WASP profile are sure to be welcomed with open arms everywhere they go is, unfortunately, a fantasy. A glance at the section in this book on Aussie slang demonstrates that there are many unflattering terms for people of an ethnic background. The label 'New Australian' is not always kind. It may imply all manner of shortcomings. There are other terms for the 'wogs' far too derogatory to reproduce here – expressions which it is hoped you will never hear as a foreign visitor or immigrant.

Racism
The influx of Oriental migrants in the 1970s, 1980s and 1990s has led to a backlash of protests and many documented cases of discrimination and even violence. The situation is one step away from the White Australia Policy supporters who, in previous decades starting with the Gold Rush of the 1850s, feared the continent was in danger of being overrun by the 'yellow peril' to its north. The anti-Asian lobby of today predicts continued migration will aggravate political and social problems. This faction of Australia's immigration debate has added Muslims to its list of socially 'difficult' newcomers, following the influx of refugees from the Middle East and other war-torn Muslim countries. However, the

government in Canberra maintains that its migration policy will continue to let in people who meet their criteria, irrespective of colour, sex or religion.

However, Australia's reputation as a relatively progressive democracy which welcomes people of all backgrounds was badly tarnished in 1997 when Pauline Hanson, the one-time leader of a small political grouping, One Nation, echoed the sentiments of the White Australian days with her criticism of migrant and Aboriginal groups. Hanson has since been jailed (and released) regarding charges of electoral fraud. Disturbingly, the ruling Liberal Party government can be accused of stealing her thunder by incorporating some of One Nation's fears and phobias into Australia's current refugee and welfare policies. By the way, Ms Hanson exited jail in 2004 and announced her new friendship for Australian Aboriginals – even appearing on stage at a music festival with an Aboriginal singer.

Franca Arena has lived in Australia for 40 years. She is a retired politician with wide expertise in the special problems of migrant communities. Arena says, 'The most recent ethnic group to arrive usually bears the brunt of prejudice. For instance, when I arrived with an influx of southern Europeans, ours was the group that suffered most. Today it is the Asian community. But on the whole, Australians are now more reasonable, more likely to admit everyone is entitled to a "fair go" and that it's a big country with room for all kinds. In my experience, racial problems and intolerance are far worse in the more overpopulated nations.'

Even the most conservative political leaders are more moderate than those of many right-wing parties in Western Europe. For all its ills, Australia remains a relatively tolerant society, greatly embarrassed by unresolved social and humanitarian issues such as the incarceration and deportation of illegal immigrants claiming refugee status.

MULTICULTURALISM

Governments try to make the most of a diverse immigrant population with a policy of 'multiculturalism'. Though the Asian community has been the focus of debate since the mid-1970s, they constitute only about 5% of the total population. More than 75% of Australians are of British or Irish origin, and 20% were born in other European countries or are of European ancestry.

For Australia, multiculturalism means the conviction that new blood brings with it many social, cultural and economic advantages. Foreigners who join Australian society are not required to assimilate – in fact, they are encouraged to be different and maintain traditions and languages while learning about Australia and improving their English language skills. Australia's publicly funded ethnic radio and television stations broadcast in 57 languages and sell subtitled foreign language programmes abroad. Government schools, colleges and universities all place emphasis on teaching community languages and offer a bewildering range of linguistic and cultural studies.

In Australian cities and larger towns, newspaper stands groan under the weight of 'ethnic' publications published at home or imported. Large, established and influential ethnic groups, such as the Italian, Greek, Lebanese, Asian and Eastern European communities, have a number of publications catering to subcultures within their communities, as well as their own social clubs, art galleries and museums, schools, churches and sporting organisations. However, studies show that many Australians remain ambivalent about the 'wogs' in their midst, claiming multiculturalism has touched their lives merely by providing a better range of restaurants.

MANNERS

Socially accepted behaviours change from country to country, and on a superficial level newcomers can find Australian manners a little surprising. For instance, Australians are great finger-pointers and if you are from a part of the world where pointing of fingers at people and things is insulting or worse, remember it is no big deal in Australia. But watch out for two fingers raised in your face – this is definitely rude! Spitting and sneezing is OK in Australia if you do it quietly and into a tissue or handkerchief. Spitting or sneezing onto the ground is very bad manners, in contrast to people of some other cultures who would never dream of dirtying a tissue then carrying it around in their pockets. Social interaction between adults and children is often relatively informal. Aussie kids are commonly on first name terms with adults in their social orbit and the old-fashioned politeness of adding 'Auntie' or 'Uncle' before the adult's name is rarely encouraged in many social groups – unless the person really is the child's aunt or uncle. Older people may prefer to be addressed as 'Mr' or 'Mrs' by younger people, but this preference is not commonly indulged by the younger people working in banks, in making business telephones calls, transactions in shopping centres and so on.

Newcomers are often shocked by the apparently informal, easy-going, even 'loose' lifestyles of the 'dinky-dis' down the road. The real differences may not be obvious for years, emerging eventually when their children adopt local manners and values. Immigrants from places with strict social or religious codes often suffer in this clash between old ways and new. Children from non-Australian backgrounds grow up to speak with Aussie accents, take to surfing, pub-going, disco-ing and other social or sporting customs considered normal for Australians but alien to their parents. A Vietnamese community leader, editor of a Vietnamese daily newspaper at Cabramatta, Sydney's suburban Saigon, summed up the problems this way: 'There are some young people with multi-coloured hair, and we don't like that. In Vietnam my children never came close to me, but here they tap me on the shoulder and say, "Hello Dad". Sometimes this goes to extremes. I once heard a boy say to his father, "Hello, mate"!'

AUSTRALIANS AND TRAVEL

A holidaying couple from abroad were touring Western Australia. They stopped for the night in a town called Denmark, noticing a Copenhagen Street and other Danish references. When they dined at a local restaurant these curious tourists asked the waiter about the reason for the place names. He didn't know, and disappeared into the kitchen to ask some old timers on the staff. He returned with the following information: 'We're pretty sure Denmark and Copenhagen are aboriginal names.'

Just a couple of decades ago, a mature Australian who had seen the world (not just Bali) was an exception. Good reasons like distance, the comforts of home, plus perhaps a fear of tackling foreigners and their languages on alien turf kept Australians to Australia. However, improved communications and an ever more cosmopolitan culture have assisted Aussies in lifting their sunglasses to take a good look at life beyond Bondi Beach. As a result, you'll often meet Aussies who have been to Alabama, Amsterdam and the Algarve – but not Ayers Rock.

Foreign travel is an obsession for recent generations of young Aussies, a breed of keen adventurers who backpack to the most unlikely places. A grand tour 'OS' (as Australians call 'overseas') is a kind of finishing school – an extension of the educational process for middle-class Australians. Yet when you encounter them sipping cocktails in New York bars or haggling for souvenirs in the bazaars of the Orient, most express supreme enthusiasm for Australia in comparison with almost any place they've seen.

Back in Australia, on radio chat shows or as taxi drivers, many Aussies will concur that 'Godzown's' is the best country in the world with top weather/beer/fashion/food/blokes, sheilas...

BLOKES

When it comes to Ocker stereotypes, there are two breeds of bloke. One is naive and Neanderthal – great for a beer and a laugh. The other embodies the toughness of the adventurer – a businessbloke with the dorsal fin of a shark beneath his grey suit, but also a guy who may take time out during his hectic week to read up on how to be a better father to his son, attend a Men's Health Seminar (annual events on a national scale in Australia) or join the neighbourhood men's counselling group. In Australia the New Bloke is also refered to as a 'metrosexual'.

The male stereotypes of Australia arise from national pride in a tough pioneering heritage: explorers conquering an inhospitable environment, macho convicts hacking their way through the bush, stockmen home on the range in the outback. That handsome, tall-in-the-saddle image blends with the anti-establishment attitude of convicts and outcast radicals from the 'old world'. Cowboys and helmeted bushranger heroes like Ned Kelly may not have been gentlemen, but they forded rivers, trekked vast deserts and often died seeking the mysteries of the island continent. Every schoolchild is taught to be proud of these aspects of Australia's eighteenth and nineteenth-century colonial history, as well as the more recent 'legend' of the Australian and New Zealand Army Corps – the ANZAC volunteers needlessly expended in a spectacularly disastrous campaign against the Turks at Gallipoli in the First World War.

Now consider that other vision of Aussie blokehood – the sensitive but tough businessman. The ubiquitous publisher, Rupert Murdoch, swapped Australian citizenship for an American passport for reasons of business rather than patriotism and remains 'dinky-di' in his ruthless, no-nonsense dealings with other companies and his own employees. His eldest son, Lachlan, is now running the local news empire. James Packer, son of another colourful media magnate and world class gambler, Kerry, is another new generation Aussie man who other blokes may privately scorn for being a rich businessman's son yet envy for this tough-minded business acumen. Both James and Lachlan are darlings of the social pages and embody many of the contradictory qualities of sporting, beefy, cultured yet canny Aussie blokedom approaching maturity.

Crocodile Dundee star Paul Hogan and international actor Russell Crowe are local heroes. While Crowe is an accomplished actor, Paul (who is getting on in years) specialised in playing himself. 'Hoges', as he is known, became a role model Down Under and famous worldwide as the thoroughly modern ocker of the cinema screen. As Mike 'Crocodile' Dundee in the highly successful movies of the same name, Hogan played the naive conman. Crowe, who is more flexible in the movie roles he takes on, is appealing to Australians for his earthy, boozy persona. Crowe has forged strong links to his adopted NSW rural community. He plays in a rock band with mates and is a family man too, in common with many less famous young Aussie blokes. Australians identify with Hogan and Crowe because they are handsome, outdoorsy, sociable, beer-drinking, rich and famous; self-made men and nice blokes too.

As in most cultures, men tend to get together to relax. This means drinking en masse in pubs, going to the footy, and letting it all hang out (beer guts too) away from the prying eyes of women and children.

While it is wrong to assume that stereotypes are the rule or that polarisation of the sexes is uniquely Australian, anyone who has stayed awhile in the outback community would soon get a picture of the more extreme characteristics. When not utterly charming, funny and sensible, both blokehood and sheiladom can be boozy, racist, anti-homosexual, violent and ugly. Expatriate art critic and New York based historian Robert Hughes now claims he wants nothing to do with his birthplace and stating (after a legal and very public media battle, over an outback car accident when he

was charged with serious driving offences) '...I shall have nothing
further to do with Australia...which with any luck I shall never see
again,' declares Hughes.

SHEILAS

The typical Australian party is said to segregate blokes at one end
around the boozetub, and sheilas (also known as 'The Girls') at
the other. Once again, putting too much faith in a stereotype can
be a mistake. A typical suburban get-together Down Under can in
fact be a sun-drenched, appetising and hugely sociable experience
for everyone; but once again there is more than a grain of truth
in the assumption that, like the blokes, sheilas are tough.
Australian women do tend to self-reliance. According to this
stereotype, a suggestion by the man of the house to his 'liddle
lydee' along the lines of, 'Ya don' mind chopping some wood for
the barbie, do ya darls?' or the knowledge that he's in the boozer
with the boys is part of the routine. The difference is that Aussie
women are just as likely to have a girls' night out as their men are
in most households. The fact is that most women with partner and
kids are likely to be in paid employment and, if they are not, men
seem increasingly aware of the value of a woman's work in the
home. A fair degree of economic and social independence has be
negotiated in most Australian relationships. Yet in Australia, the
divorce rate is high but fortunately there are so many celebrity
women in the arts, business and public service that, provided she
can earn a living and find quality childcare, the stereotype is that
working single mothers can lead a good life providing they are in
high paying jobs. More women are choosing not to have partner,
children and mortgage in their 20s. Many never have children at

all. Career and perhaps other personal goals are acceptable first priorities for modern Australian women. Kylie Minogue, internationally acclaimed (and expatriate) Aussie singing sensation, could be the 'new sheila'. Kylie may be one of the world's most successful and desirable sheilas – but she is still childless and only 'Hello' magazine seems to be worried.

But, like her masculine counterpart, the typical sheila is not always a pretty sight. The parrakeet screech of Barry Humphries' creation, Dame Edna Everage, is one of the least flattering caricatures of Aussie womanhood. Humphries' 'Frankenstein' – that jumped-up housewife whose late hubby Norm surely thanked his lucky stars that a malfunctioning prostate gland kept him in hospital and permanently away from home – rings true for some sectors of suburban life Down Under; but real sheilas and their admirers turn to intelligent, sexy female role models like acclaimed actor Nicole Kidman, Danii, Kylie and the rest.

Despite the growth of two-job families, studies showed that working wives in Australia spend about 33 hours a week more than their partners on household chores. Yet another survey showed 93% of Australian women believed men should share all the housework. The pressure is on.

Australian surveys show that most young women said they needed both a paying job and a family of their own to feel fulfilled. They want sensitive sons (who share housework) and ambitious daughters (who see themselves as social and intellectual equals to their brothers).

Certainly international feminism is indebted to feminist activists Germaine Greer and compatriots like Dale Spender. The women's movement has always been well advanced in Australia. It was the second country in the world (after New Zealand) to give women the right to vote, in 1901. However, women did *not* gain the right to stand for parliament until some 20 years later. These days, Australian state and federal parliaments have one of the highest ratios of female members in the world. About one in ten MPs is a woman, a ratio higher only in the Scandinavian countries.

'YOOF'

Australia's urban teenagers are among the most worldly-wise on the planet when it comes to shopping and sex education. Surveys indicate that most Aussie kids are also well educated, widely informed, multicultural, self-reliant and technologically aware. Nearly 70% finish high school, but their biggest problem is unemployment, which in Australia strikes 15-to-19-year olds at the rate of around 30%. Coping with change makes them value self-reliance, says the survey, and 'being in control' was nominated almost as important in measuring success as 'satisfaction with life and marriage'. According to the report, compiled from government, youth programme and advertising statistics, Australia's 12-to-18-year olds earn an average of $37 a week (mainly from weekend jobs), smoke Winfield, wear Nike, drink Gatorade and listen to Sony. Internet and computer game usage in Australian homes is high, and growing at one of the fastest rates in the world, driving mainly by youngsters' insatiable appetite for on-line and video entertainment, chat rooms and many youth-focussed services. Empirical evidence suggests they seek and get access to mobile telephones from their middle-class parents. While this can be an expensive indulgence the eroding force of peer pressure as well as parents' concerns for the young ones' safety after school or on nights out mean that a phone has become a popular birthday or Christmas gift – plus a phone payment plan that severely limits the teenager's ability to spend up big on the parental telephone account! Most school-leavers and young employed people consider that having their own phone *and* personal internet facility (via the same phone or a desktop or portable computer) is even more essential than owning their own car.

GAYS

No discussion of Australian stereotypes would be complete without the role of male and female homosexuals (gays and lesbians) in society. In bigger cities, where there is safety in numbers and a wider range of attitudes to every topic, many have 'come out' to enjoy a more or less open lifestyle. In smaller towns, rural areas and certain states, however, attitudes can be virulently homophobic and if you are gay, it does not pay to advertise the fact.

On the whole, the past decade has resulted in an accelerated acceptance of non-heterosexual lifestyles. The federal government has enacted equal rights laws making discrimination on grounds of a person's sexual preferences illegal. A former premier of South Australia, Don Dunstan, actually told a television interviewer he was bisexual. By 2008 same sex couples were regularly in the big city media talking about their romances and relationships, and many have achieved parenthood by making arrangements for artificial insemination and surrogacy in order to conceive and raise their own children. When it comes to government pensions, taxes and superannuation laws the situation is more negative. Gay couples cannot claim the various pensions, tax breaks or other government benefits available to heterosexual couples but their lobbying to change these laws is forceful.

The gay community has pushed for full recognition of the non-Australian partner in a gay couple as a 'spouse' for purposes of immigration and residency applications. After 1983, the federal government modified its rulings to give consideration on compassionate or humanitarian grounds under the immigration points system. However, the association of homosexuals with AIDS means the gay community has adopted a lower political profile, especially since the screening of migration applicants for the disease has been implemented.

The eastern capital cities – Melbourne, Adelaide and especially Sydney – have thriving gay communities. Sydney has a reputation for its vibrant scene in the Oxford Street area, which has a gay population almost as high per capita as San Francisco's. The Mardi Gras in Sydney each February is the biggest gay street festival in the world, drawing tens of thousands onto the streets and millions more in a television audience. The event boosts local and international tourism to Sydney. Yet the majority of the sightseers and television audience for the Mardi Gras is from the local 'straight' community. Sydney's current Lord Mayor, Clover Moore, is a long-term champion of the city's gay community and there is a decidely 'pink' vote that pollies at all levels of Australian politics cannot ignore.

Although only a minority of gays and lesbians find it possible to be quite open, the world of blokes and sheilas would not be the same without them. In the big cities and towns, homosexuals – open or otherwise – make a high profile contribution to arts, literature, the professions, academic life and entertainment in general.

While some church leaders and social conservatives regularly denounce them, and agitate for legislation to push gays back into the closet, male and female homosexuals of the bigger cities have their own well-publicised telephone counselling services as well as a gay clergy in some churches. There are gay pubs, clubs, performing arts groups, even travel agencies to take them to regional resorts that specialise in the lucrative gay market.

There remains a strong lobby that aims to show the danger of accepting homosexuality, championed by moral and religious organisations such as the Festival of Light. Focus on paedophilia by the media can be used to cast aspersions on the gay community, while the 'outing' of prominent public figures and their families is something of a media sport in Australia, as in other Western societies. Homosexuals are occasionally attacked by gangs of marauding 'poofter-bashers' and some murders of gay and lesbian people are clearly motivated by homophobia.

ABORIGINALS

Prime Minister Kevin Rudd's early move in government to make a very public apology to the Australian aboriginals for their treatment at the hands of white settlers was far more than a public relations exercise. The national 'Sorry Day' is set for 26 May of every year. It signifies important changes in the Aussie psyche, a contrast to times when 'abos' were considered by the white population as a subhuman under class, towards a communal guilt and recognition that decades of white abuse has brought the indigenous black population to the pathetic state so many still live in today. Like many of the world's deep-rooted problems, making improvements in the lifestyle and prospects for Australia's aboriginals will take generations, if it happens at all. According to the Human Rights Commission, 30–40% of all complaints are lodged by Aboriginal people. Those complaints usually concern the refusal of basic services – in shops, pubs, restaurants and accommodation – because of the colour of a person's skin.

The activities of Aboriginal rights activists continue to focus on whether native title (land rights) should take precedence over valuable mining and pastoral leases. It was only a little over a decade ago, in 1997, that the legal rights of Aboriginals to 'their' land had become a long-term political issue, following a series of High Court challenges and failure of parliament to resolve the debate by passing the Wik Legislation. Apart from issues like native title, and the fact that Aboriginals are imprisoned at a rate many times higher than for other Australians, it is possible to forget that Australia's genuine 'first settlers' are there at all. Even more than other ethnic groups, Aboriginals stick together in city slums or isolated in outback communities. Today the Aboriginal population (though few of these are pure blood) numbers about 300,000, though some say the real figure is more like half a million and many people identify as Aboriginal due to an Aboriginal grandparent in their family tree.

It is only since 1971 that the general census has included the native population in its survey of Australians and their living standards. A couple of years before that, people of Aboriginals and Torres Strait Island origin were granted full citizenship rights, including the right to vote. Not surprisingly, Australia has been labelled the 'South Africa' of the Pacific. Supporters of this point of view describe white Australians as passive racists, only saved from being cast into the apartheid camp by the fact that the majority of the population is white.

Respectable white society is embarrassed at the ill-treatment of the black minority by the police and other whites. Yet it is not unusual to hear such discrimination condoned – even by otherwise worldly, well-educated members of migrant minority groups who have, ironically, been victims of discrimination themselves. Their 'conventional' wisdom is that the Abos are a drunken, lazy, useless lot quite beyond help and redemption, or that governments are 'soft' on Aboriginals, giving people with sometimes vague Aboriginal ancestry preference in public service jobs and educational opportunity.

An effort is being made to apply multiculturalism to Aboriginals, too – with positive results. Aboriginal culture has become the fashion, which is ironic given that many Aussie suburbanites who wear so-called Australian Aboriginal T-shirts, invest in visual artworks or attend concerts featuring Aboriginal dance and musical expression have little contact with the indigenous people.

THE DREAMTIME

Aboriginal culture is based on the Dreamtime philosophy, giving spiritual focus to the land and with a concept of time fusing past, present and future. The peoples now known as Australian Aboriginals and Torres Strait Islanders crossed from South-East Asia more than 60,000 years ago. No one knows what the population was when the European invasion began in 1788, though it has been estimated that Aboriginals numbered at least 250,000.

OPPRESSION OF ABORIGINALS

From the time of the first arrivals from Britain in 1788, newcomers took it upon themselves to wipe out or suppress indigenous black tribes and their 'inferior' culture.

In Tasmania, the situation was so bad that Aboriginals were massacred to the point of extinction. Apart from slaughtering the blacks like wild animals and exploiting them mercilessly, the whites infected them with hitherto unknown diseases and introduced them to the corrupting influence of alcohol. By the beginning of the twentieth century, Aboriginal and especially half-caste children were exiled from their communities and trained as slave labourers and servants for middle-class whites, though this remains a controversial version of history for some white Australians.

Today the condition of many 'Abos' in country areas, shanty towns and urban ghettos is often pathetic, presenting an unpleasant example of progress-gone-haywire. Many Aborigines live on income from land royalties, mining leases or government welfare payments. These payments often assuage the guilty consciences of white Australian taxpayers, who indirectly provide

some 70% of this minority group's total income. In a landmark
High Court decision known as the Mabo case, effective ownership
of some 10% of Australia's land mass has been returned to the
natives, and, despite continuing debate and legal challenges to
clarify the Aboriginals' claims, many tribes are paid royalties in
return for the use of their land. Ayers Rock, or Uluru, the huge
red boulder which is a major tourist attraction in the desert of the
Northern Territory, is the most famous of the sites returned to the
Aboriginals in the mid-1980s by a progressive Labor
administration in Canberra, after decades of political pressure. As
a result, visits to the sacred rock are on a 'look but don't touch'
basis, and tourists are no longer be allowed to scramble all over it.
Yet the notion of owning land is at odds with Aboriginal lore.
Their idea is that people belong to the land, not the other way
around.

Government efforts to support Aboriginals' rights often lead to
accusations of tokenism by the whites and corruption by black
elders and business interests. There are at present only a handful
of blacks holding high political or bureaucratic positions.

Nevertheless, in Western Australia Ernie Bridge became the first
of his race to be appointed as a Cabinet Minister by the State
Government in 1986, while Pat O'Shane, an Aboriginal woman,
became a NSW magistrate in the same year. There are a handful
of outstanding actors, sports people and musicians of Aboriginal
origin, helping promote a more positive image of what life can be
like for those of Aboriginal background in contemporary
Australia. Despite their critics and ultra-conservative historians,
Aboriginals are politically motivated as never before, learning to

play the system with or without the help of whites who sometimes backed their political campaigns. The Aboriginal community, with the help of concerned non-Aboriginal Australians, has raised awareness of the so-called 'Stolen Generation', referring to light-skinned part-Aboriginal children who were forcibly removed from their families in the mid-twentieth century. At that time, well-meaning white Australians sought to employ, educate and assimilate these young Aboriginals to join white Christian society. While these motives may have been reasonable at that time, many Australians are now appalled to hear of such abuse. Discussions and histories of the 'Stolen Generation' have been widely aired in Australian literature, film and journalism as well as in local and international political arenas. The 'Stolen Generation' remains an embarrassing version of history for many non-Aboriginal Australians.

The plight of the native Australians is reflected in recent figures showing that they are more than ten times more likely than other Australians to have served a prison sentence – some 726.5 per 100,000 compared with 60 of every 100,000 whites. Aboriginal rights activists claim that this is proof of widespread police harassment, exemplified by a Queensland case in which an Aboriginal was jailed for three months for stealing two loaves of bread. On the other hand, the Court of Criminal Appeal has noted a tendency for judges to treat Aboriginals more leniently than other offenders.

Aboriginals are also beset with health problems often because medical treatment is not available for communities in remote locations. Alcohol abuse drags down many members of the older generation while petrol sniffing is a common pastime for youngsters. Infant mortality and disease are rife compared with other social groups while the average life expectancy for an Aboriginal is around 52 years, some 20 years less than the national average. Although unemployment is about three times that of whites, officials say that there are few complaints from Aboriginals who cannot get a job because of the colour of their skin.

Poorer Aboriginals are still fighting to obtain the basic rights – service without discrimination, adequate housing, and conveniently located health services. In many cases, discrimination in employment is the least of their worries. The cycle of poverty, drugs and crime means unemployment is an inevitable symptom of deeper social problems for many Aboriginal families.

5

Australia – How Will You Get In?

Many people misunderstand Australian rules and regulations which govern permanent and temporary immigration.

> **The assumption is that the rules exist to keep people *out*. The truth, however, is that in the past few years these rules have been reviewed and changed to encourage more of the 'right' people to come *in*.**

This chapter aims to explain how Australia's system of categories, concessions and accumulation of 'points' can work for you, to maximise the chance of success for your own application. What's more, the price you pay for this book will be far less than the time, trouble and money needed to prepare and lodge an application. It would be a pity to be rejected, with no refund for fees paid, simply because you hadn't done your homework first using our guide to Australia's immigration rules.

POLICY AND POLITICS

The federal government, which is responsible for immigration policy and must approve every application, regularly reviews the laws on immigration, in line with its political and economic concerns. With each change, the aim is to select more skilled workers and the kind of people most likely to contribute to Australia's economic growth. The aim is also to be more open to people likely to make a good life, for the benefit of both the newcomer and the nation as a whole. To be successful your application for a stay in Australia should fall into one of the following categories:

- **A holiday visit.** No intention of working – just a trip abroad, though perhaps with an eye open for business, work, educational or lifestyle opportunities, if and when you return again;

- **A working holiday.** A temporary stay presents a chance to gain work experience, live in a fresh environment, make money for holidaying in Australia and on your way to and from there;

- **Educational purposes.** Australia's educational institutions may provide equivalent or better opportunities for study than other places, while you'll also have the excitement and experience of living in a new environment;

- **Temporary residency.** Your plan might be to take a short-term job in your field of expertise, sponsored by an Australian

company or educational institution, or posted there by a foreign
company;

◆ **Permanent residency**. This is a long-term commitment to the
ideal of living and working in Australia. You may have friends
or family you want to join, you may want to live in a sunny,
relatively free, untroubled society and on this basis decide that
Australia best meets your personal needs while being a place
where your family and career can flourish.

Australia's entry rules also make it possible for people to become
permanent residents on humanitarian grounds, as refugees from a
regime or government which presents a serious threat to their
welfare.

ILLEGAL IMMIGRANTS

Overriding the rules and regulations is the law in Australia on
illegal immigrants and people working without permits. Since many
more people want to live there than Australia can accommodate,
rules regarding people who overstay their visas, or who are found
to be working in contravention of the terms of their (e.g. visitor)
visas, are tough. In recent years it has been estimated that 50,000
people live in Australia illegally. However, Australia's visa-
overstayers are far fewer than in the past due to better immigration-
monitoring systems. Each year thousands are deported as illegal
entrants or unlawful non-citizens. They may be held in on-shore or
off-shore detention centres. These are prison-like institutions which
in recent years have held up to 1,300 people in uncomfortable
conditions, mostly Asian and Middle Eastern asylum seekers. In
Australia, illegal workers and visa-overstayers are thought to cost

millions of dollars a year in government unemployment benefits to jobless residents. Yet the issue of illegal immigrants who claim to be desperate refugees is a growing humanitarian and emotive political issue. Such people face either virtual 'imprisonment' in the country, since they would probably be detected if they tried to leave, or deportation, a heavy fine or a prison sentence if they are discovered. Overstayers are excluded from returning to Australia for up to three years, whether or not they leave voluntarily. Each year thousands of people are forcibly removed from Australia because they had entered the country illegally and then were rejected for a place in the limited humanitarian category.

Visitors who inadvertently overstay their visas should contact the nearest immigration office to sort the problem out.

VISITOR VISA AND MIGRATION PROCEDURE

If you are thinking of going to Australia as a tourist, temporary resident or permanent settler, your application must be made from outside the country except under special circumstances (see Special Assistance Category later in this chapter). Over seven million visas are issued by Australia each year – so no wonder such a range of rules and fees apply.

THE COST OF VISAS AND MIGRATION APPLICATIONS

The list of migration fees is long, and in the case of applications for certain categories of permanent residency a charge is levied for each family member on the application form. If you are outside

Australia, the fees are payable in the currency of a foreign country equivalent to the amount of Australian dollars being charged for the visa. Not all fees listed below are for applications made prior to going to Australia, but in some circumstances they will be relevant for visitors or settlers *after* arrival.

These charges alter with time but, as a guide, here are some sample fees excluding the $A300 fee for government health checks which may be required.

Application fees

	$A
Tourist visa valid three months to over one year	65–200
Temporary Business Entry	65
Working Holiday	170
Temporary Residence – prospective marriage partner	600–1245
Student Visa Application	410
Sponsorship for entry to Australia for family members	400–1500
Migration to Australia – Business Sponsor	245–305
Business Owner	2450
Plus for each spouse or child over 18 with less than functional English	2555
Senior Executive	2450
Plus for each spouse/child over 18 with less than functional English	2555
State/Territory Sponsored Investor	1030
Business Talent	3585
Plus, if primary applicant has less than functional English	5270
Language Testing	150–400
Parent (migrant) plus assurance of support	2355
Aged Parent (residence) plus assurance of support	2955

NO 'FREEBIES' FOR WOULD-BE MIGRANTS

If you are serious about applying to become a permanent settler in
Australia, you must pay a fee to the Department of Immigration
and Multicultural Affairs when you lodge the application. There
are also charges for sponsors and for English education, where
relevant, which are detailed later in this chapter. Documentary
evidence such as certified copies of birth and marriage certificates
are other expenses you may have to carry, while in some cases
your employment or educational qualifications will also need to be
assessed in return for a fee (see the fee list in Chapter 6, page
128). It can be an expensive exercise and all the money is lost if
your application fails because there are no refunds.

You will not normally have access to counselling by Australia's
migration or visa officials when you apply. Unless you plan the
application carefully, it could be rejected and you would have
wasted money paid in fees, which are not refundable.

HEALTH AND CHARACTER CHECKS

Everyone who applies for a visitor visa, whether to work
temporarily or to settle in Australia permanently, is subject to
health and character checks. An applicant and his or her
dependants planning to enter under the same visa must undergo
medical examinations to prove that they are in sound health.
Criminal records may also be checked by Australian migration
and visa authorities to ensure that the people being granted a visa
are of good character. There is some flexibility in the way
Australia's 'good health and character' rules are implemented.
For example, elderly people with their only close relatives in

Australia may be allowed entry although they are chronically ill, and minor criminal offences may be discounted if the applicant has a good case otherwise to go to Australia.

All applicants for migration, or people hoping to stay as temporary residents for over 12 months, must undergo extensive medical examinations, which may cover conditions such as:

+ tuberculosis (TB)
+ hepatitis B
+ HIV/AIDS.

People infected with HIV can be refused visas to Australia, after the Federal Court confirmed in 2005 the validity of an Immigration Department ruling which had denied a visa to a PhD student planning to study in Australia.

Apart from health and character checks, age limits also apply, as in applications for a temporary residence visa for a working holiday and many categories of permanent residence applications, described in the following pages.

VISITOR VISAS

Visitor visas are usually issued within 24 hours and cover people who want to enter Australia for the purpose of:

+ tourism;
+ conducting business (negotiations or discussions – though not for taking up employment);

- visiting relatives or friends;
- pre-arranged medical treatment;
- a working holiday.

This is the entry visa you will probably need for an initial look at Australia – the people, the lifestyle, a range of vastly differing climates and locations, as well as your opportunities for career, business or investment.

The visitor visa application form, available from the nearest Australian embassy or high commission, must be completed and returned with a passport-type photograph and a valid passport.

The Australian government does not require visitors to be sponsored.

An important proviso in obtaining a visitor visa is that the applicant should not intend to take a job in Australia or start formal studies. As mentioned earlier in this chapter, if the holder of a visitor visa is discovered to be working or studying illegally, they are subject to heavy fines and will be asked to leave the country.

Extensions
Extensions of the visitor visa may be granted under certain circumstances to people who make the application before their first visitor visa has expired, although stays totalling more than six months are not normally allowed. However, visiting academics and aged relatives of Australian citizens as well as young people on a working holiday may be allowed to stay in the country under such a visa for up to 12 months.

Multiple entry visas

Multiple entry visas may be issued to people who state good reasons to be coming and going from Australia quite frequently – for instance, parents of children living there, business visitors or people planning to interrupt their stay in Australia to travel to another country and then resume their visit to Australia.

Money for your stay

There are many international banks which offer convenient accounts which you can set up before your move to Australia. Once identification laws have been satisfied, the visitor or person making a transition to a longer stay can deposit A$ cash, cheques or payroll funds from their Australia-based employer into that account. In Australia the use of automatic tellers and internet access may be free for such accounts, making them a cheap and convenient solution when compared with travellers cheques, non-Australian credit cards and other foreign exchange based transactions.

Medical treatment

If you want a visitor visa for medical treatment in Australia, a range of requirements must be met. The applicant must convince visa officials that:

◆ they can meet the costs of that medical treatment;

◆ satisfactory arrangements have been made for this treatment with Australian hospital and medical specialists in advance;

◆ such treatment is not available in their own country;

◆ the patient will receive significant benefit from such a short term of treatment in Australia;

- the patient will not pose a public health risk, because they have a contagious disease, for example.

Unless, like Britain, your country has an agreement with Australia on public health care, as a visitor or temporary resident you will not be eligible for any government-funded health treatment under Australia's Medicare system. Be sure to take out a private or travel insurance policy to refund the cost of possible medical expenses in Australia. One visit to a general practitioner costs about $A36 for non-residents and others not registered under the Medicare system, payable to the doctor at the end of the appointment. Medicare allows for a partial refund. Charges may not apply for outpatient visits at public (i.e. government-funded) hospitals. Hospitals and medical care in Australia – whether public or private – can be extremely expensive for the uninsured.

TEMPORARY RESIDENT VISAS AND SPONSORS

There are three types of temporary residency visas offered by Australia:

1. International Relations (including working holidaymakers).

2. Economic (including people wanting to live in Australia for business or study purposes).

3. Social and Cultural (covering sportspeople, artists, performers as well as secondary school-age children with relatives or friends in Australia and people over age 55 who do not wish to work during an extended stay.

If the principal applicant is granted permission to take a job in Australia, the spouse and other family members coming with them may be allowed to take jobs. However, attendance by school-age children at government schools must be paid for. This may cost $A5,000 to $A10,000 or more per child, per year, for schooling that is free for permanent residents. Private schools may cost even more.

The identification of a 'sponsor' is necessary for most types of applicants for temporary residency in non-government employment, apart from working holidaymakers.

State and territory governments may also nominate skilled migrants to work in areas where a particular skill is in short supply. In some cases, students close to completing a course in Australia will be nominated, if willing to work in remote locations where their skills are needed. Employees in Australia as temporary residents under a long-term visa usually have an agreement to stay two or three years. Australian employers are allowed to recruit specified numbers of skilled workers from overseas if the local workforce cannot meet demand for a particular skill or profession.

In recent years there has been exploitation of temporary workers from poorer nations, recruited on behalf of private businesses as cheap labour. Often from Asian countries, these employees have been tempted by the promise of fabulous wages and conditions in Australia. In some cases temporary workers are duped into working for much less money and far longer hours, with all sorts of agency fees and expenses in addition to the fear of losing their job and temporary visa if they complain. So check carefully with relevant trade union and government authorities in Australia if you are considering a temporary job. It could turn out to be disappointing.

WORKING HOLIDAYMAKERS

Unlike most categories of temporary residents, people allowed to take working holidays in Australia do not need sponsors. Rules regarding working holidaymakers are ever more generous, as Australia's popularity as a destination for backpackers grows. An estimated half a million working holidaymakers arrive in Australia each year. And what are backpackers if not tourists who can earn and spend what they earn on eating, drinking, accommodation and sight-seeing? In 2006 the rules for working holiday makers were that:

◆ they need to be aged 18–30

◆ the visa is valid for one year, but can be extended to two years if they work for three months in a specified industry.

'Specified' industries under these rules often don't provide appealing or well-paid work for the locals – but young visitors may find it exciting to try their hand in a shearing shed or as farm labourers.

Working holidaymakers can also work for six months with an employer and study for four months.

The aim is to promote international understanding by allowing young people to get a taste of life in Australia. The money earned on the strength of such a work permit is meant to help finance more travel around the country. Getting a paid job is supposed to be incidental to the whole adventure; it should not be a career move. Since youth unemployment is relatively high in Australia, people who enter under this category must also satisfy visa officials that their working plans would not threaten job opportunities for Australians.

Finding work on holiday

In most towns and cities, there are usually jobs for people willing to take casual office work. Computer skills are desirable. Register with a jobs agency after arrival in Australia and scan the local newspapers and internet employment sites. If you have a trade or profession, there are often employment agencies to match you with an employer. Remember to take documentary evidence of your training when you go Down Under.

There are also many jobs for labourers, in bars, pubs, offices and restaurants – especially in popular tourist centres – which are especially suitable for working holidaymakers. Such jobs won't tie you down if your travel plans are based on saving enough in one place to see more of the country. If you hanker for a more uniquely Aussie experience, you might consider a trip to the outback financed by work on a farm – perhaps as a 'cowcockie' or 'stockman' (Australia's answer to the American cowboy) doing such work as rounding up or moving livestock, mending fences, and so on. The ability to drive a motorcycle and ride a horse are useful skills on sheep and cattle stations.

Remember, if working on a 'casual' basis, some of the more attractive perks of working in Australia – such as paid holidays that may include holiday loading of the pay packet – will not be among your working conditions. On average you can expect to earn $A200–$A500 per week, and to spend about $A100 per day, depending on your accommodation, job and lifestyle.

Australia has reciprocal working holiday arrangements with:

Britain	Netherlands
Canada	*Japan
Denmark	*Republic of Korea
Sweden	Finland
Norway	*Cyprus
*Hong Kong (HKSAR) of the	*Germany
People's Republic of China	Republic of Ireland
*Malta	

People who hold passports from these countries may apply for a working holiday visa to Australia from any other country. Countries marked * must apply in the country in which that passport was issued. Applicants from other countries whose entry is considered of mutual advantage as a worthwhile cultural exchange and who are applying in their countries of citizenship may also be considered for places under the working holiday scheme.

Criteria for working holiday applicants

To receive the visa, you must be perceived as self-reliant, resourceful and adaptable by the Australian authorities. Only one permit for a working holiday in Australia is allowed – once you have been there under this provision, you cannot apply for a second working holiday. To qualify, applicants must:

- state that their prime intention is a **holiday** in Australia, with paid employment as an incidental aspect;

- have a return ticket, or enough money to buy one;

- have **reasonable funds** for normal living, at least during the first weeks of their holiday and perhaps while looking for work. Australian authorities in your country can advise on how much money is considered 'reasonable' when you apply, depending on factors such as whether you have friends or relatives to stay with in your travels, how much money would be left after paying for a return ticket, and so forth;

- have fair prospects of obtaining **temporary employment** to supplement the money taken to Australia for holiday purposes;

- not be responding to any **organised attempt at labour market recruitment** by an agency or employer. Pre-arranged jobs are only acceptable if they are the result of the personal initiative of the applicant;

- be **aged 18 to 30, single**, or a **married couple without dependent children**.

Whether your visit as a working holiday applicant would be of **mutual advantage** is open to interpretation by the officials in charge of such temporary visas at the time. It means that the applicant is likely to gain 'cultural understanding' through the working holiday Down Under and if that translates as getting to know the difference between a Hunter semillon and a Coonawarra chardonnay, so much the better. Most people of good health and character, with no criminal offences, are admitted under the terms of this opportunity to see something of Australia while they are young and uncommitted.

However, if you are demonstrably unable to support yourself for a short time in Australia – under the 'reasonable funds' criteria explained above – you will probably be refused a visa.

Using professional qualifications

You may have professional qualifications which you hope to use while in Australia on a working holiday. Assuming that the visa authorities are satisfied that work and career are not your main considerations in applying for a working holiday permit, your qualification may first have to be assessed by the National Office of Overseas Skills Recognition (see Chapter 6) which can take weeks or even months. An interview may also be necessary:

- if the intended stay in Australia is longer than six months;

- if the application is made outside that person's country of citizenship;

- if Australia's visa officials decide it is desirable for some other reason.

Remember the six months rule

Working holidaymakers are not allowed to stay in the same full-time job longer than six months. Anyone who does so will not be allowed a further entry permit to Australia. However, working holidaymakers are allowed to study for up to four months.

English courses

Working holidaymakers may enrol in full-time, single English courses. Part-time English courses may be taken, provided this remains an 'incidental activity' to the holiday stay in Australia. English study can only be undertaken at accredited English language institutions (those offering English language as a subject).

EXECUTIVE, TECHNICAL AND PROFESSIONAL STAFF FOR TEMPORARY EMPLOYMENT IN AUSTRALIA

Sponsorship by the prospective employer is not necessary for people seeking permission to stay in Australia for four months or less. For longer stays, the sponsor must pay for and lodge the Sponsorship For Entry To Australia For Temporary Residents Form, available from Department of Immigration Offices in Australia. In the case of senior executive and specialist staff, the application for temporary residency may be approved if a detailed case is made showing a need for such experts in Australia by either:

- the prospective Australian employer; *or*

- the usual employer overseas, with a branch in Australia where it is hoped to post that employee.

Temporary residents must pay taxes on all income earned in Australia. However, they do not have access to social welfare benefits or public health care. Citizens of countries with a Reciprocal Health Care Agreement with Australia (Finland, Italy, Malta, The Netherlands, Sweden and UK) may receive emergency medical cover under Australia's public health system. It is wise to check whether you should keep up your private medical insurance while in Australia.

Four years maximum

Applications for the temporary residence of such an expert and his or her family are normally granted for periods of up to four years, provided:

* the proposed employer provides **sponsorship** and pays the fee;

* labour market testing in Australia shows the **required skills** are not available there;

* the position is **full-time;**

* the application for the visa will **not be underpaid** in terms of Australia's industrial awards (pay and conditions);

* foreigners are **not being brought in as a substitute** for training of Australians for certain jobs, and the employer may be required to introduce training schemes for local staff;

* the applicant is not being recruited to fill an unskilled or **semi-skilled** job;

* **health and character** requirements are met.

STAFF FOR AUSTRALIAN EDUCATIONAL AND RESEARCH INSTITUTIONS

If the applicant is seen to provide enrichment of Australia's educational environment, as well as an awareness of other cultures, the rules permit entry of academic staff for temporary postings. Nomination by an academic institution is necessary and the proposed post must be relevant to qualifications and experience.

SPORTSPEOPLE AND ASSOCIATED PERSONNEL

In sports mad Australia, this category of temporary resident aims to encourage sporting contacts with stars from abroad, and to improve the sporting standards in Australia. Applicants wanting to come to Australia for less than four months do not need a sponsor, if they are coming to participate in specific events or contests, provided:

◆ they show evidence of an invitation from the organisers of the event or evidence of acceptance of a nomination to participate in an event open to contestants from overseas;

◆ they sign a declaration that on arrival in Australia they will have a return or onward ticket and sufficient funds to support themselves (and family members travelling with them) for the duration of the proposed stay.

Show or competition judges entering for less than four months do not require sponsorship.

Applicants wanting to stay longer than four months to participate in specific events or contests:

◆ need a sponsor to pay the relevant fee and lodge the application in Australia;

◆ must envisage a stay of no longer than 12 months.

Persons and teams of international standing and their personnel do not need sponsorship, and may apply directly to Australian embassies and high commissions for temporary entry to Australia.

ENTERTAINERS

Entertainers or other professional workers in entertainment industries with special talents or abilities may be allowed to enter

Australia to work for a limited period. An acceptable sponsorship must be lodged by a reputable organisation in Australia.

RELIGIOUS STAFF

People seeking visas to engage in religious duties on a temporary basis must be sponsored by an established religious organisation in Australia.

SELF-SUPPORTING RETIREES

People who wish to retire to Australia but don't have children living there are considered for temporary residency if they have reached the age of 55, have no dependent children and meet certain financial requirements as well as normal good health and character standards. They will not be issued with a permanent resident visa as in the past, however. Only a **long-term temporary visa** may be granted.

The main difference between being a permanent resident and entering on a long-term temporary visa (renewable) is that the newcomer cannot use Australia's public health and welfare facilities and must be fully insured privately On retiring to Australia, applicants are therefore expected to have enough money not to become a burden on the Australian community.

Assets
In general, those qualifying for a temporary visa as a self-supporting retiree need enough capital to invest to generate a good income, at least $A52,000 annually at the time of writing. Assets of more than $A900,000 would generate such an annual income, accordingly to Australian immigration authorities though various

combinations of pension and capital are acceptable, provided the applicant has no intention of working more than 20 hours per week and can prove they have sufficient funds to finance all their living and welfare costs.

SPONSORED VISITORS

A new category within the International Stream was introduced in 2000, to allow entry to people with relatives or a business/ government entity willing to officially sponsor their stay by providing a financial Assurance of Support. These range from $A1,500–$A10,000 per person. The bond enables the immigration authorities to recoup some of the costs of finding and removing temporary visa-holders who have stayed on illegally. The Assurance of Support (or bond), if lodged, is refunded to the sponsor after the visitor (or immigrant) exits Australia.

A *Sponsored Family Visitor* is defined as a spouse, parent, brother, sister, child, adopted child, aunt, uncle, niece, nephew, grandparent, grandchild and 'step' or adopted equivalents of these.

There are no provisions for fiancé(e)s, in-laws, cousins, friends or same-sex partners to provide sponsorship. Federal, State and Territory Members of Parliament in Australia, government agencies and local government mayors can also provide sponsorship.

A *Sponsored Business Visitor* (short stay) can only be sponsored by Federal, State and Territory Members of Parliament in Australia or by local government mayors or government agencies.

The sponsorship form is available from Australian Government offices outside Australia, the Department of Immigration and Multicultural and Indigenous Affairs or from the internet at www.immi.gov.au. It must be lodged by the visa applicant together with the visitor visa application form and the visa application fee.

PERMANENT SETTLEMENT – WILL YOU QUALIFY?

Australia has a range of rules and regulations for people intending to become permanent residents. These should be considered before lodging your application and fee because nobody wants to waste time, emotional energy and money in useless efforts to persuade the Aussies to open the door. No matter how much you want to be allowed in, take time to consider **why Australia would want you** – because that's the main consideration of the Immigration Department decision-makers. Migration officers at Australia's embassies and high commissions around the world are well-trained, flexible and often sympathetic – but an application may be knocked back long before it reaches the interview stage (if any), so you may never benefit from counselling or expert advice.

The rules under which the fortunate few who, in recent years, have been granted permanent resident visas, are continually revised to further emphasise the economic benefits migrants can bring with them. If you have professional skills currently in short supply in Australia or money and track record to build a business then the chance of you obtaining permission to settle permanently in Australia is good.

Applications for migration must usually be made from your country of residence. A visitor to Australia must depart on expiry of their visitor or temporary visa and then apply at the nearest Australian Department of Immigration Office for another visit, or permanent residence.

MIGRANT CATEGORIES

In general, migrant assessments fall into three main streams, with various sub-groups, each with their own criteria. The main streams are:

+ **Family Stream**
+ **Skilled Stream**
+ **Refugee**, **Humanitarian** or **Special Assistance**.

The sections that follow should open your eyes to your chances of success under one of these categories and the preparations necessary if you go ahead with an application for permanent residence.

FAMILY STREAM

Family migration is a shrinking but still significant reason for people to qualify for permanent settlement in Australia. By 2007 the Family Stream represented about a quarter of total settler numbers, and is likely to be further reduced because government policy favours applicants who, above all, can make a significant economic contribution. New immigration targets favoured skilled and business migrants, rather than those with a close relative in Australia. The impact of cuts to this part of the migration programme is felt most by Asian applicants, who are the biggest group of would-be Aussies who might use the family migration provision. The government now reserves the right to 'cap' the number of visas granted within the Family Stream because demand for places outstrips supply. So eligible families who have had their visa application capped must wait in a queue until the following year, when they may be granted permanent residency in the new intake.

Migrants for family reunion must be sponsored by their relatives in Australia.

♦ **The Family Stream** includes spouses, fiancés, dependent children, and parents who meet the 'balance of family' criteria, explained later.

♦ **Interdependency Category** includes people sponsored by an Australian citizen, permanent resident or New Zealand citizen with whom they have an interdependent relationship. This covers heterosexual and homosexual relationships, provided that a genuine, continuing and mutually committed relationship (excluding all other spouse relationships) is demonstrated.

There is also a **Skilled-Australian linked** category within the Skilled Stream, detailed later in this chapter. The Skilled-Australian linked stream covers extended family and non-dependants, e.g. children, parents and siblings of people living in Australia, as permanent residents.

Sponsors

Every family reunion category applicant must have a sponsor. The sponsor, who must lodge the *Sponsorship for Migration to*

Australia form (which is free of charge), must be at least 18 years old and live in Australia as an Australian citizen, permanent resident or eligible New Zealand citizen (see note above).

The sponsorship form must include **original or certified copies** of documents proving the sponsor's Australian citizenship, if he or she is an Australian citizen.

If you have a sponsor, he or she must:

◆ have been **resident in Australia** for at least two years;

◆ **provide the information and advice** you need to settle into your new life in Australia;

◆ **ensure adequate housing** is available when you arrive and, if necessary, provide accommodation for you in the first 12 months;

◆ **provide financial assistance** to meet your living expenses in the first 12 months if necessary;

◆ in some cases sign an **Assurance of Support**, lodge a bond and pay the Migration (Health Services) charge, to repay any government or charity benefits paid to the newcomer during their first two years in Australia.

The capacity of sponsoring relatives to meet these financial and housing requirements may be checked by Australian Immigration officials.

Assurance of Support
If you, as the applicant, are of working age, your sponsor may also be required to provide an Assurance of Support. If you are the mother (aged 50 or over) or father (aged 55 or over) of your

sponsor in Australia, your child must sign an **Assurance of Support** also known as a 'bond'. This document makes the sponsoring relative or Assurer liable to repay any social security benefits, including unemployment benefits, if these are claimed by the newcomer from Australian governments or charities for the first two years of residence. Most migrants in the Family Migration category require a bond to be paid by the sponsor. Recent bond charges were $A10,000 for the primary applicant plus $A3,500 for each additional dependent. No bond is required for children. The bond is refundable after two years, but the Commonwealth Bank of Australia administrative fee of $A200 for two applicants (or $A150 for a single bond) is not.

Submission of form

After the sponsor has filled in the Sponsorship for Migration form, it must be sent to you (the applicant) with any supporting documents and a number of forms to be completed and returned to the nearest Australian migration office at a high commission or embassy.

Migration rules for Family Stream applicants

The Points Test, which many applicants for migration need to pass in order to obtain permission to go to Australia, does not apply to applicants in the 'immediate family' category. On satisfying health and character requirements, their close relationship to the sponsor is usually sufficient for them to receive a visa. Here is a summary of the family relationships on which your application to become a Preferential Family migrant can be based:

Spouses

Approval for migration is **not** automatic, and spouses must first be assessed for economic status, good health and character. The authorities are aware that some Australians are paid to participate in marriages of convenience, so the spouse may also be judged on his/ her sincerity as a marriage partner if migration officers become suspicious. A one-year cohabitation rule has been introduced, and means that couples need to prove they have lived together for at least one year before making their application.

Other factors that may be considered in deciding whether partners are in a genuine relationship include:

◆ knowledge of each other's personal circumstances;
◆ financial arrangements such as joint bank accounts;
◆ joint memberships of social clubs, sporting activities etc.,
◆ joint travel.

Children

If unmarried and still part of the sponsor's family unit, children must first be assessed for good health and character. If older than 18 and independent, see the Concessional Family Category.

Parents

If sponsored parents are of retirement age or older, they are assessed for good health and character. Though aged parents often fail the medical requirements, this is no barrier in most cases unless the person's condition is catastrophic (e.g. they are permanently hospitalised or with a communicable disease). The sponsor is also obliged to give an Assurance of Support. If parents are of working age and they are assessed to have a good chance of a successful settlement in Australia, the sponsor must pre-arrange employment and, in any case, the sponsor's Assurance of Support will still be required.

Parents admitted as Preferential Family category must also meet the **balance of family** criteria which aims to reduce the high percentage of the quota being filled by aged parents wanting to join children in Australia, but with other options because they have strong family links elsewhere.

Barring migrants who through old age or lack of skills are of little economic advantage to Australia and who don't qualify on compassionate grounds because they have family elsewhere may seem tough. However, this policy reduces the burden on Australian tax-payers through government health and welfare payments. For the 'balance of family' criteria, the applicant parent must have:

◆ at least an equal number of children lawfully and permanently in Australia as overseas.

Prospective marriage partner
These are admitted at first on a temporary basis for up to nine months. Within that period, the marriage must take place and the application for permanent residency must be made. Proof of a genuine marriage (see above, section on spouses), will make them eligible for permanent residency. A fiancé must be genuinely known to the sponsor, not just coming to Australia for an arranged marriage, and the couple must have a real intention to marry. Fiancés are assessed for good health and character.

Orphans, Special Need Relatives and Last Remaining Relative
Family reunion provisions may also be extended for cases like children for adoption, certain orphans, relatives required to help overcome a serious family crisis such as death or a prolonged

illness, and wholly supported relatives over retirement age. There are also concessions for brothers, sisters and non-dependent children who are the last family members living outside Australia.

English language assessment and charges

All applicants are required to give details of their ability to speak, write and understand English. Some applicants need to prove this ability by giving details of where they were educated, the results of the Australian Assessment of Communicative English Skills test or the results of the International English Language Testing System. Certain successful applicants in the Family and Economic categories will need to pay for English language courses in Australia, except for successful applicants in the Preferential Family and certain Special Assistance migrants (e.g. refugees). For instance, a primary applicant seeking a visa under the Employer Nomination Scheme who does not prove he/she has functional English must pay $A4,080. A spouse or adult dependant must pay $A2,040 each in charges. On arrival in Australia, migrants who have paid the charge receive up to 510 hours of English tuition.

There is a scale of English charges depending on the category of the primary applicant, from $A4,080 to $A1,020 at the time of writing.

GENERAL SKILLED MIGRATION PROGRAMME

This category of Australia's migration programme is one of the most politically sensitive of the Immigration programmes. The General Skilled category has been honed and expanded in recent years, reflecting changes in world and Australian economies. Most recently the term 'regional' has been added to create new subcategories which are designed to encourage skilled or business immigrants to settle in the relatively underpopulated regions of Australia that may benefit from an economic boost. While the state and federal governments maintain the power to change the regions where settlers are encouraged to put down roots from time to time, 'regional migration' covers areas outside the main metropolitan centres of Perth, Melbourne, Brisbane and South East Queensland as well as areas outside the most populous state, New South Wales.

Employers have worked more closely with government immigration assessment centres in key countries to recruit workers where there are labour shortages. The countries targeted include Britain, India, South Africa, Sri Lanka and the Philippines. The skills and trades where Australian employers report a critical shortage include child care, plumbing, electricians, motor mechanics, carpenters and joiners, bricklayers, hairdressers and refrigeration and air conditioning mechanics. The building industry, hospitality sector and manufacturing industries reported serious shortages in trained and qualified workers at the time of writing. There is a growing emphasis on English language proficiency and a new 18-month Skilled Graduate visa to help would-be settlers with desirable qualities transition towards full migration.

Skilled Migration subcategories are the most complex of the various routes by which newcomers may gain permanent residency. However, if you fulfil the criteria, this is also the most desirable of migrant categories as far as the Australian authorities are concerned. The Skilled Migration gives the green light to some 60,000 newcomers each year – about 40% of the entire annual immigration intake.

Skilled Migration subcategories

◆ **Labour Agreement** is for applicants proving specified skills, qualifications and experience under a labour agreement. You must be nominated by an employer within the framework of a labour agreement, which provides for permanent entry of workers with skills in demand for certain industries.

◆ **Employer Nomination** allows migration of highly skilled people to fill jobs that cannot be filled from within Australia's labour force. You must be nominated by an Australian employer and have the skills, qualifications and experience matching the particular job.

◆ **Distinguished Talent** is for people who have distinguished careers internationally through special creative or sporting talents, or who can otherwise prove they have outstanding abilities of benefit to Australia.

◆ **Australian-Linked** allows Australian residents to sponsor relatives whose education, employability and skills will contribute to the Australian economy. They must be of working age and pass the Points Test. Points are awarded for skills, age and English language ability. Siblings, nephews, nieces, non-dependent children and working-age parents of the sponsor may apply under this category.

◆ **Regional Linked** allows sponsorship of skilled relatives (see Australian-Linked above) who are willing to live in less populated areas of Australia, and have the skills to obtain work in such areas. The aim is to encourage newcomers to settle in places other than Sydney and Melbourne. As an incentive to people to come to Australia under this subcategory, no points test is applied. However, the sponsors must also live in the areas designated by the government as desirable locations for new skilled immigrants.

♦ **Regional Sponsored Migration Scheme**, as mentioned, is a relatively new category which allows employers in designated regions of Australia to nominate overseas personnel for permanent residency. The employer must show the position cannot be filled locally, and the nomination must be for a full-time vacancy with a two-year work contract.

♦ **Independent migrants**, the largest category of skilled people allowed to migrate to Australia each year. People are selected on the basis of their education, skills and work experience. They are deemed to be likely to contribute quickly to Australia's economy. A points test applies, awarded for skills, age and English language ability (see page 107 on the Points Test).

♦ **Business Skills** is a category allowing migration on the basis of established skills in business and/or investment. Applicants must have recent experience running a successful business, as owner, part owner, or as a senior executive of a large company. There is a Business Skills Points Test which applicants must pass. Points are awarded for the size and sector of the business as well as age, ability in English, and assets. Extra points are awarded for sponsorship of the individual by an Australian State or Territory.

Special requirements for Business Skills applicants
In this subcategory of the overall Skilled Stream category, an assets test as well as a points test applies in some cases, while other applicants may need to show the wealth of their employer

and prove their seniority and experience. The main subclasses within the Business Skills category are:

- business owner;

- investment linked, proposing to make an investment in a State or Territory government security of between $A750,000 and $A2 million for a period of three years and to demonstrate that you have assets worth at least 50% more than the proposed Australian investment, as well as meeting criteria of age and English language;

- senior executive.

If you think you fall into one of these groups, it may be possible to gain sponsorship for your application from a regional government. Such sponsorship may smooth your path, or you and your family may prefer to retain a degree of independence, or find an employer to be a more convenient sponsor.

State/Territory Specific Migration (Business Skills)
This subcategory of the Business Skills area is a focus for the governments of Australia's states and territories. They take an active role in the selection and encouragement of businesspeople and investors who agree to live in a particular part of Australia. The governments offer support in the application process, sponsorship and a range of business information for appropriate candidates. This is covered in more detail in Chapter 13 on locations and incentives.

The sub groupings for State/Territory Specific Migration are:

- investment linked – for owners or part owners of investments and/or business; this allows business migrants to invest money in Australia for three years instead of the usual requirement to engage in a business venture;

- established businesses in Australia – which allows temporary entrants who have established successful businesses to seek permanent residence in Australia;

- regional established business in Australia – as above, plus the business is located in a region of Australia that the government seeks to develop via migration.

As owner or part owner of a business you will need to meet a range of quantitative and qualitative requirements, including:

- net assets in the business amounting to not less than $A300,000 ($A250,000 for an established Australian-located business) for two of the past four years. Your spouse's net assets in business can also be included. 'Net assets' may be:
  – equity in business
  – shares (if your shares are held in a publicly listed company you must hold at least 10% of listed shares)
  – property in your or your spouse's name, where it is clearly part of a business operation;

- you have not been involved in unacceptable business investments;

- you have been actively involved in and responsible for the overall management direction and performance of a business on a day-to-day basis for two of the last four years;

- if it is an established business in Australia, you have been resident for at least nine months of the 12 months immediately prior to your application for permanent residency;

- regional established business people must also show the enterprise had achieved annual exports of $A100,000 or annual turnover of $A200,000 for each of the two years prior to the application.

As a senior executive employee of a major business you will need to show that:

- you have been employed by a major business that has an annual turnover of at least $A50 million for two of the past four years. If you are sponsored by a State or Territory government business development agency, the annual turnover required in two of the last four years is $A10 million;

- you have been employed at the top strategic levels of management of a major business for two of the last four years, in which you have been responsible for strategic policy development affecting a major component or a wide range of operations.

However, if you have been employed by a government business enterprise in two of the last four years you cannot qualify as a senior executive in the Business Skills Migration subcategory.

There are stringent English language requirements since 2007 and extra requirements that all Business Skills applicants must meet, to convince the immigration authorities that they are genuine in their intention to settle permanently in Australia and that their future business plans will benefit the Australian economy. These requirements include one or more of the following:

- demonstrate that their proposed business activities in Australia would develop business links with international markets

- show their proposed activities would create or maintain
  employment in Australia or export Australian goods and
  services

- substitute Australian made products for goods that would
  otherwise be imported

- introduce or utilise new or improved technology

- contribute to Australia's pool of commercial and
  entrepreneurial expertise.

As an owner or part owner of an eligible investment you will need to
meet a range of requirements, including being able to show:

◆ a record of successful business and/or investment;

◆ a total of three years' experience in actively managing a business
  and/or investment;

◆ in one of the past five years you maintained direct and
  continuous involvement in the management of your qualifying
  business and/or eligible investment and that you and your spouse
  must have had at least 10% shareholding in the business, or
  investments to the value of at least $A1 million.

Furthermore, the applicant must show evidence of an overall
successful business career, have not been involved in business
activities which are not generally acceptable in Australia and
obtain the required points for the Business Skills Points Test.

Also, the applicant must at least be registered with an Australian
State or Territory government business agency and at best gain the
sponsorship (and extra points in the test) of that agency.

To apply as a Business Skills migrant, you should enquire at the nearest Australian embassy or high commission and obtain an up-to-date application package. This package will include a **State/ Territory Registration Form 927** and you should send it to the State or Territory agency in Australia in which you intend to go into business. The names and addresses of these State and Territory government agencies are on form 927.

After arrival in Australia
Business Skills migrants receive unconditional visas valid for multiple return journeys to and from Australia, usually for four years. Once in Australia as a business migrant, you will have the same freedom of activity in both personal and business terms as all other permanent residents. At the end of three years your multiple re-entry facility will usually be extended if you have spent two of the three years in Australia, or if you can demonstrate that you have engaged in a business(es) which meet the objective of the Business Skills category, as mentioned above.

The Australian government will require you to keep it informed of your current residential address in Australia for three years after arrival. You will also be obliged to participate in annual monitoring surveys regarding your business progress at 12, 24 and 36 months after your arrival in Australia. Recent survey results show that within three years of arrival almost half of the business migrants employed about four people in each of their new businesses in Australia. On average some $A677,000 had been transferred to Australia in the first three years after arrival and the average amount invested in a business was $A317,000. It appears the tough entry requirements are justified in terms of the Australian government's strategy to boost employment while improving the national balance of import to export payments. Over 60% of the new business migrants had an annual turnover from their Australian ventures, and 11% had export earnings over $A1 million. The most likely export market for business migrants is South East Asia. The top source countries for business migrants to Australia are Indonesia, South Africa, Taiwan, Malaysia, United Kingdom, Singapore, Hong Kong, Zimbabwe and Kenya.

However, if monitoring shows that no significant steps have been taken towards engaging in business within three years of arrival, the Immigration Minister has the power to cancel the right to Australian residence of the business person and his/her family.

The Points Test

Over the years many applicants had their cases assessed on the basis of a Points Test. The points test is targeted at giving the 'right' applicants maximum points.

The test is applied to only two categories of migrants:

◆ Skilled-Australian linked applicants in the Skilled Stream, who are sponsored by a relative;

◆ Independent applicants, with no sponsor.

The Points Test favours applicants in the Skilled-Australian linked category because:

◆ they win extra points for having a sponsoring relative, especially if that person is an Australian citizen, has been resident and in continuous employment for two years;

- the passmark is lower than for applicants in the Independent category.

Under the Points Test, marks are allocated, amongst other things, for:

- age (no points for those over the age of 50 or under 18, highest points for 18–29 years);

- employability, including age and skills subfactors;

- relationship to a sponsor – the fact you have a sponsoring relative wins points;

- citizenship – extra points if the sponsor is an Australian citizen;

- settlement prospects, based on whether the sponsor has been continuously employed in Australia;

- location (extra points may be awarded if the sponsor has lived in a designated locality – usually a sparsely populated area – identified by the government).

Passmarks

There are two levels of passmark:

- Pool Entrance Mark (90 for Skilled-Australian linked and 95 for Independent migrants in the Skill Migration category at time of writing);

- Passmark (85 for Skilled-Australian linked, 100 for independent migrants in the Skill Migration category at time of writing).

People who achieve or exceed the Pool Entrance have their application placed into a pool of applicants to be considered within the next 12 months. If your application is in the pool but your score falls below any new passmark, your application will be refused.

The number of points you need to pass migration requirements is **floating** – in other words, the number of points needed to 'pass' are reviewed by the Department of Immigration, according to supply and demand of would-be migrants.

For example, if there are so many people achieving the Pool Entrance Mark that the Concessional Family quota for that year is likely to be full to overflowing, the passmark is raised. If there are not enough people applying to fill the quota, the passmarks may be dropped slightly.

Those who fail to reach the Pool Entrance Mark but attain the Passmark have their application placed in a pool. Their score is compared with the next passmark, announced by the Department of Immigration during the year. If the applicant's points are equal to or greater than the new passmark, they are likely to be granted residence. If not, the applicant remains in the pool and their point score is compared with the next passmark. If the application has been in the pool and the score remains below the pass mark for 12 months, the application will be refused.

If your mark remains below the Pool Passmark on all three occasions, your application will be dropped from the pool – and is considered to have failed.

As well as the Points Test, the usual health and character checks apply, and applications may be refused if good health and character standards are not met.

Other applicants or people with special eligibility

A few people will find they stand a good chance of permanent residency in Australia because they are:

◆ former Australian citizens who have maintained ties with the country but lost their citizenship because of one of a number of prescribed circumstances (see also Resumption of Citizenship later in this chapter); *or*

◆ people who spent formative years in Australia and have maintained ties there.

HUMANITARIAN AND SPECIAL ASSISTANCE CATEGORY

This is the third main stream of the migration policy, and applies mainly to refugees, displaced persons and other applicants granted permanent residence on humanitarian grounds. The programme has about 12,000 places with a range of subcategories, some of which apply to those who don't make it under the Points Test from other categories. Refugee and humanitarian subcategories have included thousands of refugees mostly from Indo-China, former Yugoslavia, the former USSR, the Middle East and the Sudan in recent years. The Australian government is under continued pressure to review and justify the intake of newcomers in this category is perceived to be conservative in regard to assessment of people applying for immigration on humanitarian grounds.

GRANT OF RESIDENCE STATUS

People already in Australia on tourist or temporary visas may also apply for permanent migration under special circumstances. People who have studied and worked in Australia successfully may be allowed permanent residency in some cases. The visitor's family overseas may have died while he or she was in Australia. That applicant can also show strong links to Australia, which may help them make a case to stay. Or the visitor may have fallen in love with and plan to marry an Australian, or does not want to return to his or her own country for fear of political persecution. Migration officials must be convinced that each case is genuine and pay careful attention to the details during their investigations. They are well aware, for instance, that some would-be settlers try a marriage of convenience; sometimes paying money to an Australian citizen willing to wed or enter into a de facto relationship with them.

THE APPLICATION PROCESS

How long does it take?

The time taken by different migration offices to process an immigration application is variable. If you live in a place where there is no Australian immigration office, it may be necessary to send your application to a nearby country and even travel there for interviews. There have been cutbacks and staff shortages in Australian immigration offices around the world which have slowed the rate of application processing, even though personal interviews are no longer required in most cases.

Nevertheless, new streamlined points assessment procedures and other improvements, such as the immigration information sheets on the Points Test which allow self-assessment by the applicant, have improved the speed and efficiency of the service. Processing time also depends on which category you are applying for.

Requests by immigration officers for applicants to meet them for a face-to-face interview or counselling are the exception, rather than the rule.

To do all you can to encourage an early decision, make sure all relevant requested documentary evidence is enclosed with your application. To avoid delays make sure valid birth, marriage, and educational certificates, accountants' statements, and anything else the Australian government needs to decide your eligibility, are enclosed when you send in your application papers.

At the time of writing, the authorities suggested that three to six months is the average wait for approval – or otherwise – of your application, if in the Family Migration category. But it takes about eight months in most other categories. There may be extra delays due to time needed to arrange a job in Australia in advance, if this is relevant to the application, or for checks of professional, trade and education qualifications, as well as the mandatory health and character assessments.

Getting help

State and non-government ethnic advisory councils and services are available in the big cities to give advice suited to your circumstances and plans both before you finalise an application and, if successful, after you start living in Australia.

There are also some basic services provided by the federal immigration authorities to help migrants after they arrive. Most of these programmes are for people arriving as refugees or with specific English language problems, and include English courses and fee-free translator services.

For other information, try contacting the relevant trade unions, ethnic communities and professional, educational or business organisations in Australia, and of course friends or relatives already living there.

Government trade officials and state governments are represented around the world and may provide some counselling and assistance with research and planning for the move, as indicated in other sections of this book. See also the list of useful addresses for the possible sources of advice and counselling around the world.

MIGRATION AGENTS

Migration agents may provide a useful service for working people in the planning and application process for Australian migration. Their effectiveness largely depends on how closely your country of origin's government monitors migration agents. In Australia, especially for people who are already trying to extend their stay or sort out migration difficulties on behalf of someone else, migration agents may be useful. However, they have a somewhat dodgy reputation because they may not have the skills necessary to deliver an effective service. If migration agents, as a profession, are well regulated in your country and you are too busy to take on the workload of steering your application through the

Australian (and local) authorities, then it may be worth while to pay for advice about and execution of your application. However, there are many unhappy people in Australian immigration detention centres or who have been deported after spending relatively huge amounts on unreliable migration agents.

TO-ING AND FRO-ING

If and when your application for permanent residence as an immigrant to Australia is successful, you will be issued with a **resident return** visa along with your migrant visa. The resident return visa allows the bearer to enter and re-enter Australia any number of times. It is normally valid for 12 months from the date of issue of the visa to migrate to Australia in the first place. In other words, you are expected to make the move to Australia within 12 months of receiving the necessary permanent residence visa. After you enter Australia as an immigrant, the resident return visa comes into force and is normally valid for three years or the life of the bearer's passport, the maximum period for validity being five years.

This document, which allows you to come and go freely in the first three years of settlement, is useful for people in the process of restarting or transferring a business or commercial venture to Australia, selling or transferring financial assets outside Australia, or wanting to see friends and relatives in their country of origin in an emergency or simply because they are homesick.

However, the Australian authorities will not be happy to renew this resident return visa if the bearer has been coming and going to such a degree that he or she has been out of the country for one year, or more, of the past three. Your permission to stay on as a permanent resident may be withdrawn, if the authorities believe that you were in Australia for so little time that you could not have been serious about making a new life there. The authorities will consider the individual's circumstances, however – you may have had good personal or business reasons for remaining outside Australia for more than one out of three years since you emigrated.

Of course, those who become Australian citizens (see below) after migrating to Australia will not need to renew their resident return visa each time they take a trip overseas and want to re-enter Australia.

Appeals against decisions involving migrants
If your application for renewal of your resident return visa or any other matter to do with migration is refused, appeals can be made to officers of the Department of Immigration, Local Government and Ethnic Affairs in Australia. **Immigration Review Panels** consider cases on their merits and make the final decision. Fees are charged for all appeals. In 2004 tough laws were passed to prevent migration agents giving misleading advice to vulnerable people. This follows many 'vexatious' claims by migration agents in Australia and now such experts will be required by law to hold professional indemnity insurance and make public the outcomes of any failed legal attempts on behalf of clients through the industry's registration authority. The aim is to stop newcomers wasting their money on what, sadly, may be unprofessional advice from unscrupulous migration agents.

Deportation

A resident who is not a citizen may also be deported if:

◆ he or she has been convicted of any offence within ten years of arriving in Australia and is sentenced to jail for a year or more;

◆ he or she has lived in Australia less than ten years and the Minister for Immigration decides that the person is a threat to the national security.

Appeals against deportation orders may be made to the Administrative Appeals Tribunal, the Federal Court or the High Court. The federal government ombudsman may also be able to consider the case and advise on the chances of a successful appeal.

AUSTRALIAN CITIZENSHIP

You may be wanting to certify your Australian descent or citizenship in order to live there – while everyone who migrates may one day decide to take the option of becoming Australian citizens to confirm their loyalty to their adopted country. However, the move to citizenship is quite a different matter from gaining permission to move there as a permanent resident, the initial status for most migrants. There is no obligation to take Australian citizenship if it does not suit you, though it is encouraged by the government.

Rules are changing to ensure new citizens are sincere and suitably well-integrated into the society before they can officially call themselves 'Australians'. You need to be a permanent resident for four years (rather than the two years that applied before 2007). You'll need to sign a pledge of commitment and pass an 'Aussie values' test in addition to meeting sterner English language requirements. How the authorities construct the questions for the Australian values is controversial. The test, introduced in 2007, has general knowledge questions covering facts about Australian history, lifestyle and values.

There is also growing emphasis on 'functional' English skills reflected in a new language test that has also raised the bar for citizenship – but anyone who has experienced the bizarre fusion of English mixed with, say, Russian or Mandarin, as spoken by many dinky-di citizens, would have to wonder at what passes as 'functional' English Down Under. Clearly, many immigrants who have been citizens for years couldn't hope to pass the general knowledge test or the language component, but the government hopes that those with poor English will be motivated to learn more about their new country, faster, in order to obtain the privileges of citizenship.

People with disabilities or who are under 18 or over 60 are exempted from the citizenship tests. If you fail, your current visa status is not affected.

Before looking at the rules, consider what Australian citizenship entails. In contrast to permanent residents, Australian citizens:

◆ Can take out an **Australian passport**;

◆ Can **re-enter Australia** from abroad without permission or visa;

◆ Have the right to be **protected by Australian diplomatic arrangements** when overseas;

- May **stand for election** to state or federal parliaments;

- **Must vote**. Citizens may be fined if registered on an electoral roll but fail to cast a vote in person or by postal ballot at state, territory and federal elections, unless electoral officers are satisfied with the reason why that citizen could not fulfil this duty;

- May be **employed permanently in the government public service** and stand for any public office (unless that person is a British citizen, as is still the case in some states of Australia, when the job applicant has the same rights as an Australian citizen);

- Can apply for **full welfare benefits**. If they have entered under the Family Migration category, sponsors who have signed an Assurance of Support are still obliged to repay these benefits to governments or charities in full within the first five years of the migrant becoming resident.

Pledge of allegiance

Citizenship and a certificate to state the person's new nationality is granted at a formal ceremony in which people are required to pledge allegiance to Australia. A fee must be paid for the issue of such a certificate to cover the processing of the application.

To apply, a permanent resident must have spent two out of the previous five years living in Australia, excluding any time they were outside the country for business trips, holidays and so on. A permanent resident qualifying for citizenship must have spent:

- two years in Australia out of the previous five years;

- 12 months in the two years immediately prior to the application in Australia.

Also, the applicant must be of good character and over 18 years old.

LOSING AND RENOUNCING AUSTRALIAN CITIZENSHIP

Australians who have applied for, or been born to, Australian citizenship may also lose this status, with its rights and privileges, under certain circumstances. If they choose to take the citizenship of another country (other than automatically, such as by birth or marriage) Australians may have their citizenship withdrawn. It does not matter where they live when they acquire the other citizenship. On the other hand, a person marrying a citizen of another country and acquiring the additional citizenship as a 'side effect' of the marriage, need not forfeit their Australian nationality as a result, *if the law of the other country allows the person to retain their previous citizenship.* But if an Australian citizen marries a citizen of another country and then applies to assume that foreign citizenship by registration or some other way, he or she may cease to be an Australian citizen.

Renunciation of citizenship

A person older than 18 may also renounce their Australian citizenship by completing a special form and by sending it to the Department of Immigration and Ethnic Affairs in Australia, or to the nearest Australian embassy or high commission, if they are outside the country. However, the government may refuse to approve the renunciation if the person would become stateless as a result (by having no other citizenship) or if the Minister for Immigration and Ethnic Affairs considers that it is not in Australia's interest to grant the application.

Deprivation of citizenship

People may be deprived of their citizenship, inside or outside Australia, if:

◆ convicted of having provided false or misleading information, or of concealing important information when applying for citizenship;

◆ convicted in Australia or abroad of an offence committed before citizenship was granted and if sentenced to death or imprisonment for 12 months or more;

◆ their parent or guardian loses Australian citizenship, so children under 18 may also be deprived of Australian citizenship too. However, the children would not be affected if this withdrawal would leave them stateless or if they have one responsible parent or guardian who remains an Australian citizen.

Resumption of citizenship and Commonwealth citizens

A person who loses Australian citizenship for any reason before his or her 18th birthday must make a declaration within a year of turning 18 that they wish to resume that citizenship. When Australia revised its citizenship laws in 1984 the federal government approved the repeal of **British Subject Status**. In the past, this had given the citizens of other member countries of the British Commonwealth some advantage in Australia. However, this repeal of old laws will not be effective around Australia until the state governments update their legislation with regard to British subjects. As far as citizenship is concerned, immigrants from other Commonwealth countries must meet the same requirements for Australian citizenship as permanent residents from any other countries.

According to the rules on the matter, the applicant must also:

◆ intend to live in Australia permanently; *and*
◆ maintain 'a close and continuing association with Australia'.

But some people need not have lived in Australia for two years, as defined above. Provided the applicant is a permanent resident, the two-year rule may be waived if the person:

◆ is the husband, wife or widow of an Australian citizen;

◆ a child under the age of 16 included in a parent's application or if there are 'special circumstances' applying to children under 18 years of age;

◆ has spent at least three months in Australia's permanent defence forces;

◆ is a former Australian citizen or born in Australia. Such applicants can ask for citizenship again if they have lived in Australia as a permanent resident for 12 months of the previous two years.

People who have renounced Australian citizenship must wait at least 12 months before they can apply to become citizens again.

Citizenship applications from abroad

Though it is usual for applicants to be living in Australia when they apply for citizenship, and so are available for an interview to determine good character and for the citizenship ceremony which follows, citizenship can be granted to people living abroad under certain circumstances. Australian citizenship can be granted in another country to:

- spouses, widows or widowers of an Australian citizen;

- children adopted overseas by Australian citizens;

- people engaged in activities overseas which the Minister for Immigration and Ethnic Affairs considers beneficial to the interest of Australia.

Such people must have been approved for permanent residence and plan to live in Australia and 'maintain a close and continuing association' with Australia.

Other citizenship requirements

The other requirements for people hoping to be approved for Australian citizenship include the ability to speak and understand basic English; understand the responsibilities and privileges of Australian citizenship; and be of good character. However, some people are exempt from requirements regarding knowledge of English and privileges of Australian citizenship if they are spouses, widows or widowers of Australian citizens, suffer from a substantial hearing, speech or sight disability, or are older than 60.

Children born in Australia or one of its territories have an automatic right to citizenship. Children born outside Australia to Australian parent(s) can be registered as citizens under the law of citizenship by descent. The parent(s) or guardian(s) – if the Australian parent(s) are dead or no longer have legal custody of the child – can apply on behalf of the child. If the child is 18 or more, it is *not possible* for them to acquire Australian citizenship in this way.

People who have gained citizenship by descent *cannot* register their children as citizens unless the parent(s) has been legally present in Australia for at least two years at any time before the date of application for registration. However, people who become Australian citizens by other means than by descent – those who were born there – can apply to have their children under the age of 18 registered as Australian citizens by descent, whether or not they or the children have lived there.

6

Foreign Qualifications and Studying in Australia

This section is a guide for prospective:

◆ **Private overseas students**. Do you want to come to Australia temporarily, as a student? Australia actively encourages foreign students to take advantage of a multitude of tertiary and training facilities that it offers at private and state universities and colleges. Some students apply to stay in Australia as permanent residents and success may be assured if you undertake to live in more sparsely populated areas. For details of school and university life, see Chapter 12 on Education in Australia;

◆ **Professionals and skilled migrants**. Do you have qualifications, degrees, certificates or other proof of a skill, expertise or education gained which you need in order to apply for a position, or to practise your trade or profession in Australia? There is a special Australian educational body, the National Office of Overseas Skills Recognition (NOOSR) available to assist you. If you are a tradesperson, then assessment of your skills can be made via Trades Recognition Australia, part of the Australian Department of Employment and Workplace Relations.

NATIONAL OFFICE OF OVERSEAS SKILLS RECOGNITION (NOOSR)

Are you hoping to study in or to *migrate* to Australia? Whatever the grounds for your application, it is likely that assessment of your qualifications either at the Immigration Department post in your country, or by application directly to NOOSR will be necessary. NOOSR is run via the Department of Science, Education and Training. Migration authorities will advise you on whether you definitely need NOOSR's recognition of your training or expertise to work in your field. The Australian Assessing Authority relevant to your employment skills or qualifications undertakes to assess the credentials of would-be immigrants under one of the general skilled migration categories. The fee payable for non-residents is $A300 but if the assessment is required after you have arrived in Australia (for instance because it was not essential to your skilled migration application) the fee is $A145. If you are not a permanent resident but living in Australia when you apply for a skills assessment the fee is $A300.

Even if you are only going to Australia for a *temporary posting* with an employer, or as a *working holidaymaker*, you may need NOOSR's assessment in order to work in your trade or profession. Once again, authorities at the Australian embassy or high commission where the application is made will advise you if you need to check with NOOSR.

NOOSR has panels and advisory councils to check that foreign educational and training qualifications parallel the standards and knowledge expected of people practising in a particular field in Australia. Usually the Australian professional body conducts the assessments required by NOOSR, which helps Australian professional organisations to maintain uniform entry and practice standards in their field.

Often, a degree or certificate that comes from a recognised educational institution in an English-speaking country will present few complications for assessment. If you have not received an English language education, nor speak it as a first or mother tongue, NOOSR will arrange for you to be examined for your ability to speak, read and write English to a standard acceptable for that profession in Australia. The Occupational English Test or International English Language Testing System (IELTS) may be required to demonstrate proficiency in reading, writing, listening and speaking English. This test is often required by the visa application process and costs \$A150–\$A400 at the time of writing.

Growing demand for tradespeople

Thousands of people a year apply to Trades Recognition Australia, if they have trade qualifications to be assessed. There has been a major increase in immigration places for overseas-trained people in fields like nursing, engineering, computing, occupational therapy, and in many skilled areas of manufacturing, engineering and building trades. Eligible applicants are issued with an Australian Recognised Trade Certificate which is accepted nationally. You may also have overseas trade skills recognised under the Australian Quality Training Framework through registered training organisations within Australia. Contact a state or territory government vocation or training authority for information for that part of Australia.

In the case of Trades Recognition Australia, assessment may be made on the basis of a trade test including a practical and/or theory examination. You may be asked to attend an interview and English language skills are an important factor, along with documentation to prove you have served an apprenticeship and/or achieved certification in the trade. At least six years' experience is usually required of a person applying as a skilled tradesperson. In addition, some professions require occupational English as part of the assessment. This test is conducted by the National Language and Literacy Institute of Australia.

Assessment methods for professionals

NOOSR panels making assessment of professional qualifications rely on examinations or some other form of assessment relevant to the skill or profession an applicant hopes to practise in Australia. NOOSR has evolved a system of formal examinations and assessments designed by experts in Australia in the following professions:

◆ accounting
◆ architecture

- dentistry
- dietetics
- engineering
- information and communications technology
- librarianship
- medical radiation science
- nursing
- occupational therapy
- optometry
- pharmacy
- physiotherapy
- podiatry
- quantity surveying
- social work and welfare work
- speech pathology
- teaching
- translating and interpreting
- veterinary science.

Fees

Whether the applicant fails or passes, fees are charged for examinations as well as for some NOOSR literature. The table below gives a rough guide to amounts you can expect to pay in Australian dollars. Fees are subject to change without notice:

NOOSR Assessment Handling Charge	$A300
For Occupational English examination	$A300–350
Trades Recognition Australia assessment handling fee	$A355
Issue of Australia Recognised Certificate to a tradesperson overseas	$A90
Trade Test (if required)	$A270

Additional fees for recognition of professional skills may range from $A200 to over $A1,000, depending on the qualification being assessed.

Assessment policy

There is a certain amount of politics and power-play in these assessments. Australians who are already in professional, technical and other jobs requiring high levels of education or training are naturally keen to prevent their market and earning-power being reduced by competition from newcomers. Furthermore, foreign training often has aspects not covered in Australia, and vice versa. Yet Australian governments and those with the best interests of the community in mind realise that rejection of many applicants could mean missing out on an international pool of talent and expertise essential to the building up of industry and society.

Additionally, people with a non-English language background may find that Australian professionals regard foreign qualifications with some reservations. Many migrants are forced to work in less than adequate jobs, considering the standard of their education, if not recognised by their Australian colleagues through a NOOSR assessment. Even a favourable assessment is not a guarantee of professional recognition or employment in the field.

BRIDGING FOR OVERSEAS-TRAINED PROFESSIONALS

There is a federal government funded loan scheme administered by the Department of Education, Science and Training to help overseas trained professionals who are already Australian residents but do not meet requirements to practise in Australia.

This loan scheme is called Bridging for Overseas-Trained Professionals Loan Scheme (BOTPLS) and successful applicants receive loans to help pay the fees for bridging courses that may be necessary. It is similar to the HECS loans mentioned in more detail in Chapter 12 and permits the borrower to repay after graduation. The areas of study available depend on demand for certain professionals in Australia. Currently this list includes accountants, lawyers, medical practitioners, nurses and social workers. Eligible BOTPLS courses must not exceed one year of full-time study (or part-time equivalent).

Australian professions and trade organisations
Generally, the national ruling bodies of the various professions and trades require an immigrant to have their qualifications recognised by them, so he or she can legally work in that profession in Australia. Professional organisations and trade associations represent the interests of their members to the public as well as the governments in Australia. They actively lobby and advise on fees and working conditions, and enforce a code of conduct for their members.

Industry and professional websites are a good place to seek information on the professions and assessable skilled trades and their procedures. The following contact list may prove useful:

- (NOOSR) National Office of Overseas Skills Recognition, GPO Box 1407, Canberra ACT 2601, Australia;

- Trades Recognition Australia: Department of Employment and Workplace Relations, GPO Box 9879 in the capital city of each of Australia's states and territories;

- Website for the Department of Science, Education and Training: www.dest.gov.au/noosr

- Trades Recognition Australia, Department of Employment and Workplace Relations, GPO Box 9879 Canberra ACT 2601. Telephone enquiries: + 61261217456.

- www.anta.gov.au for more on Australian Quality Training Framework;

- Occupational English Test (OET), GPO Box 372 F Melbourne, Vic 3001;

- International English Language Testing System (IELTS), GPO Box 2006, Canberra 2601 ACT. www. ielts@idp.edu.au

OVERSEAS STUDENTS

Nearly 250,000 foreign students were studying in Australia, mainly attending universities and tertiary colleges located in the major cities. Many are enrolled in English language courses and the majority of people entering Australia on a student visa are from the Asian region. They contribute some $A5 billion a year in export earnings and educational institutions in Australia are increasingly dependent on foreign students for income, as government funding is limited. At some universities, such as Central Queensland University, up to 40% of students are from outside Australia while better known 'establishment' universities are comfortable with up to 30% of full-fee paying students from other countries. In Australia universities and colleges offer places to local students who mostly pay lower fees than their overseas counterparts through a government financed student loan scheme (see HECS loans on page 278 and 378).

All foreign students must enter Australia on a full fee-paying basis. There are no quotas placed on the numbers of overseas students entering the country – access is limited only by the capacity of institutions to take such students. All students from overseas are granted a multistyle entry visa to a maximum of five years.

All applicants are welcome, as long as they can meet certain academic, language and social requirements and can pay the fees. Since the number of places available at universities and colleges can be very limited, competition for temporary entry under this provision is tough. Many foreign students are motivated by hopes of points towards their application for permanent residency, after they complete their course. In 2005 some 13,312 former students gained visas under this provision (see also section Staying On, page 136). However, poor English of Australian-education overseas students has linked a surprising inability for such immigrants to find jobs in their field (see below). In addition, there has been some abuse of student visas such as working illegally and overstaying the term of the visa, so students applying from certain countries must prove their intention to study is genuine. A number of countries have been 'gazetted' by Australia's student immigration authorities as unlikely to cause such visa problems. Most of Australia's main source countries for foreign students are from gazetted countries, which means they do not need to show their application is genuine. Applicants from non-gazetted countries will need to show a high level of English comprehension and proof of qualifications – a process aimed to prove the applicant is genuine in wanting to study in Australia. (At present some 16% of students at Australian universities are from overseas and growing rapidly as universities expand to meet demand. About 75,000 more students study via Australian tertiary institutions from their home countries.) Australia has a higher proportion of foreign students attending its universities than the UK and USA, which have the largest numbers of foreign students at their universities and colleges in the world. So while Australia lags as a global educational destination in terms of numbers, it is the country with the highest percentage of non-resident students, limited only by its own small population in the tertiary places it can provide.

Admission

Would-be students must write to the institution at which they wish to study to ascertain whether there is a place for them on the proposed course. When writing to an institution, students should specify the field in which they wish to study. The institution will advise students whether they meet its academic and English language requirements. There have been complaints in recent years by former overseas students that classes were held back by the inability of some students to understand or express themselves in English at university level. Despite the financial attractions of a large foreign student body, Australian tertiary institutions are screening more seriously to ensure students have adequate English language skills. A standard visa processing fee applies. At the time of writing the (non-refundable) visa application fee for a student (temporary) visa was $A410.

Scholarships

The Australian government provides a limited number of undergraduate and postgraduate scholarships for overseas students to study in Australia. Most of these students come from developing countries under the government's foreign aid programme which is administered by the **Australian International Development Assistance Bureau** (AIDAB).

The **Department of Education, Science and Training** (DEST) administers postgraduate scholarships for students from developed countries. Scholarship benefits include full tuition, travel, and living costs or tuition only. Students interested in applying for a scholarship should obtain application forms and award conditions from the Registrar of the Australian educational institution of their choice or from any Australian diplomatic mission overseas.

Lodging your application

Australia's programme for the education of private overseas students is administered by the Federal Department of Education, Science and Training. The programme is competitive and expensive, since the policy is to charge the full cost of tuition – while students must also be able to support themselves and their dependants in Australia. Non-resident students must be studying full-time courses but are allowed to take part-time jobs (up to 20 hours a week while their course is in session – see below) only.

Applications must be lodged at an Australian embassy or high commission in the applicant's country of citizenship if requiring:

- formal studies – tertiary studies at Technical and Further Education (TAFE) college level or tertiary studies at undergraduate or postgraduate level;

- an English language course;

- occupational (on-the-job) or religious training;

- special studies at a private, fee-paying institution, for example secretarial and business colleges, or pilot training;

- study of miscellaneous subjects at a university or college of advanced education or other publicly funded institution which does *not* lead to an award of a degree or similar qualification;

- studies under exchange arrangements such as Rotary Youth Exchange between Australian and overseas educational institutions.

If you are thinking of applying as a private overseas student – or even for a scholarship to study under a fellowship or similar award – you must make it quite clear to Australia's authorities at the embassy or high commission in your country of citizenship that you:

- genuinely seek temporary entry to Australia for study purposes only;

- wish to enrol in an approved course of study at a university or college;

- will leave Australia when the course is finished, a requirement which must be agreed to in writing when you lodge an application for your temporary visa;

- have the financial capacity to meet all expenses, including the cost of the course, return fares and living expenses for the duration of your stay;

- have undertaken a medical test and X-ray examination to prove your good health;

- have taken out private medical insurance through the Medibank Private Overseas Student Health Cover facility.

Students can obtain information about institutions offering courses and educational institutions in Australia by contacting Australia Education International (contact details at the end of this chapter) from their nearest Australian embassy or high commission. Bear in mind that the Australian academic year may be quite different from that of your country, for colleges and universities. It runs from February to December, and tertiary institutions usually have semesters with short breaks in between and a summer holiday lasting about two months, following examinations in December.

Employment
Students who come to Australia on a student (temporary entry) visa are *not* entitled to take a full-time job. However, part-time work (up to 20 hours a week while their course is in session) and holiday jobs are allowed. Dependants of students of working age may be entitled to work full time.

Staying on
In most cases students must leave Australia when they finish their studies. They may apply to return as permanent residents after they return to their home country, if they satisfy the criteria for one of the usual migration categories. Yet one of the attractions for many overseas students is Australia's recent willingness to consider applications for permanent settlement, especially if the student agrees to live and work in one of Australia's less populated areas where their skills are needed. The number of overseas students permitted to stay on in Australia under the Skills Migration programme has been about 13,000 a year in recent times, and it is a boom area for immigration. However, rules about English proficiency before and after graduating are

stricter, after disappointing outcomes where skills were targeted by immigration authorities. A 2006 review of the outcomes of former students who became residents showed that many had very poor English and studied only because a particular field was 'in demand' for immigration purposes. As a result, less than half had gained employment using the qualification they gained while studying in Australia. From 2007, rules now require that more points will be given for better English language skills and relevant work experience and qualifications. Student applicants for permanent residency will also have to do a year of work experience, to prove they are really serious about contributing to Australia's economic needs by actually working in their field of study. In addition, students need to have studied in Australia for at least two years to obtain a visa. International students who are unable to meet stricter new requirements for permanent settlement or who want an alternative can apply for an 18-month Skilled Graduate Visa with unrestricted work rights.

DEPORTATIONS

Each year thousands of foreign students are deported for non-attendance of classes or working more hours than allowed under their visa. In NSW, for example, there has been closure of colleges claiming to provide courses for foreign students but actually functioning as illegal 'visa shops' for people with no intention of studying or who fail to meet study requirements of genuine courses and colleges. If a student is caught under such circumstances and deported, their chance of gaining official permission to immigrate to Australia has been virtually ruined under Australia's policies which are most unsympathetic to law breaking or illegal would-be immigrants.

The cost of study

As outlined in Chapter 12, tuition fees for tertiary study in Australia range from around $A40,000 to $A130,000 depending on the course and the university. See page 280 Chapter 12 for sample prices.

Australian universities each set their own fees and entry requirements for foreign students. They will also determine if any credits will be offered for previous study. There is a contact website at the end of this chapter for Australian universities.

ADDITIONAL COSTS OF LIVING AND STUDYING IN AUSTRALIA

Additional costs like books, union fees at tertiary institutions, and school uniforms (at high schools) must also be considered in planning your budget for living in Australia as a private overseas student. Tertiary students in Australia – except in cases of financial hardship – must pay an administrative charges of a few hundred dollars each.

The cost of living in Australia for a single student was estimated at the time of writing to be at least $A20,000 a year, plus another $A10,000 a year for each dependant (i.e. spouse or child) who joins the overseas student in Australia. These figures do not include the cost of travel to and from the country and may be offset by any money the student can earn by working part-time, within the terms of their visa.

Accommodation near major universities in Sydney and Melbourne has become 'gentrified' in recent years and rents can be high. Research by a real estate group of accommodation for foreign students in the three most popular centres for study (coastal Queensland, Melbourne and Sydney) estimated that the weekly rental costs for small student apartments, often built by private developers in partnership with local tertiary institutions, was $A120 to $A200 a week. The higher priced rooms will typically include all meals, electricity, gas and water charges.

Students on temporary visas must arrange private health insurance for themselves and their families because they can use Australia's government-subsidised Medicare health care and hospital system.

ENGLISH LANGUAGE REQUIREMENTS

In most cases, education institutions require applicants to have a knowledge of written and spoken English adequate for the level of the courses they propose to study. However, effective English comprehension and writing skills are said to be lacking among foreign students at many Australian campuses especially in courses like economics and business, where foreign students may constitute more than half the class. There is growing pressure to make English language skills tests more demanding of foreign students, to prevent lower academic standards and a resulting fall in the prestige of Australian universities. If English is not their mother tongue or the language in which they have gained their previous educational qualifications, applicants must pass the **Short Selection Test** (SST) – the official test of English language proficiency for entry to Australian courses. The test is supervised by the Australian embassy or high commission in the country where students have lodged their applications.

However, the SST will not be necessary if you are:

- A student whose first language is English;

- A student applying for undergraduate or postgraduate studies who has successfully completed secondary or undergraduate courses in an English-speaking country;

- A student who has scored 550 or more on the American Test of English as a Foreign Language (TOFL). Students undertaking the TOFL should have their scores sent directly to the Overseas Students' Office (OSO) by marking the institution code, 9193, on their test admission ticket and answer sheet, otherwise the original score report must be sent with the application form to the OSO;

- Someone who has sat the SST since January 1985 and passed. If so, simply send a copy of your certificate;

- A Hong Kong educated applicant who has obtained a pass at C grade or better in English in the GCE O level examination;

- A Fiji or Tonga applicant for undergraduate entry who has obtained a score of 50% or more in English in the New Zealand university entrance examination, or an applicant for senior secondary or matriculation entry who has obtained a score of 60% or more in English in the New Zealand School Certificate;

- An applicant who has passed the selection test for schools through the Freeman Overseas Testing Service (FOTS). However, schools represented by FOTS are only some of the many

Australian schools which welcome overseas students at secondary level.

STUDY AT JUNIOR SECONDARY LEVEL

Only nationals of certain countries can apply for entry to public (government) and private Australian schools at junior secondary level. These countries are Papua New Guinea and ten sovereign states of the South Pacific (the Solomon Islands, Vanuatu, Nauru, Fiji, Tonga, Kiribati, Tuvalu, Western Samoa, Cook Islands and Nieue). Generally, students entering (from the age of about 13 to 16, at junior secondary level) are expected to live in boarding schools, which are usually run privately and have high fees.

STUDY AT SENIOR SECONDARY LEVEL

Senior secondary students of any nationality are welcome to attend private or government schools if they can meet the English language, financial, educational, health and character criteria already mentioned. In addition, they must pay 100% of the cost of their tuition at government secondary schools or the even higher fees charged by private (non-government) schools.

Unlike students applying for tertiary education in Australia, secondary school applicants must *not* make arrangements with educational institutions in Australia directly, other than confirming a place would be available for them.

Applications should be made to the local Australian embassy or high commission which will, in turn, contact state departments of education. Applicants may nominate the non-government school of their choice and up to three Australian states or territories where they would like to attend a TAFE matriculation course or high school. Students should also indicate whether they want to complete their senior secondary education at a matriculation course run by a TAFE in preference to an Australian high school. Applicants for non-government schools must first obtain offers of a place, and include a letter from the school making this offer among other documentation in the application.

FINANCIAL GUARANTEES

When making their applications, private overseas students are required to sign a declaration stating that they are aware of the likely costs of study in Australia and that someone, the student, a parent or a guardian, has the capacity to meet these costs. A private student who cannot pay the fees or support themselves will have their stay in Australia terminated and be required to return to their home country.

WORK AND TAXES

A private overseas student is permitted to take a part-time job on a 'casual' basis (non-permanent staff and therefore having no right to holiday pay or other 'permanent' conditions) for up to 20 hours a week when their course is in session. However, they will be allowed to work full-time during vacations. But, if the student fails the course and blames the job, Australian authorities will not accept this excuse as reason for extending the stay in the country. As for tax, a student who stays more than six months must complete a **taxation rebate declaration form** and be treated as a resident of Australia in terms of obligation to pay taxes. He or she will be allowed the usual tax-free amount before the regular Australian income taxes are chargeable (see Chapter 14, page 362).

DEPENDANTS

As a rule, foreign students awarded a place at an Australian institution must go to Australia alone and apply for their spouses or children to join them later. However, it is feasible for students to apply in advance to the Australian embassy or high commission in their country to leave with their spouses and children. The student's visa application must include this request.

Dependants of student applicants may themselves undertake courses of education in Australia. However, they will have to pay the Overseas Students' Charge for formal courses leading to an award of a diploma or degree from a university, college or other institution where they hope to study.

As previously mentioned in this chapter, the spouse of an overseas student is allowed to work in Australia, though the authorities warn that this may be easier said than done – bearing in mind the delays and complications involved in gaining recognition of professional qualifications, if any, and high unemployment generally. However, overseas students hoping to take a spouse or children with them must prove to the Australian authorities that they can cover each dependant's living expenses anyway.

In the case of sponsored scholarship students, the Australian government does not pay for dependants' travel expenses although, in some cases, maintenance will be paid to the family in Australia. All dependants must leave Australia when the overseas student finishes his or her course.

Further information
Australian Department of Education, Training and Science
PO Box 9880
Canberra
ACT 2601
Australia
Tel: (02) 6283 7008
www.dest.gov.au

For a comprehensive list of universities in Australia go to
www.dest.gov.au/highered/ausunis.htm

The addresses of educational institutions may be obtained from the Australian embassy or high commission enquiries section in your country.

Taking It All With You

So you've gained permission to live and work in Australia. Now you want to know: can I and should I take it all with me?

If your 'all' features Aunty Mabel's home-made jams, a muddy lawnmower or your pet llama, the answer is probably 'no'. Yet a very clean family car, dogs and cats, or even your private airship will probably meet with a conditional 'yes'.

> **Australian red tape on customs and imports covers practically everything and should give you much to think about well before you start packing.**

Also think about whether it is actually **worth** taking certain items along at all if, in the long run, they'll be cheaper and less trouble to replace in Australia. Bear in mind that electrical goods may have to be converted to Australian standards (see pages 159 and 168) while imported vehicles may not be allowed on the roads, and other machinery may be prohibited if not complying with the safety standards of the state or territory you plan to live in. In addition, duties or taxes may apply to your belongings.

THE AUSTRALIAN CUSTOMS SERVICE

The **Australian Customs Service** is the government department responsible for many aspects of border security. Crucially for Australia and its visitors, this federal government agency administers the rules and regulations on customs and excise. It is their officers who will greet you and perhaps examine your possessions at your port of entry.

For guidance on the technicalities of Australian import restrictions and contact with the organisation(s) which can provide specific help on any special machinery or other items you hope to bring in, contact: The Controller-General, Australian Customs Service, Customs House, 5–11 Constitution Avenue, Barton, ACT 2600. Tel: Australia (02) 6275 6666. Email: information@customs.gov.au. There is a website especially for travellers to Australia.

The world has become a very security-conscious place, and anyone who travels internationally would not be surprised to learn Australia's customs procedures employ the latest technology to verify the identity of travellers and check that aircraft luggage is safe. However, customs are also aiming to prevent the possible introduction of pests and diseases to Australia, to protect the health of humans as well as the environment and agriculture.

Australia is very strict about eliminating traces of soil, straw or other matter that can accidentally bring diseases such as foot and mouth or 'mad cow' disease into the country. So far these detailed checks at ports of entry to Australia have proved effective.

SHOULD YOU BUY OR TAKE IT WITH YOU?

On page 148 there is a guide to the prices of a wide range of consumer goods in Australia, if bought new. The prices shown are in Australian dollars, and are for articles of medium to high quality.

Refer to specific information on customs regulations applying to tourists, temporary and permanent migrants about cars they wish to bring into the country, and the taxes that they may be obliged to pay or provide a surety against, later in this chapter.

Hygiene and quarantine

As mentioned, rules are enforced to prevent unauthorised animal and plant life migrating with you. In case you unwittingly carry microscopic beasties on your person, you will be sprayed on disembarkation at an Australian port ... but that's just the start. Wouldn't it be awful to send an old lawnmower and gardening tools Down Under – only to find these must be stored in quarantine for months, fumigated, cleaned and all the bills charged to you – along with whatever you forked out for shipping in the first place? An island continent needs strict rules to keep out foreign diseases and pests which could be a health risk or damage its important agricultural basis. Strict quarantine and fumigation procedures apply to all pets, cars, business or household goods you may want to

Electrical Goods		$A
Refrigerator	360 litre fridge/freezer	700
	500 litre fridge/freezer	1,000
Washing machine	Front loading 5.5kg	500
	Front loading 7kg	800
Electric range (cooker)	4 plates, grill, oven	800
Microwave	1,000 watts	200
Sewing machine	Twin needle automatic	360
Deep fryer		80
Iron		50
Hair dryer		40
Toaster		55
Vacuum cleaner	upright bag	220
Digital clock radio		25
Television set	68cm rear projection	300
	68cm flat screen	1,000
	58cm LCD high resolution	2,700
VHS video recorder		500
DVD/music system	DVD/CD, speakers AV 200 watt receiver, 100 watt subwoofer	240
Mobile telephone	$50 for phone, colour screen, internet access, built-in photo flash, text and sound, headset	for 24 month plan
Cordless telephone	with built-in answering system	129
Hand-held mobile phone/pocket PCs, rental plans also available		1,000
General household furnishings		
All wool plain rug	240 cm x 170 cm	300
Coloured curtains	120 cm printed cotton/per metre	25
Table crockery	36 piece imported English bone china	2,000
	42 piece decorated white earthenware (local)	250
	50 piece plain earthenware	100
Cutlery	43 piece stainless steel plain, 6 places	100
Bathtowel	Plain colour 60 cm x 120 cm	20
	Plain colour 91 cm x 152 cm	40
Kitchen suites	Polished round table wood 105 cm with four wooden chairs	700
Lounge suite	Three piece fabric upholstered	2,000
Dining suite	7 piece table 180cm (wood veneer) with six chairs	1,700
	Each additional chair	150
Bedroom suite	6 piece unit suite comprising 244 cm wardrobe (two pieces), dressing table, 2 bedside tables, 137 cm double bed	3,500
Wardrobe	228 cm high, 152 cm wide	700
Blankets (per pair)	Pure wool – single 182 cm x 228 cm	170
	Pure wool – double 225 cm x 245 cm	250
Sheets (per pair)	Pure cotton single 180 cm x 245 cm	90
	Double 237 cm x 245 cm	130
Motor vehicles – approximate new car prices including taxes		
Holden Barina 1.4 3-door manual		14,000
Holden Astra 1.8TS sedan		19,000
Holden Astra convertible		44,000
Ford Focus 1.8 4/5-door manual		21,000
Daihatsu Sirion 1.0 auto		14,000
Peugeot 307		25,250
Peugeot 607		79,900
Suzuki 7-seater XL-5		36,000
VW Golf GL 1.6 5-door		28,000
Toyota Echo 1.3 hatch		14,500
Subaru WRX sedan		40,000
Mazda 6 limited		28,000
Range Rover 4.4 V8 HSE		135,000
BMW645CI		196,000
Mercedes Benz E320 Elegance		120,000
Porsche 911 Carrera Coupe		189,990

Fig. 1. Sample prices in Australia.

take to Australia with you. Even your packing materials need to be free of possible contaminants, so do not use fruit or vegetable boxes, used plant pots, straw or sawdust as packing materials.

Timing

On average, new settlers do not arrive in Australia until two or three months after obtaining a visa.

Do not sell up and ship out before you have *absolute approval* from *federal immigration* and/or *customs authorities.* A state government official in London once led a would-be immigrant to believe that he was sure to win a migration visa on the strength of a job offered by that same state government. The unfortunate man sold his house, his car, packed for the big move – only to find that the federal seal of approval had *not* been given to the application. Immigration officials enforced a rule that the job had to be advertised in Australia – and when it was, someone already living there was deemed most suitable.

RESTRICTED AND PROHIBITED IMPORTS

First and foremost, you should note these goods which cannot be taken into Australia at all, unless special clearance is obtained:

- **Narcotic drugs**, including drugs of dependence of many kinds such as barbiturates, amphetamines, hallucinogens and tranquillisers which must be cleared at customs when you enter. The maximum penalty, if you are found guilty of trying to illegally import such substances, is 25 years' imprisonment and/ or a fine of $A100,000 (at time of writing) if traffickable quantities are involved.

- **Firearms and weapons**. Taking certain types of weapons into Australia is strictly policed and approval must be given if you plan to do so. Guns such as air, gas, flare, spearguns and starting pistols must be declared at customs. Importation of springbladed knives, daggers, swordsticks and knuckle-dusters are prohibited. Real or replica firearms, air pistols, ammunition, blowpipes, daggers, nunchukas, slingshots, flick knives, pistol crossbows, electric fly swatters and knuckle-dusters are included in the ban, unless imported with a permit.

QUARANTINE

The Australian Quarantine and Inspection Service (AQIS) is part of the Federal Department of Agriculture, Fisheries and Forestry. When making your **customs declaration** you must draw attention to anything you plan to take with you which could possibly contain or carry pests or disease. Commonly, foodstuffs such as preserves or favourite delicacies from another country are confiscated if detected, and people suspected of knowingly trying to sneak Aunty Mabel's apple jelly through customs can end up in court. You are required to sign a declaration saying you have no such items in your luggage, before you enter Australia as a tourist or resident. Or you can 'declare' items such as coffee, spices, biscuits or sweets in your luggage, which means allowing them to be inspected before you are allowed to bring them in and risk them being confiscated if they do not cmply with strict standards for entry. You may also be required to pay duties or other taxes for their importation.

Items of quarantine concern

Prohibited items include:

◆ Some foods, including all fresh and frozen **fruit and vegetables**; all uncanned or fresh, dried, frozen, smoked or salted **meat**, **dairy** products; whole, dried and powdered **egg** and some products with egg as an ingredient; raw unroasted nuts, raw peanuts, chestnuts and popping corn;

◆ Live **animals**, including all mammals, birds, birds' eggs and nests, fish, reptiles, amphibians and insects. The import of domestic pets is discussed on page 153;

◆ Live **plants**, including all potted/bare rooted plants, cuttings, bulbs and other viable plant material. There are processes in place, however, that enable the import of some plant material – check with AQIS in advance about import requirements;

◆ Used fruit, vegetable and flower boxes, used egg cartons, straw and sawdust are also prohibited, so don't use these to pack your goods.

Items that must be declared and inspected for signs of insects or disease, and which may require treatment before being allowed entry, include:

◆ **Food** products such as dried fruit and vegetables, noodles and rice, herbs and spices, biscuits, tea and coffee;

◆ **Animal** products including rawhide items, shells and coral, bee products and used animal equipment such as saddles. Articles of clothing, shoes, handbags, trophies, ornaments or anything else made from a protected species of wildlife may be seized under federal law. If you plan to take such things to Australia, an import permit must be obtained in advance from the Wildlife Permits and Enforcement Section of Environment Australia;

◆ **Plant** products including mats, bags and other items made from plant material, pot pourri, goods containing cereal grain or filled with seed, Christmas decorations and ornaments, and wooden articles. In planning the furniture or household effects you want to take with you to Australia, as well as when having these

packed for removal, be sure to select any wooden items
carefully. If they are found to be infested with borers or other
insect pests, quarantine officials may demand that they are
fumigated at your expense before they are allowed to join you in
your new home;

◆ **Motor vehicles**, caravans and trailers must be inspected on
arrival by quarantine officers who may request that they be
steam-cleaned at the importer's expense if found to be
contaminated with animal, plant or soil material. Also make
sure that garden tools, outdoor furniture, lawn mowers, bicycles,
sporting equipment, shoes and boots are also free of soil and
seeds, and empty vacuum cleaner bags. Motor vehicle
importation is discussed in further detail on page 157.

Finally, when packing your personal effects and household goods
prepare a list that includes all the items in your consignment, and
pack all your items of quarantine concern together, to facilitate
the import process.

Humans

People over the age of 12 months need a **Yellow Fever Vaccination**
certificate if they have travelled through or landed in an area
infected with Yellow Fever listed by the World Health
Organisation within the six days before arriving in Australia. This
applies even if there is no outbreak of the disease in the affected
part of the world while you are there. People do not need any
other health certificates to enter Australia.

Dogs, cats and other pets

Dogs and cats can only be brought to Australia from approved
countries and all animals imported into Australia require an
import permit issued by the Australian Quarantine and Inspection

Service. Dogs and cats imported from New Zealand and Norfolk Island do not spend any time in quarantine, while all other animals spend at least 30 days in a government quarantine station. There are three animal quarantine stations, located at Eastern Creek (Sydney), Spotswood (Melbourne) and Byford (Perth). Countries such as the United Kingdom, Japan, Singapore, Ireland, Hawaii, Fiji, Taiwan and Sweden have a 30-day quarantine period for all dogs and cats due to the absence of rabies in these countries. Animals coming from North America and continental Europe can also have a 30-day quarantine period in Australia, provided rabies vaccinations and testing is done at least 150 days prior to export. Information sheets are available on the AQIS website describing steps in the pet import process in more detail. Animals currently living in a country not approved by AQIS for direct importation will need to be resident in an approved country for a minimum of six months to qualify for an import permit.

Pets such as guinea pigs, ferrets, reptiles and birds are prohibited entry. Rabbits can be imported with a permit from New Zealand only. Animals arriving into Australia without an AQIS import permit will be destroyed on arrival.

Quarantine information
Australia's quarantine rules alter with time, according to the latest scientific evidence. For the latest quarantine information and the rules as they apply to animals from your country of origin, visit the AQIS website at: www.aqis.gov.au or fax +61262724494.

Alternatively, contact Australia's regional veterinary authority on quarantine via the nearest high commission or embassy.

DUTIES AND TAXES

Everything you hope to bring to Australia as a tourist, temporary visitor or immigrant is subject to customs evaluation and possibly

- an import duty,
- excise, *and/or*
- Australian sales taxes.

It makes no difference whether the goods are accompanied or unaccompanied baggage.

However there are many concessions – especially for people with a visa to stay permanently or temporarily – dealt with later in this chapter. Occasionally changes are made to the tax calculations and exemptions applied to people importing items for commercial or personal use. For full, current details of the customs rules as they may apply to your special circumstances, contact the authorities suggested at the start of this chapter.

As a rule, the following goods can be brought into Australia duty/ tax free.

- **Alcoholic liquor**. This is subject to the current rate of duty if arriving unaccompanied. However, anyone over the age of 18 entering Australia with up to 1,125 ml of alcoholic liquor, including wine and beer, can bring this in duty free.

- **Cigarettes, cigars, tobacco**. As above, unaccompanied goods of this kind are subject to the current rate of import duty. People over the age of 18 arriving with up to 250 cigarettes or 250 grams of cigars or 250 grams of tobacco may bring these through customs duty free.

- **Articles purchased outside Australia or at Australian duty-free shops.** An individual traveller may bring in $A400 worth of goods (not including tobacco or alcohol), and $A200 if under the age of 18. This category includes cameras, electronic equipment, leather goods, perfume, jewellery and sporting goods.

- **Articles that a person outside Australia** has asked you to take to a person in Australia. These are subject to import duties and taxes.

- **Goods sent as freight**, and goods sent directly to Australia from shops on your behalf would also be subject to regular import duties and taxes.

- **Currency $A10,000 or more**, or equivalent in foreign currency notes and coins, must be reported on departure.

Personal effects – exemptions for tourists and migrants

'Personal effects' (the things you take in your own luggage) are duty free providing they:

- are your own property;

- arrive on the same aircraft or ship on which you travel;

- are suitable and intended for your own use;

- are not intended for 'commercial purposes' (sale, rent, hire, etc.);

- are not imported in commercial quantities;

- do not exceed a purchase price of $A400 per person or $A200 per person if under 18 years of age. This amount excludes tobacco and alcohol products but may include fur apparel and perfume. Members of the same family (husband, wife, children) who live in the same household and are travelling together may combine their individual duty free concessions.

Customs rules allow family groups, including children under the age of ten, to club together to make the most of the concessions applying to individuals, but of course people under 18 cannot claim the concessional rate or exemptions on cigarettes, tobacco or alcohol declared as their 'share'.

Duty free personal effects are, in the jargon of Australian customs authorities, 'articles of the type normally carried on your person or in your personal baggage including jewellery and toilet requisites, wristwatch, cigarette lighter etc. but not electrical entertainment appliances (DVDs, mobile phones, etc.), binoculars, laptop computers, exposed films of your travels, photographic cameras, video cameras, personal sporting requisites including sporting and camping equipment.

Tourists and temporary residents may import cars and other machinery provided they convince customs officials that these are for their own use while in Australia. They may be obliged to lodge a cash or bank surety redeemable when the imported item leaves the country. If you do not take the car or other item with you when you leave the country, it will be necessary to pay the amount of duty assessed.

People who object to the customs charges made on their belongings can appeal to the senior customs officer stationed at the port or airport of arrival.

Motor vehicles, caravans and trailers imported by tourists and temporary residents

As a tourist or temporary resident, you may bring a car, caravan or trailer into Australia for up to 12 months without paying duty. For this concession to apply you will need either:

- a **Carnet de Passage en Douanes** from an overseas organisation which has a reciprocal arrangement with the Australian Automobile Association, *or*

- a cash or bank security equal to the amount of duty and Goods and Services Tax (GST) otherwise payable.

The vehicle is subject to the general safety standards applied to all vehicles on Australia's roads and waterways (contact the relevant state government or motoring organisation in Australia) and must fulfil the usual quarantine and hygiene regulations. If the vehicle is stolen, damaged or destroyed while you are in Australia you should notify customs authorities at your original place of arrival. All fittings and accessories imported with the car, caravan or trailer must also be exported with it.

Additional concessions for migrants and returning residents

Certain duty free concessions apply only to people coming to Australia to take up residence for the first time or permanent residents returning to resume permanent residence. However, duty free concessions on alcohol, tobacco, electronics and other new articles do not apply to unaccompanied effects.

Unaccompanied luggage – exemptions

There are certain items which can arrive as unaccompanied

luggage, and duty free allowances for those coming to make their homes in the country are generous. Unlike tourists, people with permanent residence are allowed to import their belongings as unaccompanied baggage without paying the usual import charges, providing all the other conditions (relating to hygiene, quarantine and so on) have been met and that these are not 'controlled' (firearms, food, plant material).

The following general concession categories apply to immigrants:

◆ any personal belongings, furniture or household goods which the importer or importer's family have owned and used for 12 months before departure for Australia;

◆ goods on which sales tax has previously been paid in Australia and which are being sent back there;

◆ furs and other clothing that the owner and importer has used for at least 12 months before departure;

◆ sporting goods such as non-motorised bicycles;

◆ motorcycles without sidecars;

◆ motor vehicles, caravans, and boats subject to special conditions;

◆ plant, equipment or machinery, all subject to conditions given later in this chapter.

Commercial equipment – special exemptions for immigrants

Secondhand machinery, plant and equipment such as lap top computers which you may want to take to Australia for use in your job or business is duty free if:

◆ you have come to Australia for the first time to take up permanent residence immediately;

◆ the goods are the importer's personal property. Naturally, it is best to produce receipts, examples of your work, or other proof to show customs officers in case they ask for evidence;

◆ you can convince the customs authorities that you will be using the goods for the purposes for which they are intended;

◆ during the first two years in Australia the items are not sold, hired, mortgaged or otherwise disposed of. The two-year period specified begins from the time you start using the equipment for their intended commercial purpose. Any storage period for the goods inside Australia does not count;

◆ you lodge a cash or bank surety to guarantee use of the equipment for its intended purpose by you in Australia for at least two years.

However, if machinery, plant or equipment is owned by a company or partnership, or if the individual owner is not over 18 years old, duty must be paid at the regular rate.

Carnets may be obtained for temporary duty-free entry of goods that are subject to international agreement. You are advised to contact your local Chamber of Commerce or business organisation for application details for this exemption, covering items like goods for exhibiting sporting events, professional film and television equipment.

Also, some types of machinery in this category are subject to licensing controls in Australia, so it is advisable to check with customs authorities in the state or territory where you plan to import, before taking the trouble and expense to transport them Down Under. For instance, you are not permitted to bring in radio transmitters, including cordless telephones and citizen band (CB) radios, which do not conform to Australian standards. An import permit will be required for such items. For further information on the kinds of radio transmitters permitted, contact:

The Secretary
Department of Transport and Communication
PO Box 132
Belconnen
ACT 2617, Australia

Motor vehicles

In Australia you will find that taxes on imported vehicles are high, making many models considered quite ordinary abroad expensive and exotic in Australia. The list of new car prices (see page 144) is a guide to what you could pay for a car comparable to the model you may be thinking of shipping to Australia. Do not assume that a vehicle that seems to be an identical model to one already available in Australia conforms with Australian Design Rules (ADRs). Before you decide if it is worth transporting your car, truck or any other motor vehicle to Australia, it is wise to consider whether it:

♦ conforms with Australian **Design Rule requirements** (ADR), as enforced by the motor registration authorities in the state or territory where you will be living. If in doubt, check with that state or territory government or your present motoring organisation, if it has contacts in Australia. Necessary safety features which must be fitted to all cars driven in Australia include seat belts and head restraints on front seats, that the vehicle be right-hand drive (if it is left-hand drive, it may not be permitted on public roads);

◆ meets requirements of Australia's **Motor Vehicle Standards Act**, administered by the Vehicle Safety Branch of the Federal Department of Transport and Regional Services. These standards cover safety and emissions and any modification your vehicle may need;

◆ meets **other registration requirements** of the state or territory where you plan to live, again through the particular government or a motoring organisation.

If the car conforms to Australian rules then an Import Approval will be required to bring the vehicle into Australia.

Together with customs and shipping charges, it can take many months and thousands of Australian dollars (or the equivalent in the currency of the country where the transport company is based) to send a vehicle Down Under. Wherever it comes from, and whatever its condition on departure, you could be charged for steam-cleaning, quarantine inspection, wharfage and storage in Australia as well as delivery charges to take it from the docks to prepare for driving in Australia. If the car exceeds the high valuation threshold applied by customs authorities in assessing sales, taxes and duties (see below), that expense will be even greater. This amount, plus whatever you might sell it for before you leave, might pay for purchase, lease or hire of a suitable new vehicle in Australia. Alternatively you may own a unique 'collector's' vehicle, in which case Australia's Specialist and

Enthusiast Vehicle Scheme (SEVS) may apply if your vehicle fails to comply with the ADRs.

Guide to importation

Privately owned passenger vehicles or motor cycles
The customs clearance of a privately owned motor vehicle or motorcycle is subject to:

- Letter of Compliance (to ADRs) and completed Import Approval documentation;

- payment of import duty and consumer tax at the rates which apply to your type of vehicle on the date you import it into Australia;

- authorisation from the Federal Office of Road Safety;

- quarantine clearance.

It costs $A50 to apply for Import Approval. However, if you ship your vehicle *before* receiving an approval and your vehicle arrives *before* the application is processed, an approval cannot be issued.

'Transaction Valuation Method' of new or second-hand privately owned vehicles
Valuation is normally assessed on the actual purchase price, plus cost of any modifications or work, less depreciation, converted to $A at the exchange rate on the date of export.

The above method is used where it can be shown that:

- the actual purchase price was in a bona fide sale where the price was not influenced by any other factor;

◆ the vehicle was purchased to be exported to Australia.

Depreciation
A depreciation allowance for the period of personal ownership
and use may be allowed, at the rate of 5% for the first completed
calendar month and 1% for each subsequent month, to a
maximum of two years (28%).

Ownership and use period
The period is determined by documentation in the importer's
name, and is the time from the vehicle being registered overseas,
or the date the owner takes delivery overseas, whichever is the
later, up until the time the vehicle is handed over for shipment to
Australia or the owner departs the overseas country, whichever is
the earlier.

Conversion to Australian dollars
The purchase price is then converted to Australian currency using
the official rate of exchange on the day of import.

'Alternative Method of Valuation' of privately owned new or second-hand vehicles
The Alternative Method of valuation is generally based on an
assessment of 40% of the full price of the vehicle in Australian
dollars. The vehicle's potential sales value in Australia by a qualified
vehicle valuer, less overseas freight and insurance costs for its
shipment to Australia and any other non-dutiable post-importation
charges, such as customs duty and sales tax. This method applies to
vehicles bought after 2 March 1988. A previous set of guidelines
applies to even older vehicles, while yet other guidelines may apply if
you are seeking to import a vehicle that is not supplied in full
volume but for a 'specialist or enthusiasts' market.

Quarantine
To prevent diseases, noxious weeds and insect pests being brought
into Australia, quarantine authorities will inspect all vehicles on
arrival. Your car should be steam-cleaned before shipping and all
soil and other dirt should be removed from all surfaces before you
send it, in order to pass through quarantine.

Rates of customs duty
The taxes that may apply to your vehicle include customs duty,
Goods and Services Tax (GST) and Luxury Car Tax (LCT).
Luxury Car Tax is levied on vehicles valued over $A57,000. Here
is a broad guide to current tax rates on a range of commonly
imported vehicles.

	Customs duty %	*GST %*	*LCT*
Cars < 30 years old	15	10	May apply
Cars > 30 years old	NIL	10	May apply
Campervans and mobile homes	10%	10	May apply
Motor cycles	10	10	Does not apply

Shipping your vehicle – other considerations

♦ If the vehicle is **left-hand drive**, what would be the cost and
viability of converting it to right-hand drive, as necessary under
Australian regulations?

♦ **Shipping charges**, including after-arrival handling charges and
clearances.

♦ The **cost of similar new vehicles** in Australia. Again, you may
discover this through a motoring organisation in Australia or in
your present home, via state or territory government motor
transport authorities, or simply by perusing the new and used

car sale advertisements of Australian newspapers in the reading rooms of the nearest embassy or high commission, or at a state government office abroad.

◆ Whether **spare parts and repairs** to your vehicle would be readily available in Australia. Again, this is information available through motoring organisations, and could tip the balance in favour of buying a car there. See Chapter 10 for more details.

◆ **How long it will** take before the vehicle joins you in Australia, if it is to arrive after you do.

◆ If the car is to arrive before you, the amount of **customs surety** you will be obliged to pay (sometimes the entire value of the vehicle – see the guidelines below) before it can be released to you.

◆ Vehicle registration and insurance costs required by the state or territory of Australia to which you plan to move. You need to check registration issues and costs with the relevant state or territory government's transport department to ensure it will meet their requirements. Vehicles can be temporarily driven on Australia roads while the carnet that covers it is valid in the vehicle's country of origin.

Consider the age and condition of the vehicle generally in the light of the points made above about conforming to design and registration regulations and Australian road conditions mentioned in Chapter 10.

Yachts and other craft

Tourists and temporary residents may bring a yacht or other craft to Australia for up to 12 months (or longer under certain circumstances) without paying duty on it.

However, you may be required to lodge a cash or bank security with customs, equal to the amount of duty otherwise payable.

A separate booklet, entitled *Yachts and Other Craft*, is available from customs offices or via the Australian Customs Service website.

If you are taking up permanent residency, customs duty and tax will be payable on the vessel.

Caravans, trailers and boats

As a migrant or returning resident you may bring a non-motorised caravan, a boat and non-motorised box, boat or similar trailer to Australia, duty free, providing:

◆ You have personally owned and used the caravan, boat or trailer overseas for the 12 months (or more) before your departure for Australia;

◆ You can satisfy customs that you have come to Australia to take up or resume permanent residence immediately;

◆ No member of your family (husband, wife or children) has brought a caravan, boat or trailer to Australia within the last three years using this concession;

◆ You lodge a cash or bank security with cstoms that you will not sell or dispose of the vessel in Australia within two years – this security will be equal to the amount of duty otherwise payable on the vessel. *And*

◆ The vessel conforms to one of the following specifications: Eligible boats include:

sailing boats, which do not exceed 1,000 kg unladen weight, do not have any means of motorised propulsion (including an auxiliary motor) and are not of a deep keel type;

motorised boats, which do not exceed 7 m in overall length or 2.5 m in width at any section, and which do not exceed 800 kgs unladen weight without drive units and transmissions or 1,250 kgs unladen weight with drive units and transmissions;

other boats, which are propelled by manual or pedal power.

Final formalities for clearing a vehicle at customs in Australia

When the vehicle arrives at an Australian port the importer must produce documents including a passport, driving licence, bills of sale, purchase papers, registration and insurance records for Australia, service records, log books and shipping documents. Vehicles imported before the arrival of the importer will only be released on payment of security covering customs duty and sales tax as stated already.

Quarantine experts will inspect the vehicle carefully on its arrival and, if traces of animal or vegetable matter are found, may order steam-cleaning.

TEMPORARY RESIDENTS AND VISITORS

You should be able to take the things you need during your stay into Australia free of import charges for a temporary job posting, as an overseas student, working holidaymaker or for any other reason. However, you must satisfy customs officials that any household items or other items are for your personal use and not for sale. These items must also comply with rules on quarantine, hygiene and not be otherwise outlawed.

You will be asked to sign an undertaking to remove such items again within 12 months or longer, depending on your visa and any extensions you get to it. However, a financial guarantee – cash or documentary – may be necessary as a surety. This is based on the sales taxes or import duties which apply to the goods you want to take with you to Australia. If customs officials decide that you or the goods do not qualify for any concessions, the normal GST or import duty will be charged.

Electrical appliances – Australian standards

It may not be worth the trouble and expense to take along electrical equipment and household appliances to Australia. Apart from the size and weight of such goods, consider whether they conform with the standard Australian electricity supply, at 240 volts AC (50 hertz). If not, they may be dangerous or impossible to use. If not modified correctly, they may be explosive.

For colour television, Australia uses 625 line PAL. But even sets designed for PAL will only be able to receive television broadcasts in VHF, so international models with a VHF option are the only televisions suitable for Australian conditions. High definition digital TV is being introduced to Australian homeviewers. If in doubt, check with electrical retailers and authorities before you leave and, on arrival, have appliances checked by local electricity (or gas) authorities before you use them.

ARRIVING IN AUSTRALIA

Getting your visa for Australia is half the battle. For newcomers, the complexities of packing, deciding what to take and what to leave behind, then finding a place to live and work will be important in making the most of your adventure Down Under. Clearly these are personal matters which depend on your particular circumstances and whether or not you have the help of friends, family or business colleagues smoothing your path to Australia.

Because Australia is a country of immigrants, it leads the way internationally in settlement programmes which are often supplemented by support networks, advisory centres, clubs and charities run by the ethnic communities themselves. Other migrants of your own background are often the most reliable safety net for emotional – if not financial – support and advice. Apart from the list of organisations included at the back of this book, the Department of Immigration will also be able to put you in touch with clubs and societies for people from your part of the world in the part of Australia where you plan to live.

Other government programmes for newcomers

The Department of Immigration, Local Government and Ethnic Affairs funds and staffs the following support programmes for migrants and temporary settlers:

◆ **Migrant resource centres:** autonomously managed by migrant communities to provide counselling, help with contacts and solve problems that newcomers encounter in Australia. There are over 30 such centres at the time of writing, mainly in the large cities;

- **Welfare assistance:** settlement support and counselling are also provided at state and regional offices of the Department, giving advice and practical assistance to individuals as well as to other agencies working with newcomers. The focus is on refugees and other recently arrived immigrants with genuine financial problems;

- **Grant-in-Aid scheme:** these grants are allocated by the government to needy new settlers such as refugees. As mentioned in previous chapters, the majority of migrants are expected to be financially independent from the time they arrive. Furthermore, a sponsor may be obliged to sign an Assurance of Support so that any welfare claims made from a government or charity must be repaid by the sponsor;

- **Telephone interpreter services:** Australia leads the world in this cheap, efficient interpreter service available 24 hours a day throughout the country for the price of a local call. Telephone operators speaking a range of community languages can answer questions or provide advice on medical or legal problems, social welfare, accommodation, police, education, or any other matters concerning the non-English-speaking resident;

- **Translation service:** the Department has translation service units in Sydney, Melbourne, Canberra and through the telephone interpreter service in other cities. Migrant settlement documents will be translated for free, though a fee may be charged for other services;

- **Adult migrant English programme:** teaching English to migrants of non-English-speaking background English to prepare them for jobs or further education.

8

Housing and Property

Australia is a big country with plenty of land, where almost any home-buying fantasy can be accommodated – provided money is no object. You may dream of a sturdy brick bungalow fully equipped with swimming pool, tennis court, barbecue area and lush gardens down to a private beach. An ultra-modern high rise penthouse could be your ultimate living space; on the other hand, perhaps, a plot of land on a tropical island would do nicely. All are attainable Down Under, where home ownership is enjoyed by almost 70% of the population – one of the highest rates in the world.

Naturally, it is necessary to know where, when and how to strike a balance between a sound investment and a property that makes you happy. Unless you are a student with plans to live in a university or college, or are staying with friends and relatives at least at first, be sure your expectations and arrangements for a place to live are well made and realistic. Even if a contact or employer has made and confirmed an offer to supply housing on arrival, you may soon want to enter the real estate market independently as a buyer or investor.

Property prices galloped ahead then crashed in the late 1980s. By 1994 prices were on the rise and took a decade to plateau, in 2004. During 1997 interest rates fell to their lowest historical levels for decades and have stayed low. A sound economy and competition by financial institutions to lend money for mortgages has meant that home loans are around 7.5%, but predicted to rise over the next year or two.

There is no tax relief for owner-occupiers, unlike some countries such as the United States, although tax deductions apply to investment property.

Many first time buyers – including migrants – are moving away from coastal areas in pricey Sydney and the second most expensive city, Melbourne, to other capitals or to far-flung new suburbs where it costs less to realise the great Aussie home-ownership dream.

There is a $A7,000 First Owners Home Grant funded by the government for those who have not bought a home before but with the average home loan at about $A190,000 in 2003, with monthly loan repayments at $A1,300, buying a residential property in Australia is a costly long-term commitment. In fact, according to the Real Estate Institute of Australia's statistics, the number of first time buyers is falling – especially among people in younger age groups. If you decide to buy a home in Australia and pay via a mortgage, expect to devote a large chunk of your income to housing repayments. The mortgage is the largest item of typical household expenditure in Australia with 27% of family income required to meet the average home loan repayments.

Relative to other countries, Australia's big cities can be very, very expensive for housing and property. In 2006 Sydney was ranked the world's 19th most expensive city, the only Australian city in the top 50.

On the other hand there are plenty of homes for sale that look cost-effective if you are moving to Australia. Hobart, the capital of Tasmania, and Darwin, in the Northern Territory, are Australia's least expensive capital cities in which to buy or rent a home. Some of Australia's towns and cities are ranked among the world's most liveable cities – thanks to the political stability, low crime rates, good human rights record, quality health and education services, pleasant climate and the low chance of natural disasters and terrorist attacks.

WOT'S IN A NAME?

Australians live in some pretty strange places, but don't laugh – you too could end up living in Winji Jimmi, Kangy Angy, Tom Ugly's Point or Wobby Beach. However, suppressing a giggle at Aussie place names will be the least of your problems on arrival in Australia. The language of real estate is a whole new aspect of Ausslang, and it's worth perusing the common terms and abbreviations listed at the end of this chapter to help decode property advertisements in Australia's local newspapers.

Never mind what it's called – where is it anyway? Of course, obtaining a map of the city or region where you plan to live is vital before you head off, as are the names and addresses of local real estate agents. You can start the search for a home well before you even decide definitely that Australia is for you. Major property agents in your nearest capital city may be able to advise you directly, if they have Australian offices, or could supply the names of an international property agency with branches or associated companies Down Under. And of course there is the internet, providing virtual details of more up-market properties for sale via local real estate agencies. They can provide listings of commercial and domestic property for sales, auctions or rentals as well as counselling on locations.

RENTING A PROPERTY

Despite high land prices, some residential rental prices have fallen due to a glut in houses and, particularly, flats built to take advantage of the recent real estate boom. Most people will decide to rent before they buy, getting to know the locality as well as finding jobs, schools and social life as part of the process of discovering whether Australia is for them in the long term.

Figure 3 shows a guide to the weekly rent you might expect to pay on a typical capital city family home.

Rents are considerably cheaper outside the big cities, due to less demand. Rent control is not widespread in Australia, and has been abolished entirely in Tasmania and Western Australia. In other states, control over rents in residential premises does not apply to new premises or tenancies.

	3-bedroom house	Vacancy Rate
Sydney	532,000.00	5.70%
Perth	450,000.00	34.00%
Canberra	380,000.00	7.80%
Melbourne	377,000.00	6.20%
Darwin	350,000.00	25.00%
Brisbane	326,000.00	5.20%
Adelaide	285,000.00	3.60%
Hobart	277,00.000	6.50%
Australia – Median	425,285.71	13.43%

Source: Real Estate Institutes around Australia

Fig. 2. Changes in capital city median house prices during 2006.

Many Australian families are being forced to stay longer in the rental market due to the significant rise in house prices over the past decade, which has outstripped increases in wages over the same period. This helps ensure rental demand remains strong for good family properties, despite the over-supply in some inner city areas of smaller apartments. Another important reason for a tight rental market in some popular locations is **Capital Gains Tax** (see Chapter 14). This is levied at the personal or company's standard tax rate on sale of an investment property other than the house or unit which is the owner's actual residence, and only one such residence is allowed per owner. Naturally, most rental properties in Australia are investment properties that attract this Capital Gains Tax. Stamp duty on buying and/or selling properties depends on where you live because it may be levied by state governments. Stamp duty can be another significant additional financial hurdle for homebuyers and investors. On a typical first home costing $A250,000 stamp duty will be an extra $A10,000 in some states. However, NSW, the most populous state, scrapped stamp duty on lower priced properties in 2004, to help first time buyers but raised taxes on the sale of investment properties and land. Finding a deposit of (typically) around 10% of the property value and servicing a mortgage of several hundred thousand dollars are the other costs of switching from being a renter to a home-buyer. Council rates and water charges are also the responsibility of the home owner.

However, there is a federal government taxation incentive known as 'negative gearing' to people who lease out investment properties for less than their mortgage repayments on those properties. Taxpayers are able to claim this shortfall as a loss which they can offset against other income but it is only beneficial to people in high tax brackets.

It is illegal for property owners to discriminate against a would-be tenant on the grounds of sex or marital status or because they are pregnant, under the federal government's Sexual Discrimination Act.

Commercial property

Unless you insist on luxurious fittings and sweeping views of local waterways and beaches, commercial rental rates are modest compared with prices in the world's biggest business centres. However, Sydney is now one of the most costly cities in the world for prime office space. But on the whole, relatively low commercial and industrial rentals mean that workplaces are generally more spacious than in many Western societies.

Prime locations in Sydney or Melbourne are more expensive than any other Australian city. The space in large commercial buildings and complexes is let by the square metre and, like the domestic rental sector, finding a vacancy can be a competitive business, especially in places where the market is tight.

The only business premises subject to rent control are buildings and tenancies in existence before certain dates, some decades ago.

Looking for a place to live or work

The best places to start, if you plan to rent a house or business property in Australia, are local newspapers and real estate agents. They have shopfront listings with photographs of premises for sale or rent. Real estate agencies are often signposted and advertised as **realtors** with details of current properties on their websites. Private as well as agency rentals are advertised in the newspapers while university or college student unions have bulletin boards or magazines listing rooms, flats or houses to let on a share basis.

Many real estate agents specialise in property management and know exactly when and where a property is coming up for lease. In the housing market, short leases are sometimes available, and a private agreement may mean that after it has expired the owner will allow you to stay on a weekly or monthly basis. But usually a first lease is set at six months and is extendable depending on whether you and the owner can agree on rent increases. Properties are let either furnished or unfurnished, the former normally being more expensive. When renting somewhere to live, the terms and language of the lease is normally clear enough so paying for legal advice should be unnecessary.

However, if you want to rent a **commercial property**, it is probably best to take the advice of a solicitor. Commercial leases are more complex and may be negotiated at a set rental for longer periods. Such leases may be 'sold' to a new tenant approved by the property owner (and the local zoning authorities, depending on the type of business and if it is to change) when the current tenant decides to move before the lease expires.

In addition to real estate agents and newspapers, state and territory governments often keep **registers** of serviced industrial land while, at local government level, **zoning restrictions** may stand in the way of using a property for a particular business or industrial purpose; it is best to check with these authorities for information and advice about your proposed rental.

The payment of **council rates** is not usually an additional expense for the tenant, since this should be accounted for by the landlord. However, tenants are responsible for paying electricity, telephone, gas and similar connection and upkeep charges. An **inventory** of items in the property – especially if a furnished house or flat – is usually drawn up along with the lease. It is advisable to check this list of furniture and fittings carefully before you sign, to make sure it is accurate.

Putting up a bond

Renting a home in Australia will normally involve the payment of a bond as well as rent, often amounting to four to six weeks' rental, as well as a month or so of rent in advance. This could add up to hundreds – even thousands of dollars, so be prepared. Failure to vacate the premises leaving furniture and fittings in reasonable condition (meaning 'reasonable' wear and tear) may give grounds for the landlord to draw on the bond you lodged on taking the lease, to pay for replacements and repairs. Similarly, all or part of the bond may be forfeited if the tenant defaults on payment or conditions of the lease.

BUYING PROPERTY

Property values have fluctuated markedly in Australia since the 1970s – rising, falling, then zooming upwards again. Riding the real estate rollercoaster is usually a safe enough bet, however, since most properties more than hold their own against the inflation rate over a few years, and some lucky people can make a fortune if buying and selling in the right place, at the right time.

> **People who want to immigrate to Australia are generally expected to show their commitment to their new country by buying a place to live.**

If coming from a country with a good exchange rate in comparison with the Australian dollar, purchasing a home in Australia is one of the most attractive prospects of the move. However, if you must borrow money to buy a home, it is not possible to raise a full mortgage unless you are a high income earner who can show the lender a stack of assets to cover your housing loan.

In addition to the agreed price of your new home, you should budget for a **solicitor's fee** (which depends on how complicated the transaction is) and **stamp duty**, as mentioned on page 175 which is a tax paid by the purchaser to some state governments. In the case of first home buyers, some states will waive all or part of the duty and in Queensland there is no stamp duty at all while in NSW it applies to more expensive properties and investment properties.

AUSSIE HOUSING – FROM HUMPIES TO HIGH-RISE

There are a multitude of architectural styles adapted to Australian conditions – from the aboriginal 'humpy' or 'lean to' which are very practical timber or corrugated iron constructions to constructions of glass, timber, marble and concrete which are the last word in contemporary styling. Steeply sloping building sites are common in the beautiful coastal suburbs where many people live, and building difficulties usually result in terraced apartments or multi-level houses.

In tropical areas or those subject to flooding, houses may be raised on stilts or constructed with storage and garaging below and the living quarters above.

Australians have growing respect for their historical heritage, with much attention paid to the preservation, renovation and classification of appropriate buildings. Hence you will pay more for a **Federation** (early nineteenth century) cottage of wood or sandstone than for a brick bungalow built in the 1980s, and the presence of an old leadlight window or stone fireplace increases a home's beauty (and value) in the eyes of many Aussie beholders.

City and suburban housing

In real estate terms, the choice in city and suburban housing is generally between an **established** property – one that is already completed and previously inhabited – and **project** or **estate** homes bought from the drawing board for new suburban developments. In inner city areas, terraces or townhouses comprising one or more storeys and attached to other such buildings are common, as are home units, also known as apartments or flats. Undercover parking or garage areas are important features of Australia's sprawling suburban streetscapes, especially on the coast, where there is a danger of the salty sea air rusting the metal. Sea air also damages any external metallic features of a house or flat. Ugly rusty smears or flaking paintwork from metal balcony railings are, like the Hills clothes hoist and barbeque out the back, part of the seaside streetscape.

'Average' homes – established or brand new, whether houses or flats – will have three or four bedrooms, often more than one toilet and bathroom, a separate laundry, and plenty of low maintenance outdoor living area, such as balconies, but not much garden. Detached suburban houses occupy more and more of the site as the Aussie enthusiasm for extensions and renovations drive more people to upgrade their home rather than move. 'Room for a pool' is common in Australian real estate jargon, and means you can expect a garden with room for outdoor entertaining. However, in more expensive areas of the large cities, where land is at a premium, there is an unfortunate trend to build, pave and generally 'use' every available inch of the site. In waterside locations this tendency to put a huge building on smallish land is not only ugly, but causes storm water and associated pollution problems when it rains, with less green space available to absorb water.

While there has been a flurry of interest in rainwater tanks, solar heating, recycling of 'grey' water and other environmentally-friendly measures, most Australian homes rely on electricity and natural gas for power and air conditioning is common.

Where land is more scarce, as in central metropolitan areas, high rise flats and townhouses – often most elegant and attractive – can offer marvellous views and usually feature at least one large balcony, private courtyards and off-street, two-car parking facilities. The plusher home unit developments feature swimming pools, tennis courts, sauna baths and gymnasiums since many Australians aspire to having their sporting luxuries at home, even if they must share them.

Homes in outer suburbs of major cities have been criticised for being too large and environmentally insensitive as the owners and tenants aim to live in a luxury setting within their means and sacrifice larger garden for extra rooms to house electronic entertainment areas for the family.

Housing out of town

If you plan to move into the countryside, do not take it for granted that the property will already have running water, sewerage, electricity and telephone cabling. Septic toilets, rain water tanks, onsite electricity generators and dirt roads are what you can expect if 'going bush' to live on a farm or otherwise get away from it all. Enduring drought conditions in many parts of the country mean that water restrictions have made rural life rather tough in recent years.

FORMS OF ENTITLEMENT

There are a variety of forms of ownership applicable to property in Australia:

Freehold estate (fee simple)

This is the most common and desirable estate entitlement, and means that the owner has exclusive right to the use of the property and no one but the Crown (federal government) can interfere with that right. The government may be able to serve an acquisition order to buy up all or part of the property for, say, road works, or there could be other complications you should check on, if considering a freehold, such as an easement to the state sewerage and water supply authority (meaning that the government has the right to lay pipes on that land).

Leasehold estate

This is the next best thing to a freehold. A person may lease property from a government or from a private owner of a freehold estate. For instance, in the Australian Capital Territory it is generally not possible to buy a freehold, and 99-year Crown leases are the norm for home owners.

Other forms of leasehold may be a life entitlement which may be specified in a will referring to the property of the deceased.

Documents of title

In the case of freehold ownership, one of two documents may be issued by the government – **certificate of title** or **strata title**.

♦ **Certificate of title** is usually issued by the state or territory's **Land Title Office**. It keeps a record of who owns each particular piece of land and the relevant document is called certificate of title. The government keeps the original while the owner is given a copy. This copy, along with mortgage documents if a loan has been taken to buy the property, is usually filed at the Land Title Office. Each successive owner of that piece of land is mentioned on the certificate of title. If the owner decides to lease the land, this transaction must appear on the certificate. If the land is sold, the certificate becomes the property of the new owner. Freehold title, as proven by the certificate of title, means that the current owner has rights over the land and whatever is above it – literally, from the centre of the earth to the sky. However, mineral rights to such a property are reserved by the Crown.

◆ **Strata title** is a document showing ownership of part of an allotment of land or of a 'piece of air' (stratum). It normally applies to home units and shows that the owner has a share in the land surface and whatever lies above it. Each owner of a unit, flat or apartment on the land block has a copy of the strata title. Maintenance of common areas, like driveways and gardens, is the responsibility of all title holders for that property and subject to 'fair and reasonable' rules. Strata title holders must agree to these rules, which are enforceable.

◆ **Company title** is the old-fashioned and increasingly rare entitlement to property on which flats have been built – the predecessor to the strata title. It is sometimes more difficult to raise a bank or building society mortgage on this type of ownership, due to its greater complexity. Broadly, company title means that the right to occupy part of a property is via shares issued by a company which owns the property. The buyer acquires shares in the company.

Obtaining a home loan

Savings banks and building societies provide most of the finance for housing in Australia, through partial mortgages on the purchase price. Since financial deregulation, the level of interest rates hardly varies between banks and building societies.

Prospective owners must raise a proportion of the price, known as their 'deposit', themselves. The necessary deposit is around 10%

of the total amount, but personal equity amounting to only 5% of the price may also be acceptable to some lending institutions. Banks and building societies lending over 85% of the purchase price require mortgage insurance, depending on the amount of the mortgage.

Though it is sometimes possible to obtain the deposit through a finance company or 'second mortgage', banks and building societies will usually refuse to fund the deal if they know about it or have not approved it themselves. There is no fixed loan limit. The most important criterion is that the borrower can afford the repayments and that the property is conservatively valued in case it needs to be sold in a hurry to pay back the mortgage provider. The affordable maximum in terms of repayments (which determines the amount of money borrowed in the first place) is usually calculated as no more than 30% of his or her post-tax monthly income. The buyer must provide proof that he or she has the stated income, though in Australia many families are paying far more than a third of their income on the mortgage.

Some financial institutions offer low start and fixed rate loans but the spectre of rising interest rates means that these can be risky forms of finance for the home buyer.

The terms of home loans are usually 30 years, or before the buyer's retirement age (60 years for a man, 55 for a woman).

Apart from banks and building societies, federal, state and territory housing authorities may provide finance, often through insurance or superannuation organisations. Life assurance companies, mortgage brokers, credit unions, solicitors funds and finance companies may also be helpful in raising the money you need to buy a home or another property.

AUSSIE REAL ESTATE JARGON

Prop. cl. Dandenong sol 2b'rm det. cnr bv. Lge ver. wiwo cpbds, all elfs., f/covs., ven blds incl . . . What does it all mean? Who would ever guess that the above is an advertisement offering a property for sale which, according to the vendors, is close to Dandenong (outside Melbourne, in Victoria), solid, two bedroomed, detached, on a corner, and built of brick veneer? Or that it features a large verandah and walk-in-walk-out cupboards? Included in the price are all electric light fittings, floor coverings and Venetian blinds.

Australian real estate advertisements are often couched in a special language which can be frustrating for Aussies – so how is a new resident to cope?

The brief Real Estate Dictionary in Figure 3 may be useful when you start scanning newspaper advertisements and agency brochures, looking for a property to buy or rent. As you'll see, in Australia they call a sitting or drawing room a 'lounge', the WC is a 'toilet', and interior cupboards any number of things.

Whether you are looking for a house to live in or a place to do business from, the list includes the fixtures, fittings and features which are typically Australian. It also indicates the kind of heating, floor covering, cooking, laundry and other arrangements people usually expect to find in a property.

alc	alcove	elfs	electric light fittings
awso	all weather sleep out	elev	elevated
appr	approximately	encl	enclosed
avail	available	estab	established
Av	avenue	exh fan	exhaust fan
		ext	external
bal/blce	balcony		
bsn	basin	f/covs	floor coverings
bath/bathrm	bathroom	feat	features
bh	bath heater	fitts	fittings
b'fast	breakfast	flr	floor
bib	built-in bath	fluor lts	fluorescent lights
bics	built-in cupboards	f/wire doors	fly wire doors
bir	built-in wardrobe	f/wire scrns	fly wire screens
br	brick	Fwy	freeway
bus	business	fr drs	french doors
bv	brick veneer	frt	front
		f/furn	fully furnished
cl	close to	f/tld	fully tiled
crpt	carpet		
crpt sq	carpet square	g.l.	galvanised iron
ct	cement tiles	grdn	garden
ctr	cement trough	grge	garage
cnr	corner	gbh	gas bath heater
conc	concrete	g cpr	gas copper
crt	court	g htr	gas heater
Crs	Crescent	ghws	gas hot water service
crtns	curtains	g spc htr	gas space heater
		gds	glass doors
dep	deposit	govt	government
det	detached	Gve	Grove
d'ette	dinette		
dng rm	dining room	htr	heater
dbl/dble	double	htg	heating
dbss	double bowl	holl blds	holland blinds
	stainless steel sink	hs	high school
df	double fronted		
dt	dressing table	incl	including
Dr	Drive	ins	insurance
		int	interest
E	east		
elect	electric	kit	kitchen
elHWS/ehws	electric hot	k'ette	kitchenette
	water system		

Fig. 3. An Aussie real estate dictionary.

lam	laminex	sep	separate
lge	large	shwr rec	shower recess
lp	linen press	sgle	single
LA	Listing Agent	sf	single fronted
lu	lock up (as in LU grge)	sh	sink heater
lnge	lounge (i.e. sitting room)	so	sleep out (enclosed verandah)
		sol	solid
mins	minutes	sav	stock at valuation
mod	modern	sss	stainless steel sink
mort	mortgage	sstr	stainless steel trough
mos	mosaic	stv	stove
mth	months	St	Street
N	north	tce/trce	terrace
ncs	nearest cross street	timb	timbered
		tld	tiled
o/o	owner occupied	trzo	terrazzo
ofp	open fire place	tct	terra cotta tiles
ono	or nearest offer	thru	through
op	off peak (as in hot water)	t'out/thru' out	throughout
opport	opportunity	toil	toilet
opp	opposite	tbiw	triple built-in wardrobe
Pde	Parade		
parq	parquetry	ven blds	venetian blinds
ped bsn	pedestal basin	ver	verandah
p a	per annum	v/fl	vinyl floor
p m	per month	v/tls	vinyl tiles
p w	per week	vol	volume
Pl	Place		
pol fir	polished floor	W	west
prop	property	wb	weather board
purch	purchaser	wir	walk-in wardrobe
		wiwo	walk-in-walk-out
qual	quality	wipantry	walk-in pantry
		w/minster	Westminster (a carpet-style floor covering)
rec	recess		
ref	references	w/w	wall to wall
req	required	wk	week
rend	rendered	w/ends	weekends
rd	road	w/m	washing machine
rm	room	w/shed	woodshed
rch	rotary clothes hoist	w/shop	workshop
rotis	rotisserie	w i	wrought iron
rc	rough cast		
		yr	year
S	south		

Fig. 3 (continued).

Playing Down Under

NATURE – THE MIXED BLESSING

Fans of Australia agree you can't beat the local sun, sea, bush, snow and water sports for a good time. But whether you are at home or on a day out, sunburn, the flies, ants, mozzies (mosquitoes) and other biting insects make the outdoor life a mixed blessing. The aromas of exotic sun screens and fumes of bug killing sprays are as evocative of a dinky-di day out as surf boards on the roof rack and a well-stocked eskie (box for keeping drinks cold) by the barbie.

The lure of the barbie

Inland, as well as on the coast where most people live, Australia is remarkable for the proliferation of public barbecue places. It is hard to find a large or scenically located park without built-in facilities for cooking and picnics. Many Aussies carry a charcoal-burning portable barbie in their cars – just in case they are overcome by the urge for a sizzling steak or some hot, juicy king prawns in the great outdoors.

However, clearing your space of the previous occupants' litter can be a chore. Australians are not the tidiest people on Earth, though in some places you can't see the kangaroos for the bins. On a sunny Sunday 'arvo' every family and their dog seems to be out and about. City beaches, or local dams, rivers and public swimming pools are often full of other people flocking to enjoy themselves. Those hoping to discover an isolated picnic setting with vacant facilities (tables, benches, fireplace, toilets and car parking) can be in trouble. But on weekdays when there are no school holidays, beaches and bushland in population centres are reliably quiet and empty.

Going camping

Similarly, camping grounds in national parks in the bush or by the sea tend to be frenetic during weekends, school vacations or on public holidays – and peaceful the rest of the time. Australia's national parks usually have thoughtfully organised facilities for campers, while rangers from the local parks and wildlife service drop by to keep an eye on things. Private campgrounds and caravan parks are generally less inspiring although there are plenty of them.

If you yearn for splendid isolation – or a cheap family holiday – Australia is the place to enjoy the great outdoors. If you plan it carefully, you might not see any other humans for days – just possums, kangaroos, wallabies, lizards great and small as well as emus, kookaburras, magpies or shyer creatures like koalas, echidnas and wombats.

POLLUTION, WATER SHORTAGES AND THE ENVIRONMENT

Sadly, there are also places where wildlife and even humans have been driven away by pollution. Apart from the more conventional concern about the greenhouse effect, denuding of rain forests, and levels of smog in Sydney (which can be greater than in London, Tokyo or New York), Australia has recently woken up to water pollution, and in the coastal capitals everyone seems to be talking about it.

City beaches are the most spectacular case of environmental damage wrought by sewage and storm water pouring into the ocean. No longer is it true that Aussies can go for a dip at any time, anywhere. The awful truth is that bathers may catch ear, nose, eye or throat infections linked to the effluent disposed miles out to sea, and brought in with the tides. Surfers joke wryly about catching a 'brown trout' instead of a wave.

Port Phillip Bay in Melbourne, St Vincent's Gulf, Botany Bay, some areas off the Tasmanian coast, the Tuggerah Lakes near Wyong in NSW, Victoria's Gippsland Lakes, and Western Australian waters including Shark Bay also caused concern due to water pollution in recent years, though most local water authorities are trying to improve the situation. The Murray-Darling River system running through NSW-Victoria's vital agricultural belt is dangerously depleted of water due to shortsighted use of land for irrigation over the decades and is an ecological wasteland in many areas due to high salinity. There is a marine desert off Gladstone in Queensland not far from the famous and ecologically sensitive Great Barrier Reef. Development of housing and tourist resorts along the coast are jeopardising wetlands, salt marshes, sea grass beds and mangrove areas, which are vital nurseries for marine life. Governments around Australia are hardpressed to reverse the damage of decades by changing arrangements for sewage disposal. Additives in certain boat paints are also killing marine life and unbalancing the ecology of waterways. In the worst affected areas, dangerous levels of pesticides have been found in fish – as well as more obvious signs of pollution like foul smells and rubbish in the water.

River systems and dams serving major population areas on both south-east and south-west coastal regions of Australia are at an all-time low. Suddenly, drinking and household water shortages have become a fact of life for city people as well as for people who live in 'the bush'. In Sydney water restrictions have been in place almost since the start of the twenty-first century. By 2005 householders face $A220 fines for hosing hard surfaces or watering their gardens unless during hours and days stipulated by the government.

Acting locally

Individual state governments are responsible for keeping waterways clean and dams adequately filled if for drinking purposes, yet the debate on the local environment is now a political obsession at every level. It's one thing for industrialists and 'green' politicians to argue the pros and cons of a new pulp mill or hydroelectric scheme – but when the nippers can't have a dip at the local beach without bringing home the dreaded lurgy (an infection), political heads must roll. Public pressure now demands radical measures to clean up the worst affected areas and avert further panics because water pollution has got out of hand. Government and Opposition politicians everywhere are responding with strategies to present their 'green credentials', the environment competing with the economy as key issues for law-makers and voters. Whether long-term improvement is achieved by so much public debate is, sadly, a question that future generations of Australians – and immigrants – will need to address.

AVOIDING BUGS AND BITES

Even if you are not a fan of the great outdoors, living Down Under means putting up with numerous creepy-crawlies. Unlike countries with cool climates where only mice and rats survive indoors all year round, it is common for humans to share their homes with a multitude of bugs. A bush garden will even harbour the odd snake or goanna and some find their way inside. No need to panic – mostly these are harmless and keen to find their way outside again. Giant toads occasionally descend in plague proportions in the tropical north of the country. Known as cane toads, they can grow as big as a cat. Although they are not toxic to humans, they are ugly, noisy and unpleasant to squash underfoot, especially now that they have begun to invade many moist dark areas, including gardens, and have devastated many local species.

The presence indoors of assorted species of flies, ants, spiders, moths and cockroaches doesn't mean that the human occupants are slobs who leave a lot of exposed food around, though it helps to keep cupboards and surfaces scrupulously clean and store as much food as possible in the refrigerator. Hot weather and bright lights are especially attractive to insect life – and the reason that wire mesh outside doors and windows is standard. Some people take insect repellent as part of their essential picnic, beach or gardening kit.

Most insects are harmless, though there are some poisonous spiders which include the Red Back, Funnel Web, White Tail and Trap-Door spiders. They lurk in dark corners like garages and garden sheds, as well as in the bush. In addition, mosquito bites in most places are no more than an itchy nuisance, though in some parts of Queensland and New South Wales these can lead to outbreaks of the infamous Ross River Fever. There is no cure, but it is not fatal. The effects last as long as two months when patients usually make a spontaneous recovery.

The reptile population

Australia has a wide variety of lizards, many quite weird and even angry-looking, but none are venomous and only the largest – the estuarine salt water crocodiles of northern Australia – are dangerous. Since these 'crocs' can be people-eaters you should not swim randomly in the creeks, rivers or waterholes of northern Queensland and the Northern Territory. There are many perfectly harmless reptiles, despite their fierce appearance. For instance, Blue Tongued lizards are commonly found in suburban gardens and are useful for keeping snails and other pests at bay. The most dangerous of Australia's snakes are the Brown snake, the Tiger snake, the Taipan and the Death Adder. However, these creatures are extremely shy and unlikely to be a hazard unless threatened. Similarly, the large lizards known as 'goannas' which forage for scraps of meat by the barbecue at home or in the bush should not be teased or approached because they can be aggressive. They are formidable fighters with a nasty bite and vicious claws. Fortunately, young Australians are taught at school about dangerous wildlife in their environment although newcomers of all ages should learn what these creatures look like. If you are keen on bushwalking or have young children, in particular, it is important to know how to react in an encounter and to be able to administer first aid treatment.

Marine menaces

Sharks abound in the coastal waters of Australia, although most popular coastal beaches have lifeguards and surf patrols to monitor their presence. Many beaches use shark netting to keep the monsters away. At patrolled beaches, when an unwelcome fin is spotted, shark alarms will alert people not to swim in the ocean. Similarly, beaches may be closed if the number of jellyfish is high. It is not uncommon to see blue bottles or other types of stinging jellyfish washed up on sea shores – indicating that a nasty sting is in store for a bather and keeping out of the water is the best strategy until the tide washes the stingers into another direction.

In northern Queensland coastal beaches and rivers are closed to swimmers during most of the summer months due to the presence of the box jelly fish. This species can deliver a sting which proves fatal, especially to young or elderly victims. As with land creatures, you will need to learn to recognise the types of sealife which are poisonous. Apart from the box jelly fish, the most dangerous sealife you might find swimming beside you or underfoot in Australia's warm tropical oceans are the Portuguese Man o' War and the stone fish of the Great Barrier Reef. Rock pools in eastern Australia are sometimes inhabited by the blue-ringed octopus. Venom from any of these may be fatal.

Bushfires

Inland and coastal Australia are notorious for grass and bushfires. This is a growing environmental worry and blamed on a diverse but perhaps related range of factors – global warming leading to drought, over-grazing, tree clearing, replanting with non-fire resistant species and so on. It is imperative for people starting a fire in the bush to do so only when and where signposts permit and common sense prevails. High winds can easily cause a so-called 'safe' campfire to spread out of control. Smokers should never throw smouldering matches or butts out of car windows into the scrub. Anyone who has seen the forests of charred tree stumps – not to mention the terror of actually being caught in a bush fire – knows the consequences.

CITY LIFESTYLES – THE CONSUMER LANDSCAPE

More than 60% of the population live, work and study in Australia's southern and coastal cities – from Brisbane south to Sydney, then Melbourne, and west to Adelaide and Perth. Australia is said to be the most suburban place in the world.

Beyond the compact high-rise of city centres, there are millions of bungalows with gardens, backyard pools, tennis courts and barbies.

> **Suburbanites usually have easy access to enormous air-conditioned shopping centres, known as 'malls', pronounced to rhyme with 'halls', as well as communal swimming pools, sports fields, parks and children's playgrounds.**

Sydney and Melbourne, home for three to four million people each, cover about the same amount of ground as cities like Greater London or New York. From the air you can see wave after wave of detached bungalows with swimming pools, as the suburbs spread along the coast and inland, hemmed by the mountains.

FOOD AND FOODIES

At a café in Florence, Italy, a blond Aussie breasted the bar. 'A cup of cheeno, mate', he told the man behind the espresso machine. What the youth desired was 'cappuccino'. Though unable to pronounce it, he was sufficiently multicultured to know what he was talking about. Australians are accustomed to espresso machines, barristas and a long menu of coffee-based beverages. In fact, city-living Aussies enjoy access to a most cosmopolitan range of food and drink and are even selling unique home-grown products – such as crocodile, emu and kangaroo meat – to adventurous gourmets abroad.

This happy state of affairs has been largely achieved in no more than a decade or two. Many not-so-new Australians remember a time when it was difficult to buy anything but basic beans, peas, carrots and beef in Australia. But be prepared: in some places circumstances have not changed much. In remote country towns you can expect cafés offering 'Chinese and Australian' menus – meaning sweet 'n' sour pork served with slimy potato chips or a hair-raising take on ubiquitous Thai favourites. Don't ask why the curry is 'green'! While excellent continental and other ethnic speciality food shops abound in big towns, the notorious 'Australian' cakeshops and milkbars still lurk in remoter locations, serving cups of cheeno made with Nescafé, dry lamingtons (sponge cake coated with chocolate and coconut), greasy chiki rolls (grated vegetables wrapped in batter and deep fried) and similar horrors of post-colonial Aussie cuisine.

Many newcomers are fooled by the myth that in Australia everyone eats steak for breakfast. Though it is cheaper than in most other developed countries, most people either can't afford to eat prime cuts three times a day – or wouldn't want to swap their 'breakie' of muesli for a steak, anyway.

> **What most Aussies can afford to do is eat out. Restaurant dinners are a national obsession.**

The American influence is increasingly apparent in suburbs and along highways. McDonalds, Kentucky Fried Chicken, Pizza Huts and their Aussie imitators abound, serving quick meals and takeaways.

The upmarket food industry is flourishing also due to high disposable incomes, plenty of rural capacity to produce the necessary ingredients, and ethnic cooking styles imported by newcomers or brought back home by adventurous restaurateurs.

Melbourne, Sydney and Adelaide have reputations for the best quality and highest number of restaurants per capita. Italian, Greek, French, East European, Spanish, South American and Middle Eastern cuisines flourish. There seem to be Thai, Chinese, Japanese, Indonesian or Malaysian restaurants in every main shopping centre. Many cities have impressive 'China Towns' rivalling those of the larger American cities. Most Australians know and love the varieties of South-East Asian and other

Oriental cuisines, due to prevailing high standards and low prices. Thai and Chinese food are to Australians what Indian cuisine is to the English, or Mexican to the Californians, and learning how to use chopsticks is a useful skill for both adults and children.

Aussie cuisine
There are a few restaurants specialising in bush cooking, using ingredients considered great tucker by Aboriginals. Exotica like roast witchetty grubs served on a bed of alfalfa sprouts with peanut sauce, emu egg omelettes, and sweet pies made from little known native fruits like quandongs are the result of a fad that caters more for tourists than local foodies.

Though you sometimes find Kangaroo à la King on local menus, the national emblem is the exception rather than the rule while crocodile is mainly an option for diners in Queensland and the Northern Territory, where these reptiles abound. Despite the fact that the emu – a leggy, ostrich-like bird which shares Australia's Coat of Arms with the kangaroo – has been approved for consumption nationwide as 'poultry', emu meat is mainly of interest to tourists or the export market. However, there is a more conventional 'Australian' cuisine – featuring the wonderful local seafood like crayfish, barramundi, John Dory and jumbo prawns as well as exotic tropical fruits. The recipes and presentation at top restaurants are usually a fusion of French, Italian and Asian styles.

BOOZE AND SMOKES

Liquor and cigarettes are among the most heavily taxed consumer goods in Australia. People commonly stock up on beer, wine, spirits and tobacco before yet more taxes are piled on by the Canberra government in its annual budget.

Australians are not huge drinkers and smokers, despite their boozy image. Smoking is banned by airlines on all internal flights, on buses and in restaurants, except on the pavement outside.

As for alcohol consumption, Australians drink less than the citizens of most European continental countries, though significantly more litres per annum than people in Britain, the USA, Canada and Japan.

Licensing laws

Licensing laws are less puritanical than in some Western societies, though not as liberal as in many parts of Europe. The cost of a liquor licence means that many Australian restaurants post a B.Y.O. (Bring Your Own) sign and charge a small amount for 'corkage' (opening bottles and providing glasses). This is a great advantage, since restaurant wine menus can be pricey. Pubs and liquor retail hours have been liberalised in recent years, though the rules vary from state to state. Beer, wine and spirits can be bought by people over the age of 18 from licensed shops, pubs or restaurants. Hotel (pub) trading is usually from 10am to 10pm Monday to Saturday and from noon to 8pm on Sundays.

Discovering Australian wine

More than a century ago fine wines started being produced in Australia. As long ago as the Vienna Exhibition of 1873 the 'Bruce Juice' up for tasting (actually Hermitage from Victoria) won first prize. When the European judges were informed that the wine was Australian, they thought again. Such wine could only be French, they insisted – and gave first prize to someone else.

Nowadays the Australian product is accepted internationally as excellent quality. In Britain, French wines were pushed out of the ten most popular wine brands for the first time in 2003, with Australian labels holding seven out of ten places. A US brand was in first position but the Aussies are confident they will soon be dominant in this key international wine market. The US and Canada are also getting to know the pleasures and keen pricing of Australian wines through a strategy of aggressive marketing. Much time and effort has been invested to make sure the world knows the Aussies are good for more than a beer and a barbie. At home, the market for wine is as big as it is for beer and far more prestigious. Australians are increasingly well-educated about wine varieties and many middle class homes feature wine storage facilities, a measure of success for wine as it edges out beer as the nation's favourite alcoholic beverage.

Driving tours of winegrowing districts are ideal for getting to know Australia's regions and their wines. The major producers have cellars and vineyards around the country where restaurants, accommodation, picnic and barbeque areas as well as children's playgrounds are sometimes provided, encouraging visitors to linger. Many interesting wines produced by family-run or boutique wineries are a pleasure to visit, and may have excellent restaurants as well. Buying wine from the cellar door is not as cheap as most of the large retail bottle shops, but far more fun if you like to see the countryside and meet the winemakers.

The main grape-growing regions – the Barossa, Coonawarra and
Clare Valley districts of South Australia, the Hunter Valley
northwest of Sydney, the Rutherglenn area of Northern Victoria,
and the Margaret River and Swan River Valley of South-Western
Australia – produce wines to please even the most pernickety
European palates. The wine labels are similar to those of France –
Chardonnay, Semillon, Cabernet, Cabernet Sauvignon and Shiraz.
However, each of Australia's wine-producing regions has built its
reputation on just a few styles. So it is best to do your homework
before you taste and buy. Most styles are robust compared with
the wines of Europe, and can be a surprise to the nose and
tastebuds.

In Australia, appreciation of the quality and quantity of the local
product is such that it naturally dominates the domestic market.
Table wines in the Australia-invented 'bladder' box are so popular
that some local 'grog shops' and 'bottle-Os' seem to be
constructed of them. Unpretentious but quaffable plonk is
certainly as good value for money as local table wines available in
France, Germany, Spain or Italy, though it is not as cheap due to
high taxes. Australian sparkling wines, however, can be an
inexpensive delight at a third of the price of the French original,
and a bottle of passable bubbly can be had for close to the price
of a bottle of table wine, or even a sixpack of beer.

Beer
The Aussie economy is sometimes said to ride on the sheep's
back, yet it seems that white fluffy stuff isn't always associated
with Aussies of the four-legged variety. The Aussie wine-boom
notwithstanding, beer remains as popular as Paul Hogan. Like
Hoges in one of his famous advertisements, the joke is on the

wine-drinkers as lovers of the amber nectar stand around in wine cellars slurping from a 'tinny' and watch while wine tasters spit out mouthfuls of whatever they are drinking.

Each state and even region produces a range of beers. Hot weather provides a perfect excuse to drink the stuff like water, served so cold you can barely taste it. People take home crates of beer in bottles or tins (known as 'slabs'). In pubs beer from the tap is poured into huge and often iced glasses called schooners (pints) and middies (halves), except in the more farflung country regions where blokes are served beer still in the can or bottle. A few years ago only sheilas or 'poofters' would expect to drink from a glass, but these days in urban pubs it is acceptable for women to drink direct from the bottle, just like their blokes.

Throughout the land, pubs make a feature of their beer gardens. Though many inner-city establishments have no more than a concrete square to call a 'garden', drinkers and diners flock outdoors whenever possible, in the sun or under the stars.

KANGAROO KULTCHA

Patriotism is a multi-million dollar industry. Aussies happily fill their homes and wardrobes with paraphernalia usually aimed at tourists but appreciated most at home.

> **Painters and commercial artists spearhead the New Patriotism, their vision of Australia inspired by brash, cosmopolitan city environments as well as the physical joys of surf, sun and bush.**

Jewellery, clothes, handbags, even kitchen canisters abound with the splashy designs in the colourful style of Sydney artist Ken Done, while earthy Aboriginal motifs are high fashion – whether displayed on the wall, a hair clip, or someone's sweater. Most people wouldn't think twice about sporting a T-shirt depicting their city's new entertainment complex, or a sweatshirt thick with koalas.

Performing arts

Despite the popularity of local soap operas on television, there are plenty of live shows to keep people entertained in the big cities. As in most affluent societies, there is no shortage of opportunities for people to enjoy ballet, opera, music and any other entertainment they fancy. Smaller centres also have regular music on the itinerary for leading local and international artists. Australia's geographical isolation has sometimes been cited as a barrier to the introduction of fresh ideas in the arts, but there are also advantages: Australians have been forced to rely on local entertainers and so a vigorous cultural life has evolved. Opera, ballet, modern dance, theatre, classical and all varieties of contemporary music have strong followings.

Interest in the visual and performing arts is fostered by governments at federal, state and local levels. Corporate sponsors also like their names associated with 'culture' and pour in millions of dollars to fund performances. The general public has money to spend on entertainment so theatre, concert promoters and art galleries vie with one another to attract an audience. Stars from other countries find it increasingly worth while to include Australia on their itinerary and not just for the money. Many leading artists from around the world combine their performance itinerary with a holiday Down Under. Some even keep homes in Australia, particularly along the sophisticated and attractive east coast. Record shops and libraries in most cities and many towns are as well-stocked with local and imported music and video materials as any other wealthy Western society. Facilities for performances have improved vastly in the past ten years, with major cities opening large entertainment complexes and concert centres.

The Sydney Opera House

No culture vulture visiting Australia should miss the Sydney Opera House. Its acoustics are not perfect and its famous sails are already falling to pieces – requiring regular repair work costing millions of dollars – yet as a venue it is comparable with La Scala in Milan, Carnegie Hall in New York or Covent Garden in London. The calibre of productions and standard of Australian opera, ballet and orchestras performing there are often as good as anywhere else. Nevertheless, the wondrous outlook over Sydney Harbour as you sip champagne – or a cup of tea – at the interval is as much part of the pleasure as the performance you came to see.

The arts in the state capitals

Most state capitals have their own theatre and opera companies, dance troupes, music academies, symphony orchestras and so on. Melbourne has the most vigorous theatre life, with conventional, fringe and comedy performances rivalling New York or London for standard – if not for choice. It also has a swank performing arts complex that rivals Sydney's Opera House in many respects, except harbour-side location.

A sense of humour is an essential part of the emerging Aussie theatrical tradition, and Melbourne in particular is known for its comedy performances.

Pop arts
The home of popular culture in Australia is the leagues club and casino. Leagues club are run by the Returned Servicemen's League or local football associations. Suburbanites flock to these often gigantic edifices, which can afford to stage extravagant variety shows thanks to gambling, bar and restaurant revenue. On a Friday or Saturday night, there may be two or three entertainments going at once. You can foxtrot in the ballroom, bounce around at 'dance parties', watch live shows over a drink or simply play the pokies (poker machines). The larger casinos also offer good theatre as well as restaurant facilities, to attract a wider audience for the various forms of entertainment that help them turn a profit.

Music
On the pop music scene, Australia has plenty of singing celebrities. Midnight Oil and Kylie Minogue are almost as well-known on the international touring circuit as they are at home. Over the years, Aussie performers have vied with one another for names and sounds fans find witty, ideologically correct, or simply intriguing: Johnny Diesel and the Injectors, Greedy Smith, silverchair, No Fixed Address (an Aboriginal group associated with promoting the land rights for their people) and even Harold Holt and the Sharks (named after an Aussie Prime Minister who disappeared in the 1960s, swimming near Melbourne). A strong following for heavy metal, blues and jazz notwithstanding, Australian music is noted for its affinity to the laid-back sounds of the American West Coast. On stage and disc, singers often adopt American accents.

The Australian touch
However, growing national pride and the celebration of over 200 years of cultural fusion has resulted in a new independence. Home-grown acts – be they musicians, dancers, comedians or thespians – draw heavily on local colour, politics and folklore expressed with a twanging Aussie accent. Barry Humphries' Dame Edna has plenty of competition in Australia – which is probably why she so rarely shows her face Down Under.

Fillums

Local films (pronounced 'fill-ums') export Aussie culture around the world, to the point where, in some places, the labelling of a film as 'Australian' means it must be at least interesting. Hollywood stars like Russell Crowe and Nicole Kidman have helped promote the image of Australian actors internationally. Dozens of feature films are produced annually, from deadly serious historical classics like *Picnic at Hanging Rock* to zany romantic comedies like *Crocodile Dundee, Strictly Ballroom, Priscilla, Queen of the Desert, The Matrix* series, *Bootmen* and *Rabbit-Proof Fence*, to name a few box-office success stories. Sydney's privately owned Fox Studios provides facilities for film makers of local origin as well as for international projects seeking cost effective but world class production capacity. Recent large feature films include P J Hogan's *Peter Pan* which was filmed at Warner Bros' Roadshow Studios in Brisbane. *Star Wars* and *Matrix* features and *Anaconda II* have been produced at Fox Studios in Sydney. To the credit of some states and the Canberra government administration, film commissions and government finance corporations help channel available public and private monies into the industry, while there are tax breaks available to certain commercially managed film investment funds. However, a stronger Australian dollar in recent years and tougher competition from overseas has put a dampener on the Australian film production business, with previously booming studio complexes experiencing quiet times in the mid-2000s.

Literature

Any who assume Australia is a nation of philistines, please note that more books are read per head Down Under than in what are supposed to be the more literary countries like Britain. The recently published *Oxford Literary Guide to Australia* and the *Oxford Companion to Australian Literature* celebrate this coming of age in Australian writing.

The best known authors often combine the art of fiction with their personal philosophy of what it means to be Australian. Nobel prizewinning Patrick White was and posthumously remains the grand old man of the local literary arts, followed by thinkers such as Edmund Campion, Richard Hall and Frank Moorhouse. In the footsteps of Thomas Keneally whose *Schindler's Ark* became the Hollywood film *Schindler's List*, Peter Carey also won the prestigious international Booker Prize for his novel, *Oscar and Lucinda*. As in visual arts, Australia's unique landscape is inspiration for fiction writers as well as biographers, economists and historians. Aussie culture can also be identified through the influence of non-Anglo languages, customs and values. So novelist and multi-media personality Clive James, another non-resident but strongly identifying Australian based in London, describes the post-Second World War immigrant influence like this: 'The post-war European influence was crucial. It was as if the whole population changed...(and) it would be quite common now to have a young poet, for example, a female who grew up in a house and heard German, Slovenian and has a very wide range of references... it increases the emotional vocabulary of the language as well as the words.' The contribution of Asian and non-European languages and experiences of the latest influx of immigrants is also leaving its mark on how Australian arts and writing evolves.

MEDIA

The Australian Broadcasting Corporation (ABC) and a handful of privately owned networks dominate the market for television entertainment. Hundreds of radio stations – ABC, community or university-based as well as commercial stations – put even the most remote places on the air. There are proposals which, through the cable-pay TV option and new Aussat satellites, could allow Aussies a choice of up to 60 television channels by the end of the century.

So far, most capital cities each have three commercial channels and one public (ABC) channel with digital television recently introduced. The commercial stations of major cities offer all-night television and round-the-clock movies. There is cable and satellite TV aplenty. Insomniacs who have no television or live in smaller centres without 24-hour programming can always turn on to a range of all-night music and chat shows on the radio.

As in most Western societies, television is a competitive business, and the commercial channels are perceived as gold mines which in recent years have switched owners in a continuing game of musical chairs.

Apart from the crass reality TV shows, soapies, game shows and comedies of British, American or local origin, Australian broadcasting is strong on sport. Most big international events, such as Wimbledon tennis, world boxing, cricket or European football, can be seen live or repeated on terrestrial channels as well as a satellite station devoted to sport.

News and current affairs shows are also very popular, though the content is often of a parochial or particularly puerile nature. As (non-resident) Australian philosopher and writer, Germaine Greer, observes: 'I hate what they (TV reporters) do after a bomb outrage – running around looking for bits of people to interview'.

Ethnic broadcasting

In most big cities, Australians have a unique entertainment opportunity unheard-of in most other countries – ethnic or 'multicultural' broadcasting. Despite the fact that Australia's multicultural programme-makers are said to be so good that they even export their shows overseas, there are plenty of critics of this publicly-funded television facility. As the mouthpiece of Australia's large Italian community, newspaper *Il Globo*, declared: 'Basta. Enough... The SBS has offended the Italian community with idiotic, dated and offensive contents of its programs ... it repeated ad nauseam films of the lowest category about prostitutes, pimps, drug addicts, the alienated, Mafia criminals, terrorists, scandalmongers, emphasising corruption, obscenity and blasphemy ... SBS was managed by Anglo-Saxons insensitive to community needs ... Their idea of local coverage was contests of spaghetti eaters with their hands tied behind their backs ...'. Meanwhile, many English-only speakers of ethnic origin object to the fact that some radio programmes have no English segments at all.

However, most SBS viewers appreciate that it brings foreign 'Art' films to the suburbs, while the world news coverage is generally superior to the more parochial fare offered by commercial and ABC channels.

An Aussie accent

On the airwaves, no effort is made by many popular broadcasters and public personalities to suppress the Aussie nasal twang and fractured grammar. The success of political as well as media personalities these days owes much to that bloke/sheila-in-the-street approach. The trend to an 'Australian' sound among radio and television presenters means that people struggling with the English language or simply accustomed to hearing BBC tones may not understand much of what is said. Furthermore, the accent is 'catching' and anyone who has lived in Australia for a few months will almost inevitably end up with an Aussie accent and a colourful new vocabulary (see Chapter 15: The Slanguage).

Newspapers can be similarly impenetrable. Headlines and reports in the mainstream press are full of colourful local slang. What would a newcomer make of newspaper headlines like: POLLY BUCKETS BENT POLICE? (Translation: A political figure reveals some nasty secrets about dishonest policemen.)

Newspapers and magazines

Newspapers and magazines written in English and other community languages proliferate. However, production standards, photography, journalism and advertising techniques are often less slick than counterparts from abroad, especially in the country areas.

Nevertheless, Australia's news and current affairs media provide excellent services. Considering the time difference (it's the middle of the night in Australia when it's midday in Europe) and geographic isolation, Australia is well-catered for in terms of international news. Words and pictures reach newspapers, online news services, radio and television almost as soon as they happen in countries of origin.

At the last count, Sydney and Melbourne each had two major daily newspapers; Brisbane, Darwin, Hobart, Perth and Adelaide one each, and most other cities and larger towns at least one. In addition, the suburbs and shires usually have privately-owned local papers while internet-based versions of major news outlets offer a choice of free and paid-for information.

In terms of print media, there are two daily newspapers available nationally for news and advertising every day – *The Australian* and *The Australian Financial Review*, plus a number of business and general political weekly magazines including *Business Review Week* and *The Bulletin*. As well as stridently local magazines such as *The Australian Woman's Weekly*, *Woman's Day*, *Dolly* and *New Idea*, there are radio and TV programme magazines plus Down Under editions of *Vogue*, *Cosmopolitan* and *Time*.

Control of the commercial broadcast and print media is in comparatively few hands. Little has been done to loosen the hold on media of Rupert Murdoch (News Ltd.), which controls some 60% of the print media. That other bastion of Australian news, the Fairfax organisation (John Fairfax & Sons), as well as Kerry Packer's stable of publications and television interests, have flourished. Australia's media chiefs are often blatantly mixed up with political events and openly use their publications or programmes to influence events. Yet media bias is a burning issue only for a minority of politically aware Australians. The rest ignore it, or use 'media bias' as an excuse for apathy about 'important' issues 'cos y'd be a mug to believe everything in the news, wouldn't ya?'

TELECOMMUNICATIONS

Due to size, scattered population and isolation from its main trading partners, as well as the high standard of living, Australians have lavished much money and energy on acquiring the best technology to keep in touch with one another and everyone else. Australians have embraced both mobile telephones and e-mail more passionately than most developed countries: on a per capita basis around 80% of Australian households have a mobile phone. Australia's national telephone company, Telstra, is partly privatised with plenty of 'mum and dad' investors in its shares. It is in hot competition with Optus and a range of niche players in the Australian telecommunications industry such as Hutchison Orange and Virgin Mobile.

Mail and e-mail
Australia Post has sole responsibility for distributing and delivering all standard national and international mail, though some of its minor divisions, like parcel delivery and courier services, have been sold to private contractors in recent years and run express mail services. Australia Post provides its 'priority paid' facility for next-day mail deliveries inside and outside Australia (applying to addresses in Britain, the USA and a

number of other countries with frequent flights from Australia).
Now the popularity of e-mail, faxing, scanning, mobile phone
technology and other new technologies means the so-called 'snail
mail' is declining in importance for the typical household and
businesses.

SPORT AND HEALTH

*'If you exercised and dieted and lived like me for one month, you'd
be really fit . . .'.*

*'Look mate, if you worked and drank and ate like me for one **day**,
you'd be dead – so who's fit?'*

The dialogue from an Australian cartoon summarises the national
schism of sport and indolence, washboard abdominals versus giant
beer belly. Sure, many Aussies are obsessed with achieving and
maintaining the Bondi Beach Lifesaver Look. They revel in all
things physical – from mountaineering, barefoot water skiing,
bungy jumping, triathlons, you name it. On the other hand, you
can sit on Bondi Beach all day without seeing more than a
handful of people with The Look.

Around half of Australian adults are estimated to be overweight
or obese, while more than 15% of the population are thought to
be drinking alcohol at dangerous levels. The incidence of child
obesity has risen to disturbing levels with television, computer-
focused pastimes and fast food to blame. Adults may exercise no
more than their arm muscles (lifting tinnie to mouth, pulling
poker machine handles, pressing mobile phone and computer
keys) in their leisure hours. Heart disease is the nation's biggest
killer due to an over-rich diet, smoking and lack of exercise.
Dieting and plastic surgery are big business. People are seduced

by the easy fix of a suntan, equating it with good health but the incidence of skin cancer among Australians is the highest in the developed world.

Despite the disappointing reality that most Australians leave serious sporting activities and physical workouts to the professionals, a recent survey had some good news – Australia is second only to Japan if you want to live to a healthy old age. According to the World Health Organisation, the average Japanese can expect 74.5 years of healthy living and Australians tend to survive around 73 years before ill health strikes and an irreversible decline sets in. This looks quite good compared with nearly 72 healthy years in the US and only 70 years for the average person living in the UK.

Sport as 'art'

Detractors of the great Aussie sporting life (which, as discussed, involves mainly armchair participation for the average person) say that being good at sport is the nation's way of alleviating its massive inferiority complex about a poor cultural life. Take away Australia's reputation as a winner in international tennis, swimming, athletics, cricket and football of various flavours and there's nothing left, culturally speaking, say the critics.

Other experts give a kinder alternative view of the national affinity for sport. They argue that sporting themes and events provide unique and rich inspiration to artists, playwrights, dancers and an array of creative people from fields other than sport. According to Richard Cashman, author of *Sport in the National Imagination* and associate professor in history at the University of New South Wales, sport and the arts go hand in hand in Australia. Sport in

Australia just might be more meaningfully cultural than in any other country. Since hosting the 2000 Olympics, 2003 World Cup Rugby and an array of other international tournaments in recent years, supporters of the 'sport as art' viewpoint say that Australia's artistic community has found funding and enthusiastic audiences though sport. The Melbourne Cup, a horse race of world standing run each November, is a fine example of how a sport has become a community art form. People dress up, gamble, party, go to long lunches, create amazing hats for the occasion – all around the country, not just trackside at Flemington Racecourse where the nags actually do their stuff.

Sport is an obsession for the mainstream media. News and features about sports events and sporting experts are a mainstay of many 'general' news publications and current affairs shows. By contrast, business news, art sections and foreign news are relatively low profile. Arts bodies and their supremos complain publicly that the 'real' arts (music, dance, theatre, opera, art galleries, etc) get a poor deal from government because there are fewer votes in 'elite' pursuits. They argue that theatre seats, concert tickets, and entry fees to major art shows can be expensive in Australia due to lack of government subsidies. In sports-mad Australia, governments certainly seem to shy away from too close an association with so-called highbrow cultural activities. But retirement brings freedom for many politicians. Once in high-profile attendance at sporting events, as *ex*-politicians many can and do indulge their passion for public performances of opera and classical music without being accused of elitism.

Sport as 'motherhood'

Sporting heroes and heroines are Australia's own royalty and win accolades such as Australian of the Year with great frequency, since sport is a bit like motherhood in Australia, so who can knock it?

Olympic gold medal winning swimmers like Ian Thorpe and (now retired) track and field athlete Cathy Freeman are highly esteemed by the Australian people. They have integrity and are therefore a magnet for political and commercial organisations who hope that a little of the good stuff will brush off on them. Sportspeople are regular front page and celebrity column news. Their popularity with the public can resonate for years with consumers, long after their lucrative mid-career promotional and advertising contracts have expired. Celebrity sportspeople have carefully managed 'retirement' careers that may include stints as models, actors, fashion designers and promoters of a variety of goods and services.

Sporting options

Walking is the number one regular physical activity Down Under. Next in popularity – during the summer months, at any rate – is swimming, though aerobics, yoga, Pilates and cycling are also popular ways for Aussies to let off steam and keep fit. Of the team sports, football and soccer, then golf, tennis, netball, and basketball are popular physical activities and of course cricket also has a keen following.

Some kind of team sport is mandatory for middle-class children everywhere, and parents spur their budding athletes on to ever greater achievements at weekend matches and inter-school tournaments. However, there is plenty of evidence to suggest that love of sport is not innate in children. Worse still, they may have spent years lazing with their parents by the television rather than going to a park and throwing a ball around. At the extreme end, some kids – like their counterparts in other wealthy nations – may even have to be bribed with computer games and other toys and treats to attend training and perform on the playing field. So watch out if you are moving your kids to Australia, there is no guarantee that sporting lifestyles will be a way of life for them just because the climate and conditions are good for it!

It's just not cricket

Cricket is the main summer sport, while many versions of 'footy' dominate the airwaves and news stands in winter. The most popular football games in Queensland and New South Wales are rugby league and rugby union. Though most team sports have a time and place in Australia, due to immigrants of so many backgrounds, the Australians have evolved their own brand of football – known as **Aussie Rules**.

The game is most popular in Victoria, South Australia, Western Australia and Tasmania. Australian Rules emerged in the mid-nineteenth century. It has evolved since the days of Irish immigrants to the Victorian goldfields, who based their game on Gaelic football and Hurley. Admirers of the game say players are wonderfully fit and macho while detractors claim this breed of football is one of the most uncouth ever played, one step up from mud-wrestling. There are 18 men to a side, and the aim is to put the ball between four posts. Nobody gets sent off and the injured are left where they fall. Punching, kicking, or hitting the ball with any part of the body is allowed. The only no-no is tackling below the knee or above the shoulder. Victorious hulks hugging each other in the mud, blood spattered losers being dragged from the field by their mates – these are common sights in news reports of the day's big game.

SPORT AND GAMBLING

Unlike political, environmental or cultural events, sport can be relied upon to stir fierce emotions. Fans often prove their obsession by putting their money where their hearts lie, laying bets as gestures of loyalty, sporting spirit – or simply for the thrill. Armchair athletes abound and having a flutter (gambling and betting) is part of the Great Australian Way. As mentioned, the Melbourne Cup every November brings the country to a halt for a few minutes while the big race is run. There's hardly a club, office, shop or school where 'sweeps' on the current crop of top 'nags' running at the Flemington race course aren't organised while everyone waits breathlessly by the radio or TV for the result. For some state governments, poker machines and gambling-related activities also help fill state coffers via taxes that apply to casinos, clubs and betting shop operators. So while most politicians condemn gambling from a moral standpoint, they are having a bet each way – if you can't beat 'em, tax 'em.

Sport meets entertainment

There are also more offbeat betting opportunities: cane toad races in northern Queensland, dwarf-throwing contests in certain regions, and send-ups of posh 'Pommy' socio-sporting occasions, like the Henley-on-Todd regatta at Alice Springs. This particular 'boat race' is a farcical version of the Henley-on-Thames affair in England. In Pommyland's original version, champagne and real water flow. However, the Todd River is a very dry place in Central Australia where the favourite thirst quencher is, of course, beer. The locals of 'the Alice' lay bets, drink and keep themselves entertained watching the hordes of hairy legs (shorts are *de rigueur* in the desert heat) bearing 'boats' along the Todd course. The similarly facetious Beer

Can Regatta at Darwin features vessels made of emptied, flattened tinnies – though they do actually float on water in this Ocker send-up of the prestigious sailing events of Mother England and elsewhere.

However, Australians don't need a display of sporting prowess or a race to provide an excuse to try their luck. The combination of a convict history and the need for entertainment in very basic working and living conditions has led to the invention of many betting games. Two-up, played with coins and still outlawed in most Australian states, is a good example. Betting shops and casinos, legal or otherwise, are part of the lifestyle for many Australians who like to mix gambling with social activities.

TIME OFF

Australians value their leisure time, and public holidays are sacred. There are one or two public holidays which apply in some states and not others. However, the list below shows the National Public Holidays which Aussies can rely upon in planning their long weekends and vacation schedules:

New Year's Day	1 January
Australia Day	26 January
	(the actual anniversary of Cook's
	landing in Botany Bay in 1770)
Good Friday	variable
Easter Monday	variable
ANZAC Day	25 April
Queen's Birthday	variable (long weekend, usually June)

Labour Day	variable (long weekend, usually October)
Christmas Day	25 December
Boxing Day	26 December (except South Australia)

ESSENTIAL SIGHTSEEING

While you are Down Under, whether as a visitor, student or on a permanent basis, there are certain 'must-sees'. Ironically, many Australians have not been to more than a few of these world famous places – but then it is a big country and can be expensive as well as time-consuming to get around.

Temporary visitors and tourists with a foreign passport and outward ticket can take advantage of a discount on internal air fares offered by the major airline companies Virgin Blue and Qantas-Australian Airways in order to encourage overseas tourism. The airlines offer other special deals on internal flights to visitors.

Apart from the beauties of Sydney and the attractions of the **Great Barrier Reef** on Australia's eastern seaboard, you should try to include **Alice Springs** and **Kakadu National Park** in your Australian itinerary. Kakadu Park is an outback wilderness with pools and waterfalls which is protected by World Heritage Listing. Tours run from Darwin, in the Northern Territory. The highlight of any Alice Springs visit is massive **Ayers Rock (Uluru)** and observing its colour changes as dawn progresses to sunset. Though tourists are no longer allowed to make the strenuous climb up the rock to see the Aboriginal rock markings for themselves, the general atmosphere of Australia's 'red centre' is a special experience and is in sharp contrast to the tropical island life of Queensland, for example, or the sophistication of Melbourne and Sydney.

In the west, the thriving city of **Perth** and its environs should not be missed if you want a coast-to-coast impression of life in Australia. A slow drive between **Melbourne** and **Adelaide** is a great Aussie experience, with a remarkable rocky coastline and historic towns, winegrowing regions and nature reserves in between. The new rail and road link from Adelaide to Alice Springs is also a good trip for the more adventurous.

Australians on holiday tend to drive to seaside towns near their home city, if they live in a suburban centre. Perhaps the ultimate Aussie beach resort is **Surfers Paradise**, on Queensland's Gold Coast. The hotel, casinos, and holiday apartment skyscrapers tower over the beach and the area features some fabulous theme parks for kids of all ages. 'Surfers' (as the town is known) is a small-time Manhattan with its high-rise water frontage – plus the miles of surf and palm trees. There is a large range of eco-tourism destinations around the continent, as well as many islands and sub-tropical resorts particularly along the east coast of Queensland and NSW and off Western Australia.

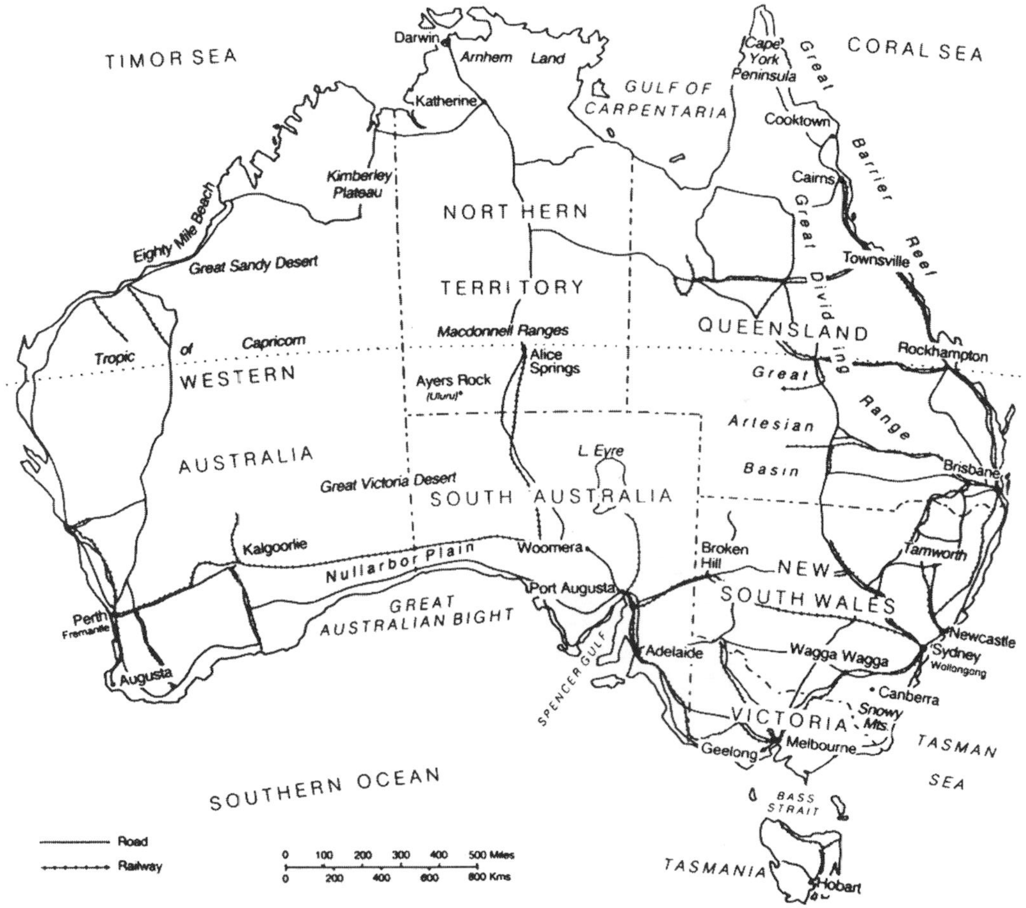

Fig. 4. Map of Australia.

10

Driving in Australia

PLEASURES, PROBLEMS AND THE POLICE

Wide open spaces make Australia a fine place to drive. In remote regions, as well as the cities and towns, long distances between destinations are to be expected. It's nothing for an Australian to drive for an hour or two simply to call on people or find a picnic ground. Sensibly, major transport routes are designed to include rest areas, speed ramps and other conveniences for cars and drivers obliged to cover long distances, rather than for the considerations of pedestrians, kangaroos or koalas crossing (of which more later).

City driving

In bigger centres or at key crossroads, traffic snarls, bottlenecks and problems are usual. Regional governments, responsible for maintaining and planning roads, are often slow to commit the vast sums needed to improve traffic links and may wait for the federal government to step in with finance or loan approvals until action is taken. Sydney, for example, lived for decades with hellish peak hour jams on its famous coathanger Harbour Bridge. Now the harbour tunnel has relieved the bottleneck but cynics say this won't solve the problem for Sydney and more underground road tunnels are opening to reduce congestion in Australia's largest city.

Country living

On country roads it can be risky to dawdle along gawping at the scenery, just as it is to cover too much ground too fast. Driving hundreds or thousands of kilometres (often through the night), eagerness to arrive at long last, plus the unchanging scenery and straight roads that seem to go on for ever, may reduce the ability to see other vehicles and to judge their speed.

Expressways and tollways

Main city and tourist routes feature six to eight lane **expressways** with speed limits of up to 110 kmh – the Australian term for super-highways known as motorways in Britain, autoroutes, autobahns and autostradas in continental Europe and freeways in the United States. All speeds and distances are stated only in kilometres in roadside signs and on maps for Australian roads. Occasionally, **tolls** are levied to help cover the expensive business of highway building and maintenance over a vast continent, usually by private infrastructure consortia. Such privately operated roads are referred to as 'tollways' or 'motorways'. Lighting is sophisticated on major arteries and usually adequate elsewhere. Tollways, and expressways in particular, feature emergency telephones at regular intervals for use in case of a breakdown though the popularity of mobile phones means that a driver will often have a phone in her or his own vehicle (providing it is in range).

DRIVING ON MINOR ROADS

Though the standard of Australia's 16,000 km national highway system linking major towns and cities is high and ever improving, the isolation, perpetual roadworks, bushfires, floods or droughts can make tarred and sealed roads inaccessible. Minor routes are sometimes no more than rock and gravel. Even Australia's north–south link, the 3,000 km **Stuart Highway** from Adelaide in South Australia to Darwin in the Northern Territory, was at last sealed with bitumen and suitable for heavy traffic as late as 1987. After bumping along a dirt track for a few hours, it is little wonder that nuts and bolts – of occupants as well as the vehicle – come loose. Driving unsealed roads requires great care, skill, patience and preparation for the threat of being stranded in the middle of nowhere with a cracked axle or universal joint, at least until the next car comes along. Despite the popularity of four-wheel drive vehicles, dirt roads remain a danger. Even if the vehicle can cope with rough tracks, the driver may not be skilful enough to provide a safe ride!

Koalas crossing

Most roads are well signposted to warn of unexpected bends, treacherous conditions or flooding. Uniquely Aussie wildlife signs pop up near bushland areas. They may look cute with their message like 'Kangaroos 5 km' or 'Koalas Crossing' above silhouettes of the beasts. However, they are not merely there to protect the wildlife from cars. Large animals like kangaroos or wallabies moving at speed across or along a road are a real danger to cars and their occupants, and can cause serious accidents if one emerges suddenly from the scrub, taking a driver by surprise. Vehicles in rural areas are often fitted with large 'roo bars in case they strike an animal, to minimise damage and provide some psychological protection to the person behind the wheel. An unprotected car colliding with a kangaroo or wild pig at high speed is unlikely to escape unscathed, and the damage can often be considerable.

Air conditioning

Just as most of us wouldn't dream of driving without good interior heating and windscreen demisters in the colder climes of the Northern Hemisphere, air conditioning is an essential luxury for the average family car Down Under and a standard feature for most Aussie-bought vehicles. It enhances the ability to sit out a traffic jam or drive long distances in searing temperatures. Also, think about colour – dark coloured vehicles absorb more heat than lighter coloured ones. Even in the coastal cities which benefit from a sea-breeze, summer temperatures regularly soar to 40 degrees – and if you leave your car parked, you may well return to find it's at least 45 degrees inside and the steering wheel is too hot to touch.

Be prepared

Given the long distances and sparse facilities in country areas, it's advisable to carry extra water and even fuel for your car on long journeys. Each year there are several rescues of travellers to remote places who have had misadventures when extra fuel and provisions would have been handy. Many outdoorsy types with extra boot space stick to the 'have barbie – will travel' principle, always carrying a portable barbecue and bag of charcoal – just in case they run into that extra-special spot for a swim and some food in an idyllic beach or bushland setting, or if they are too weary to drive on. But you don't need expensive equipment – a 'billy' (metal pot with a wire handle) and some kind of improvised grilling rack will do the job, and is what most rural Australians use.

But be certain that you don't light a campfire in a **bushfire zone**, or when fire danger is high. The golden rule is never, never leave until every last spark has been extinguished, preferably by covering the embers with dirt or sand. The danger of starting a bushfire is ever-present in the Australian bush. For the same reason, never throw your cigarette butt or matches out of the car window – it's the easiest way to start a fire which could cause serious loss of life and property, and an offence punishable by heavy fines.

ROAD RULES

The Motor Registry or Road Transport Authority for the area where you plan to visit or live can provide all the information you'll need about driving rules. Familiarise yourself with these as well as signposting which apply. Bear in mind that while the general laws of motoring around Australia are fairly uniform, and similar to those of most Western societies, some aspects could be totally alien to first-time drivers there.

Just as driving conditions alter around the country, so do the rules which apply in the states and territories of Australia. Each is responsible for writing and administering its own road law, and the police forces co-operate to exchange data about criminal and traffic offences across borders. Stiff fines, jail terms and licence suspension are among the penalties for drink-driving convictions and causing an accident by breaking a road safety or traffic regulation (see next section). For other more minor driving offences like speeding, most states employ a **points system**. A driver's points are deducted according to the magnitude of each traffic offence. If all points are lost by an individual within a certain time period, the licence is withdrawn as punishment.

Driving interstate

From state to state the changes in road rules may be small, though on matters like priority at intersections these differences can be dangerous, so it's wise to obtain the Highway Codebook for both the region you mainly drive in and elsewhere, if you plan to drive interstate. Basically, all states and territories adhere to the 'keep to the left' principle, the driver sitting to the right of the passenger as in Britain. Picking up hitch-hikers is not recommended in most places – and is illegal in some states.

Using seat belts

Australia was one of the first countries in the world to introduce compulsory seatbelt-wearing, and steady falls in road deaths since the 1970s demonstrate the wisdom of this law. Traffic police don't think twice about stopping a car if the driver and passengers are not strapped in properly. Fines for each offence may be imposed (though this varies slightly between states). It is compulsory to wear a seatbelt whether you are in the back or front of the car, though there are exemptions: passengers in taxis, for instance. Small children must wear a special seatbelt and it is illegal in most cases to carry a baby or toddler (pre-school child) who is not in a special harness and child seat. To encourage compliance with this law, some state transport departments rent child seats and baby capsules since they are expensive to buy.

SPEED LIMITS

Despite some major traffic jams in big cities at peak hours, Australian roads and conditions tend to be fine and clear – but beware of an urge to break the speed limit. For example, living out your Grand Prix fantasies on the spectacular S-bends of Sydney's eastern suburbs by the harbour may be hard to resist. However, traffic policing is tough and the road accident toll remains unacceptably high in most places. Before you can say 'New Australian' a cop car could be looming in the rear view mirror, sirens blaring. Speeds are measured in kilometres per hour, and cars are usually required to have speedometers which provide a reading in these terms. In built-up areas – defined as those with street lighting, curbing and guttering – the speed limit is between 40 kph and 60 kph. Outside built-up areas, as on country roads and highways, the general speed limit is 80–100 kph and 110 kph on expressways. Speeds of more or less than these may apply and the motorist is told by frequent restriction signs showing the highest speed applicable in that zone. In the vicinity of schools the speed limit is 40 kmh during school arrival/departure times, typically 8.30–9.30am and from 2.30–4pm.

UNDER THE AFFLUENCE OF INKAHOL

Stamping out drink-driving to reduce road deaths is a national obsession. The legal blood-alcohol limit is 0.05 to 0.08 per cent of alcohol per 100 ml of blood, depending upon the state or territory and each enforces an individual set of regulations, fines and drivers' licensing laws.

Random breath testing is the main road safety weapon. In recent times, only Scandinavia and Northern Ireland have more fanatical crusades to eradicate drink-driving offences. Critics of the policy say the campaign to stop people mixing drinking with driving is also a political ploy. They say it is cheaper for the state governments to run emotive publicity campaigns and provide more 'booze buses' (breath testing units) than it is for them to build wider, safer roads which might also improve road safety. Publicity campaigns to eradicate drink-driving are relatively cheap but effective. Shock-horror TV advertising remakes the point about drink-driving to each new generation of 17 year olds allowed to hold a licence. Australians may be willing to live with even tougher drink-driving laws in future and it appears that driving while under the influence of alcohol has become socially unacceptable at last. The only exception of major concern remains the propensity of young people to get behind the wheel with too many drinks or other substances affecting their judgement. Sadly, car accidents are still the biggest killer of Australia's teenagers.

INSURANCE AND REGISTRATION

The states are responsible for the building and upkeep of their often extensive urban and outback roads. Car registration fees paid by owners form part of this budget. 'Rego' (registration fee) comprises road tax, a roadworthiness test and a minimum car insurance requirement for third party injury. Third party insurance is compulsory throughout the country though progressively higher levels of car insurance, as well as driver insurance, can be bought. The average cost of third party insurance (to cover other cars and drivers in case you are at fault in an accident) for a typical family sedan is around $A500. Details of licence laws and registration for vehicles brought into Australia from abroad are also provided in the section on licensing for drivers from overseas later in this chapter.

Remember: foreign insurance policies are generally *not* applicable in Australia and it is illegal to drive a vehicle, caravan or trailer on any public road unless at least third party (bodily injury) insurance is in force to cover that vehicle, caravan or trailer effective in the state or territory where it is to be driven.

General car insurance

The insurance premium is calculated by private or government insurers on a zonal basis, depending on the address of the registered individual or business which owns the vehicle. Usually, risk of accident, theft or damage is considered to be greater, and premiums therefore higher, in city or urban areas. People temporarily importing vehicles into the country are advised to extend their insurance for full cover in Australia.

Temporary visitors

In most states and territories, temporary residents and visitors are exempt for up to 12 months from paying vehicle registration fees as long as the registration of that vehicle remains valid (unexpired) in the country of origin and the vehicle is exported when they depart. As soon as possible after the vehicle has arrived in an Australian state or territory, it must be inspected by the nearest registration authority to make sure it is roadworthy. For this concession to apply, a temporary visitor will need either:

◆ a *Carnet de Passage* or other evidence that security has been lodged with customs authorities in Australia (see Chapter 7);

◆ a cash or bank security equal to the amount of GST (Goods and Services Tax) and LCT (Luxury Car Tax) otherwise payable. These taxes are briefly explained later in this chapter.

MOTORING ORGANISATIONS, PETROL AND ROAD SERVICES

Most Australians belong to private, state-based motoring organisations. Some 60 to 75% of car owners – twice the rate in Europe – find it pays to join the motoring organisation in their state or territory and benefit for roadside services in case they are needed. The efficiency of the breakdown and rescue services provided by these associations is among the best in the world. Mechanics are at the scene within an hour of a member's telephone call to their base. Due to the high market penetration, annual fees for roadside service at around $A60 per vehicle are low in comparison with motoring organisations in other countries. Touring information, including hotel guides and maps, telephone advice as well as access to the motoring organisation's mechanic to check a used car the member is proposing to buy, are other advantages for members.

Buying petrol

Petrol prices can rise or fall a few cents from place to place, and there is a discount war between service stations, especially in big cities. The cost of unleaded petrol is around $A1 per litre at the time of writing. LPG, diesel and other grades of petrol are also available at Australia's service stations, as are spare parts and autoelectrical and mechanical assistance.

On day trips and driving holidays, the petrol stop can serve multiple purposes. But beware – the standard of comfort and service diminishes with the distance from civilisation. In the long hauls between towns, a hamlet often consists of a couple of petrol pumps, a garage where you pay for the petrol and (maybe) a pub. The 'restaurant' and other facilities in Australia's isolated areas can be truly appalling, especially if the motorist is accustomed to the hi-tech finesse of American or European road rest centres.

BUY IT THERE OR BRING YOUR OWN?

If you're thinking about buying a car or any other vehicle in Australia, new or second-hand, high protective import duties on fully imported vehicles combined with the historical weakness in the 'Pacific Peso' against the currencies of major vehicle-exporting nations means that car prices are steep. However, tariffs and duties fell steadily from the late 1980s as the federal government tried to implement a 'sink or swim' policy for protected local car manufacturers and so car prices have fallen. A stronger Australian dollar in 2002–3 should also benefit people buying imported cars. From a mid-1980s high of 57.5%, the size of the tariff on fully imported cars has fallen to 10% in 2005. There is GST (Goods and Services Tax) of 10% for cars that are bought new and imported to Australia for sale or for the use of the owner who is coming to live in Australia on a temporary or permanent basis.

Considering prestige value
Given these high taxes and tariffs, if you are considering whether or not to pay the transport costs for a luxury or exotic car, bear in mind that it might be sold for a profit or at least have your import costs covered when you want or need to buy a new car

yourself. The market for prestige imported vehicles in Australia is vigorous and they dominate the expensive end of the market. Cars which don't rate a second glance on European roads – like BMWs, Mercedes, Porsches and Citroens – may turn heads in Australia because everyone knows they can cost a small fortune. However, servicing and spare parts can be tricky and expensive for such models, one more factor to consider if you're trying to decide whether to take yours with you or to buy one there.

Around 12% of all the new cars sold in Australia are imports, but profits are high enough to keep the dealers smiling. The price of imported cars starts at around $A30,000, while a Rolls Royce will set you back a cool quarter of a million dollars brand new. Overall, Mercedes-Benz is the most popular of the imported status cars, followed by BMW, Volvo, US-made Ford, Mazda and Jaguar.

Four-wheel drive
There has been a trend in suburban Australia since the 1990s to four-wheel drive vehicles. Jeeps and 'sports' vehicles are becoming popular with both inner city macho types and middle-class families, as the ultimate protective vehicle against encounters with other cars, or if you want space for five or more passengers.

Going for value
Apart from wholly Australian-made models, Japanese or other imports from the Asian region represent top value for money. The companies which build or assemble vehicles at plants in Australia are Toyota, Mitsubishi, Holden and Ford. The last two are long-established as the biggest-volume sellers on the new and used car market in Australia, providing easy access for repairs and parts at most car shops and garages. A locally assembled car costs at least

$A14,000 new though some tiny models are slightly less. A typical family sedan is around the $A30,000 mark. See Chapter 7 for a more specific list of new car prices.

Buying a second-hand car

Due to the high cost of new cars, the second-hand market is often worth investigating. Classified advertising sections in local newspapers are heavy with car advertisements placed by owner-drivers and licensed dealers. By the early 2000s, the used car market was dominated by Japanese models under five years old and easy to service in Australia as well as the locally made vehicles. Most big towns and cities have second-hand car dealers concentrated in a particular area. Car auction rooms also provide opportunities to pick up a vehicle minus the dealer's profit margin, though mechanical checks are your own responsibility.

If you're planning to buy a used car in Australia, it is wise to join the regional road service organisation first so you can use one of its qualified mechanics to run an impartial check on a vehicle you might decide to purchase, in case it's not all it's hyped up to be.

Apart from obvious mechanical problems or other defects like rust, buying a stolen or debt-ridden car is also a trap to be avoided. As a safeguard, all car dealers and auction rooms are obliged by law to provide title guarantees proving the vehicle is free of debt and not stolen. If you are buying privately through the press or other contacts, legal points like these should be clarified first.

Being cautious

Car salespeople can be as slippery in Australia as elsewhere in the world, especially in highly competitive markets like Sydney's 'magic mile of motors' along the lengthy stretch of Parramatta Road. If possible, try to test drive the car by yourself, without a salesperson at the wheel. When closing a deal with a used car dealer, never put your signature to a purchase form until it is fully filled out and do not agree to a deal offering a free vehicle check. For this 'free' check will only be carried out after your signing to the purchase document, and you could find yourself stuck with the vehicle irrespective of faults discovered. Even a purchase agreement subject to a satisfactory mechanical check should not be signed. Unless the terms of what you mean by 'satisfactory' are well defined, there could be an ugly squabble with the dealer over the repair of any faults which do come to light.

Anyone foolish enough to pay a deposit and sign a purchase agreement before the mechanical testing is done risks losing their money if they decide to scrap the deal. Some states stipulate a 'cooling-off period' in the used car warranty, giving the buyer an option to return the vehicle within a certain period should it not be as represented by the dealer. Often used cars bought from dealers and costing more than a few thousand dollars will have some form of mechanical warranty as well.

THE LICENCE – FOREIGN AND AUSTRALIAN DRIVERS

Usually, a driver from abroad is allowed to drive on a current foreign or international licence for a 'period of grace' – after which he or she must take a local licence as a resident of a state or territory. Though many states do allow newcomers to get behind the wheel for a few months on the strength of a foreign licence and no testing, it is a good idea to take the initiative: study a summary of driving regulations from your local roads and traffic authority on arrival.

Most states and territories license Australian-resident drivers for three to five years at a time and a licence fee is imposed on each renewal, as a revenue-raising tactic by governments. If you obtain a licence in one Australian state or territory, it is valid everywhere you drive inside the country. Similarly, if you are convicted of an offence, fined, or otherwise penalised in one place, such convictions or unpaid fines are also on record wherever you go. Sophisticated computer systems in transport and police departments mean that the authorities will eventually catch up with you at the address on your licence.

Diplomatic exemptions

It raises the hackles of many citizens that foreign diplomats and their dependants are immune from the obligation to pay the price of their traffic offences since, as representatives of another government, they cannot be sued. People on diplomatic passports may be able to get away with non-payment of fines and minor offences, but there have been some cases of driving incidents causing a political fracas between Australia and the country represented by the offending diplomat (or family member). Agitation continues for this aspect of diplomatic immunity to be tightened.

11

Health and Welfare in Australia

A DELICATE BALANCE

Recent Australian governments have tried to minimise the massive
financial burden on tax-payers of health and social security
benefits. On the one hand, Australia is one of the most highly
taxed societies in the world, and its citizens may therefore expect
that, when the proverbial rainy day comes around, a generous
public welfare system will back them up. The counter argument is
that with its aging population, significant unemployment rates
and economic uncertainty the cost of a healthy, publicly financed
health and welfare system would be too much for Australian tax-
payers to bear. Many people prefer to be more moderately taxed
while financing their own future needs for pensions and medical
services. Despite the political tensions, Australia's hybrid welfare
system appears to be in working order after the many changes and

cuts of the past decade. Government welfare agencies are augmented by a range of charities that help keep destitute people off the streets to a fair extent, especially in comparison with other Western societies.

Australia's social security system is a complicated 'user-pays' concept, whereby tax-payers make a substantial contribution towards their own health and welfare needs while they are in paid work. For those without financial support, there is a skimpy safety net readily available if they can prove they have little or no financial assets or income. Into this category of welfare recipients fall some aged citizens, chronically unemployed, students, people with injuries or disabilities that prevent them working for a living or paying for medical attention.

The main federal government organisation responsible for implementing government policy on welfare payments is known as Centrelink. Centrelink has many shop-front offices around Australia's towns and cities, as well as telephone and internet information in a range of languages, or with translator services if applicable.

Medicare is the government-funded health and medical system, administered by an organisation of the same name, Medicare, also with many shop-front offices around the country. Unlike the welfare system of payments, Medicare's subsidised medical and hospital services are available to new settlers and some categories of visitors and to all Australian tax-payers, who pay for the public system via a taxation levy and various other measures covered later in this chapter.

WELFARE SERVICES AVAILABLE TO NEWCOMERS

Refugees and certain categories of temporary residents may be able to receive some welfare assistance while all migrants and most visitors with visas for longer than six months have the right to use the Australian public hospital and medical system.

However, given that the main immigration focus is on encouraging permanent settlers who can bring money, expertise, talent and other economic benefits to Australia, it follows that tax-payers are not footing the bill for 'immigrants' welfare and pension needs.

Sponsored newcomers, either in family or economic streams, *cannot* access any welfare benefits until they have lived in Australia for two years in most cases. This waiting period is extended to ten years for an age pension, when certain pharmaceutical costs and other allowances are provided to eligible people subject to income and assets testing. The person or organisation signing an Assurance of Support is liable to repay any benefits the sponsored party may have received via Centrelink, charity, local or state government. In the case of migrants who are the parents of such a sponsor, any official Assurance to the migration authorities means the son or daughter who signed it must cover all the newcomers' expenses in Australia for the specified period.

INTERNATIONAL SOCIAL SECURITY AGREEMENTS

There are bilateral treaties in place with Britain, New Zealand, Austria, Canada, Cyprus, Malta, Spain, Ireland, Italy, The

Netherlands, Portugal, Denmark, Germany and the USA. These effectively guarantee welfare benefits, and particularly an age pension, to people who migrate between Australia and these countries. International Social Security Agreements were also signed but had not officially commenced at the time of writing between Australia and Belgium, Chile, Croatia and Slovenia. So if you are thinking of migrating to Australia from any of these countries, such an Agreement should benefit you by closing any gaps between your pension entitlement in your country of origin, and what you would be normally entitled to if you stayed in Australia until reaching pensionable age.

Partner countries in Australia's International Social Security Agreements share responsibility for welfare payments with Australia. Both countries make concessions in their social security rules so that people can access payments for which they would otherwise fail to qualify, for instance because they do not fulfil requirements like citizenship, minimum contribution record, past residence record and current country of residence.

Australia will equate social security periods in Agreement countries with periods of Australian residence in order to meet the minimum qualifying period for Australian pensions. The other countries count periods of Australian residence as periods of social insurance in order to meet their minimum qualifying periods for payment.

Usually both countries will pay a part pension to a person who has lived in both countries. If you have lived in Australia for 25 years you will receive a full age pension and a proportion of the full pension is payable if you have been resident in Australia for less than 25 years. The idea is that the Agreement country will top up the pension for a person who does not qualify for the full Australian pension based on their residency period in that other country.

Australia has additional ways of determining if a person should receive an age pension apart from the period of time as a resident. Measures of personal wealth and the ability of the aged person to generate their own income in retirement (see 'How Rich is Too Rich?' below) may cancel pension entitlements. For instance, unlike some European countries where national insurance is every tax-payer's entitlement at retirement, no matter how wealthy they may be, in Australia this is not the case because assets and income tests are applied.

HOW RICH IS TOO RICH?

Most pensions and benefits are subject to 'means testing' of income and assets. These tests decide how much the family or individual will receive from the government in the form of pensions, pharmaceutical benefits or other benefits and allowances if they are disabled, unemployed, studying full time and so on. For example, in the case of the age pension (to which citizens of some European countries may be automatically entitled) some 30% of Australians are considered too wealthy to receive any pension at all, though they would be eligible for other concessions and benefits for living and travel expenses as well as medicine. Many allowances and government pensions are reduced if a person has more than $A250,000 in assets ($A150,000 if they also own their own home) or earn more than $A62 a fortnight.

AGE PENSION AND RETIREMENT INCOME/BENEFITS

Here's how it works with means testing of Australia's age pension:

Single pensioners: A full age pension is available to a single person with assets of less than around $A150,000 apart from their family home (these assets may be shares, superannuation funds, investment property) and who has pretax income up to $A60 a week from work, share dividends, rent and so forth. The single rate of age pension is about $A280 a week. For every dollar of income above $A60 a week, the pension is reduced by 40 cents. For every $A500 in assets above $A150,000, the pension is reduced by $A1.50.

Married couples: A full age pension is available to a married or de facto couple with assets of less than around $A220,000 apart from their family home (these assets may be shares, superannuation funds, investment property) and with pretax income up to $A100 a week from work, share dividends, rent and so forth. The married rate of the age pension is some $A400 a week. For every dollar of income above $A100 a week, the pension is reduced by 40 cents. For every $A500 in assets above $A220,000, the pension is reduced by $A1.50.

Other welfare benefits are calculated on a similar basis, deducting pretax income and assets from the pension entitlements so that payments are not made to people who can conceivably cover their own costs.

UNEMPLOYMENT BENEFITS

These are *not* available to new migrants or new residents but it is handy to know what the safety net consists of if you and yours one day fall on hard times. In 2004, single people with no children received $A385 a fortnight if aged over 21. A couple can claim $A347.50 each. Singles with children receive $A416.40. Full-time students, aged 18–24, may receive the Youth Allowance of $A175 to $A420 a fortnight. All these allowances are means tested as already mentioned.

HEALTHCARE IN AUSTRALIA

Here are some basic terms to help explain Australia's government and non-government funded health services:

♦ Medicare is the name of the federal government's public medical benefits organisation. On arrival in Australia to take up residence, you will need a Medicare card. If you are a card-holder and need to visit a doctor, Medicare will refund by cheque or in cash (if you queue up at a shop-front Medicare office) certain basic medical fees charged by general practitioners and medical specialists;

♦ Medicare is funded by a 1.5% Medicare levy collected via the income tax system. There are other Medicare-related tax incentives and penalties, detailed in the section 'Public or Private Health Cover?' later in this chapter;

♦ Medibank Private is the name of the government's own private health fund so don't confuse this with the name 'Medicare'. Like other private health funds, Medibank Private struggles to cover its costs despite the push to encourage people on higher incomes out of the public system;

◆ Private Health Funds compete with Medibank Private in offering insurance cover, which will pay for medical, dental, alternative therapies and private hospital costs not covered by Medicare system. Most private health funds offer a range of insurance plans;

◆ The Pharmaceutical Benefits Scheme is a government-funded programme that works alongside Medicare to help pay for drugs and other treatments a doctor may prescribe. Most benefits are available to low income earners subject to means testing of income and assets. For everybody else, there is a partial subsidy in the price of certain prescription medicines, which is also funded through this Scheme. Pensioners pay around $A4.00 for most prescription medicines while the general public pays $A25 per prescription or more if they wanted a particular brand of drug.

Medicare does not provide:

◆ Repayment to the patient of a doctor's charge that is higher than the schedule fee, though private health funds may cover this;

◆ Accommodation and treatment if admitted at a public hospital as a private patient (i.e. with the doctor of your choice);

◆ Accommodation and treatment at a private hospital;

◆ Prescription medicines. These are subsidised to some degree by the Pharmaceutical Benefits Scheme described above;

- Physiotherapy, dentistry, podiatry and other allied health care services *except* for people with certain chronic conditions (see below);

- Medical repatriation;

- Funeral costs.

PUBLIC HOSPITALS

Though their services are mostly 'free', the public hospital experience in Australia can be a nightmare. In some locations public hospital facilities are very stretched and waiting times as an emergency case or an outpatient can be frustratingly long. You cannot choose the doctors who attend to you and there is plenty of paperwork as you are moved from section to section, which can be another problem in a perceived emergency.

Small children are generally dealt with promptly to ensure they do not need immediate treatment for life-threatening illnesses. Some big city hospitals are forced to turn away ambulances from time to time, because they are so seriously over-crowded with emergencies and people queuing for treatment. Despite the funding shortages, Australia seems likely to maintain some level of free hospital service in future, and most users of the public system eventually receive good quality care. The professional staff at public hospitals, no matter how stretched, tend to be friendly and well-trained.

VISITING THE DOCTOR

You may prefer to visit a private doctor because waiting times at public hospital outpatient departments can be lengthy or there may not be a hospital close by if you become ill. At each visit to a general practitioner or medical specialist you will need to show the Medicare card that covers you and any dependents. You pay the doctor for the visit, and then mail or visit a Medicare office to receive your refund of the 'scheduled fee' for that type of medical treatment or consultation.

Some medical practitioners 'bulk bill', which means that patients do not have to pay any money when they visit because the doctor bills Medicare direct for their payment. Those practices or clinics that do bulk bill usually have a focus on the needy or are in areas where many patients cannot afford medical treatment. Most doctors in Australia avoid bulk billing for sound economic reasons – the schedule fees that the government pays them are not high enough to cover the cost of their time, practice costs and expensive medical indemnity insurance they need (in case a dissatisfied patient takes legal action for malpractice) *and* make them a profit.

PUBLIC OR PRIVATE HEALTH COVER?

In Australia, deciding whether to rely solely on Medicare and the public system or to pay for private health insurance is a no-brainer for most middle and high-income earners.

The good news is that there is a 30% income tax rebate for individuals and families taking out private health insurance. This rebate aims to encourage most citizens *not* to rely on government-funded health services. The bad news is that you will help fund the public system anyway through a 1.5% levy on your gross taxable income, whether or not you have private health insurance.

In addition to the Medicare levy, higher income earners must also pay the Medicare tax surcharge of 1% *unless you already have basic private health insurance* in which case the Medicare tax surcharge is waived. A high income earner is defined as someone with taxable income and fringe benefits over $A50,000, which is not much more than the average wage. The Medicare surcharge threshold is a more generous $A100,000 for couples with no children or one child, rising by $A1,500 for the second and each subsequent child.

So do your sums. If you are an uninsured couple earning a combined income above $A100,000 a year you will pay upwards of $A2,500 (that's the 1.5% Medicare levy plus 1% Medicare surcharge) towards the government's health system, whether you use it or not. By comparison, hospital-only insurance can cost as little as $A1,000 for family private hospital benefits (depending on the provider) a year, including that aforementioned 30% tax rebate to reward you for taking private insurance. Remember, this family will pay $A1,500 a year anyway in Medicare levy so may as well receive basic private hospital insurance rather than pay the $A1,000 Medicare surcharge for no specific benefit.

Whether or not you have private health insurance, there is a modest tax rebate for tax-payers who incur high medical expenses after any Medicare rebates and health fund payments are taken into account. To claim this rebate you need to carefully track of your health costs during the year and collate the bills to see if you are over the threshold for the tax break at the end of the financial year. Not surprisingly many people just don't bother to keep records so they can't claim the tax break.

In 2004–2005 Medicare was extended to provide allied health services such as dentistry, podiatry and physiotherapy for people with chronic and complex conditions. These benefits will apply only to restricted cases, such as diabetes, heart disease, asthma, cancer and kidney disease. The new Medicare rebates are limited to five services a year where the family doctor refers a patient to an allied health professional.

Below is a table of recent Australian private hospital charges for common surgical procedures. While the same operations may be provided free at a public hospital, there can be long waiting lists or limited resources in an emergency.

Figures representing the most frequent range of costs for operations/procedures

Childbirth	$A5,000–19,000
Coronary bypass	$A17,000–32,000
Hip replacement	$A19,000–32,000
Appendix removal	$A3,000–9,000

Source: Medibank Private

PRIVATE HEALTH COVER

For the tax reasons already given, and to avoid large hospital bills as a private patient, many higher income earners opt for a basic hospital insurance package with a private health fund. The lowest cost insurance packages feature excess levels of several hundred dollars per hospital admission, to be paid by the patient. This excess payment is a complicated issue best explained by health funds, but put simply it means that the nominated dollar amount is the most that the insured party will pay for a hospital stay, with the health fund paying the rest. As you can see from the table above, common operations/procedures at an Australian private hospital are expensive. If you want the operation at a time and hospital of your choosing rather than waiting on a list for public hospital treatment *and* you want the surgeon or specialist of your choice, then private health insurance becomes attractive. Since most healthy people cannot predict if and when they will need an operation in hospital there will be a trade-off between a higher excess payment by the patient and a lower insurance premium.

As mentioned, a basic hospital cover package for a family cost around $A1,000 a year with an excess of $A400 a year per family member or up to four hospitalisations a year. After that, the fund pays for private hospital and many related expenses.

The alternative strategy might be to pay for top hospital cover, which can be around $2,500 annually per family (about half that rate for single people). Top cover generally means just that – no procedures are excluded and you will have few out-of-pocket expenses if you go to hospital. In addition, you may want 'anciliary' cover for non-hospital provided healthcare, eg. dentistry, optometry, alternative therapies, physio, podiatry, gym membership – the sky is the limit, provided you are willing to pay. An employer may provide health and hospital insurance as part of your job package, which can make some of these decisions easier but not much cheaper in the long run. In any case, the idea is to shop around. Do your sums and estimates, and remember that while Australia's medical and associated providers are high quality, for all but the very poor and Australian war veterans who get unlimited free treatment, your best plan is to stay healthy!

Imagine a bad year for a hypothetical family with, say, four hospital in-patient stays by various family members as the result of a major car accident. In this situation the insured family would pay no more than $A1,600 from their own pockets for hospital services (plus the $A1,000 insurance premium). All up, that's $A2,600 to be paid to the private health fund for hospital services that *may* be had free in the public system. Remember, this family also pays $A1,500 a year towards public hospital care through the Medicate levy. This brings the total health insurance bill for the family to $A4,100 in a 'bad' year – or $A2,500 if no claims are made at all because no family member needs to be hospitalised in that year. Yet there are compelling reasons to consider private insurance – required procedures may not be done in time due to waiting lists, or with relatively inexperienced doctors. Also, operations deemed non-essential may not be available to you unless you become a private patient.

Education in Australia

As a newcomer to Australia, you should know the right to education may be universal but it is certainly not 'free'. Among the national priorities, it may seem that there is less emphasis on education than in some other prosperous societies. Educational facilities are excellent for those who can afford to buy them – however the government funded 'safety net' system for schools and universities is basic compared with standards in some other developed countries.

This chapter is a guide for permanent or temporary residents intending to educate their children in Australia and for people of any age thinking about continuing their education when they go to live in Australia. Australians are required to go to school from the time they are six until they finish junior high school at about the age of 15. However, the pressures of a specialised and consumer-focused society – not to mention unemployment and fear of narrow job choices for those making an over-hasty exit from school – mean young Australians commonly continue in formal education well into young adulthood if they can foot the bill or if they are in a position to take out study loans and work for a living while attending courses.

However, youth unemployment is a problem area in an economy where the job market has been quite strong for trained workers. University and tertiary college entry rates are fairly static among Australians due to the steady rise in the cost of education and dwindling government funds over recent years. Ironically there has been a recent surge in the market for full fee paying students on temporary visas, as covered in Chapter 6. There is also a degree of snobbery about young people who embark on trades and non-professional courses when they leave school. In 2004 the government announced expanded migration targets and a fresh approach to apprenticeships and trades training for resident school-leavers to help meet the demand from employers for skilled metal, manufacturing and engineering workers in short supply.

THE POLITICS OF EDUCATION – MONEY, MONEY, MONEY

As with many other developed countries, Australia is in the process of dismantling the old welfare state ideal of tax-payer funded 'free' education for all. Potential welfare recipients among the aged (pensions, health) and the young (education, health) have been obliged to rely on their own finances in recent decades by economically conservative governments. The idea that an increasingly large middle-class population should fund their own retirement via superannuation savings in their working years is now uncontroversial in Australia – but the notion that the cost to tax-payers for educating the nation's smaller proportion of young people should also be strictly contained, with the best education reserved for people with the means to pay for it, remains cause for heated debate. Opponents of the move to a user-pays system say that it is in the interest of all tax-payers to fund a better standard of education for the community, and the current generation of decision-makers are promoting a selfish attitude despite benefiting from tax-payers' largesse a decade or three ago when they attended 'free' Aussie schools and universities. Supporters of the new approach argue that, by imposing significant financial hurdles, both students and their families will take education more seriously. Fewer university places will mean higher standards academically, and that there remains an adequate safety net for the genuinely financially disadvantaged.

University funding

In 2003 an OECD report found that Australia lagged in terms of public investment in universities in the years 1995–2001, compared with 32 other countries. Public investment in universities fell 11% in Australia, compared with an average growth rate of 21% in other OECD countries. Public investment in Australian universities lagged behind Japan, Korea, Slovakia, Italy and the UK. More Australian universities rely on income from the private sector than any country surveyed, except Korea, Japan and the US. Australian governments may counter this with their own numbers about how they are maintaining a high level of spending on university education. Figures vary but it seems that nearly a third of all people who applied for university places each year are rejected simply because there are not enough places. Since 1988, Australian universities have moved from a 'free' system funded entirely by tax-payers to a user-pays model where some degrees cost $A150,000. Indications are that the trend to more expensive post-school education will continue, so expect to dig deep into your pocket if tertiary education for you and your family is a priority.

Unsurprisingly, the Australian university system is increasingly reliant on business sponsorship and, even more heavily, on foreign students who pay full fees. Around 13% of university revenues come from some 210,000 foreign fee-paying students. Over 70,000 of these are currently undertaking Australian university courses without leaving their homes, mainly in South-East Asian countries. The other 140,000 or so live on or near their campus as temporary residents of Australia and, for many, eventual immigration to Australia is an important goal (see also Chapter 6) because there are concessions in the points scoring and application process for would-be migrants educated in Australia.

Schools funding

Primary and secondary schools are experiencing funding cuts and shortfalls under a complex financial arrangement between states and the federal governments. You can rely on passionate debate in the lounge rooms of suburbanites and others concerned with educating Australia's children to the highest standard. Meanwhile, economic success for many families means working a little bit harder to pay for a religious or higher quality private education. Private school enrolments are growing due to parents' willingness to pay ever-higher fees. Governments around the country are committed to funding these choices for fear of angering the electorate and of putting greater pressure on the under-funded government system, which would be overburdened if many struggling private schools closed.

The standard of a school's existing facilities has little or no bearing on how much money it receives from the public purse. Everyone feels hard done by, some parents complain they pay taxes to support public schools while paying thousands more each year to educate their children at their non-government school of choice or vice versa. Other Australian tax-payer groups moan that they help foot the government's bill for their kids to attend government schools then pay almost as much again in taxes to support children at private schools.

Despite recent measures that effectively sell education to students with the money to pay, Australia's system of university entry is still a good part meritocracy. As ever in Australia's short history, the children of recent immigrants seem to work the hardest and perform the best. The serious 'nose to grindstone' approach to learning by many young people from the Asian regions means they dominate university entrance exams at the end of the high school years – but even so their parents may have invested heavily in private schools and/or private tuition along the way. Investment plans are available to anxious new parents so they can save for private school and full fee university education for their children. Grandparents commonly help out financially. To enrol your child (at birth, preferably) in a big name private school can also cost hundreds or even several thousand dollars in application and other fees, which are not refundable. For the top schools, demand far exceeds the number of pupils they can educate, so entry examination and interviews are commonly used to select children with the best academic, musical or sporting abilities.

SCHOOL DAYS – WOT'S AN OLD SCHOOL TIE GOOD FOR?

Anyone intending to move their family to Australia will probably have to canvass the pros and cons of private schooling versus a government school education.

Official figures vary but almost a third of school-age children are sent to preparatory, primary and secondary schools runs by religious, community or other non-government organisations. About 20% of enrolments are in Catholic schools and 10% of children go to other non-government schools which foster a range of religious, community and educational belief systems. Depending on where you live in Australia, the proportion of children attending non-government schools will be much lower or higher due to social and other pressures on parents to follow the local trend.

Confusing for many people from the UK in particular, the term **public school** in Australia means government school (open to the general public and usually obliged to take people within its defined geographic area). Non-government schools are usually termed **private schools**.

Private schools
Private schools in Australia can be divided into four categories:

- Catholic church-run establishments. Catholic schools are subsidised by the Church though, with a few exceptions, these are not considered luxurious or academically elite;

- other religion-based schools including Church of England, Muslim, Jewish, Hare Krishna, Anglican, Baptist, Christian Scientists and so on;

- non-denominational schools, perhaps with an educational or community philosophy in mind, such as Steiner or Montessori methods of education;

- 'establishment' schools (which may be of any or no denomination). These charger higher fees, have long histories, illustrious old boys/girls, excellent facilities, and are general over-subscribed and therefore very selective, using entry examinations and interviews to screen candidates and their families.

All private schools have the right to accept or reject pupils on the basis of academic or religious/philosophical criteria.

Private versus public schools

The broadest difference between public and private schools is that public schools are mostly non-selective – which means any child in the local area, whatever their religion, level of academic achievement or special needs, has the right to attend a public school. Suspension rather than expulsion from the school is reserved for the more serious cases of misbehaviour in government schools (with police or social services experts looking into extreme cases) since every Australian child is entitled to an education at the public's expense. By contrast, many private schools can and do pick and choose their pupils and have a reputation for promoting discipline.

The range of subjects, quality of teaching and extra-curricular activities make the best of Australia's 2,500 or so private schools stand out. The pupil-teacher ratio may also be lower in the better-endowed schools. Many private schools are single-sex especially in high school while government schools tend to be co-educational.

The old school tie

Despite the high cost of private education in Australia, there is relatively little snobbery about which primary or secondary school an adult attended – though this may change if governments continue to finance already well-heeled schools of the private sector while failing to adequately resource many public schools in need. In the job market your trade or professional qualifications really count, as well as career achievements and personality, rather than any old school tie. At a personal level, the footy club you played for in your youth and the location of your last holiday are more likely to interest people than the name of the school you attended.

The opposite may be true when getting to know the parents of school-age youngsters. If your kids attend well-known private schools this could make quite an impression. ('How can they afford that? Those kids must be so smart that they are on scholarships...Ahhhhh, the parents *both* work full time, that's how they do it!')

The lack of deep snobbishness about where an Australian was educated is due to the fact that, unlike in some countries, children usually do not emerge from the system with obvious signs of where they went to school via accent, dress code, politics or other homogenous characteristics. This is because private schools in

Australia are usually for day pupils rather than for boarders. Boarders, if they are catered for at all, are usually in the minority. Their parents live on far-flung agricultural properties or are working abroad for long periods.

So the predominance of day schools in Australia means relationships forged at school are of limited intensity compared to influences drawn from home and their community. Private day education in Australia will naturally create a strong social framework for children and young adults but it does not usually produce the close, club atmosphere of a boarding establishment.

School costs and fees

Public (government) schools cost a few hundred dollars a year per pupil to attend. This includes a voluntary contribution to the schools' Parents and Citizens fund-raising group (around $A200) annually plus excursions, books and uniforms.

Equipping a young child for school can cost around $A200 a year at a public school, rising to an estimated $A350 a year for high school. Incidentals, such as excursions, choir, band, sports and so forth may be around $A200 a term, rising with the age of the pupil and facilities offered by the school.

School uniforms are mandatory at most public and private schools, but the official dress code at a private school may be strictly enforced and conservative in design compared with public schools. A school wardrobe for a public school child may cost around $A50 a year if clothes are available second hand, but outfitting a child for a private school can cost hundreds of dollars each time new sizes are required.

Better public schools will have relatively good facilities due to the fund-raising efforts of parents and support of the teachers. Parents groups often pay for improvements such as extra teachers, new buildings, sporting or art facilities and computer aids. Often funds donated by the parents groups at activities such as school fetes, dances, and chocolate drives are matched by government grants. If you settle your family in a relatively prosperous area where many parents are likely to have the motivation and time to work for the school community, the school is likely to be better funded. The uneven system of government funding means the opposite is true if your neighbourhood has a low employment and a high proportion of people with financial priorities other than the local school.

For Australians without strong religious or philosophical beliefs that steer them to choose certain private schools, the public school down the road is usually satisfactory. Investing in Shirlene's ballet lessons or fixing Brett's buck teeth may seem a better investment than spending thousands of dollars on private school fees. Parents may also prefer to pay for coaching to help pupils with key subjects and save for the increasingly expensive university years, where fees for some degrees are now as high as for 12 years at private school!

Many **private schools** can be very expensive though some newer establishments or those run by Catholic or other religious local community groups may be very dependent on government funds and charge relatively low fees, around $A3,000 to $A6,000 a year at secondary (high) school level. Fees are on a scale rising from kindergarten to primary and secondary school. The establishment 'brand' name schools will charge $A12,000 to $A17,000 for each year of high school education (upward of $A20,000 annually for boarding pupils) with books, uniforms, music lessons, some sporting fees, excursions and other equipment costing extra. Fees are usually payable per term but many schools offer discounts for prepayment. In addition, parents at private schools are also expected to donate their time and certainly additional money to help fund-raising activities. As at any public school, a private school's fund-raising functions will naturally reflect the interests and socio-economic status of the families involved.

Some private schools offer academic scholarships that may be assessed by examinations and interviews, or themed as music, drama, art or sporting scholarships. Some private schools means test the scholarships, which means the discount on school fees depends on a pupil's parents' taxable income.

State and federal governments effectively means test all parents as well, allocating funds to schools based on residential addresses of families with children attending that school. This calculation relies on official statistics about average income by postcode or zip code. With this approach, it is irrelevant what facilities the school has already. Despite the high fees and 'luxury' facilities offered by many private schools, governments feel obliged to help parents who have chosen private education for their children. It is a chicken-and-egg situation for, by helping private school parents, there is less money left in education budgets for government schools that appear to have difficulty providing adequate equipment and teaching. Meanwhile, a growing proportion of Australian parents choose private education, if they can possibly afford it, for fear of a second-rate result at the local government school...perpetuating the cycle. An obvious solution and one that appears to be under consideration by some state and federal governments is that funding for education should increase sharply. In the meantime, newcomers to Australia can expect to join the queue for quality education and pay the price.

HOURS, COURSES AND FACILITIES

The school day, whether at a public (government) or private establishment, is on a par with standard working hours in Australia, though shorter at both ends. There is no long 'siesta' as in some countries, nor are classes commonly stopped after lunch – they start at about 9am and continue with breaks at mid-morning and lunch, then more classes until around 4pm. For schools, the academic year starts at the end of January, has three or four terms with holidays of two to three weeks in between, depending on the state or territory, and ends in December for a long summer holiday of some six weeks. Public holidays punctuate schooldays as well.

Food at school

Parents are expected to meet all the children's mealtime needs while they are at school with prepacked snacks and lunches brought from home. Larger schools have canteens selling lunches, morning teas and snacks to the children at a small profit. Usually a parents' group will organise the canteen as a small business, and profits are donated to the school. Parents volunteer to help run the canteen, which is a great way for newcomers to an area to get to know people from the neighbourhood and understand the life of the school.

It is estimated that a growing proportion of Australian school children are overweight, spending too much time in front of computers and televisions and preferring to buy chips, lollies and ice creams if school canteens offer them. However, there is growing pressure at government and community level for schools to withdraw from sale those fatty, sweet snacks that sell well to children but are of poor nutritional value. Inexpensive sandwiches, fruit, pasta, sushi and nachos are frequently among the choices at many Aussie school canteens and considerable imagination may go into creating an interesting and nutritious menu.

Studying, playing and teaching

School children are expected to do homework and may volunteer or are obliged to attend extra recreational or academic activities outside the regular 9–4 school day. By the time a student reaches high school their day can be quite long. Outdoor sports, in particular, are popular and time-consuming additions to regular classes, in a land where the climate encourages all the physical pursuits under the sun.

Languages, computer studies, music lessons, arts and crafts are explored during the typical Australian government school education. As students move through pre-school, primary and secondary school levels, the learning methods rely on discussions and research rather than parrot-fashion repetition of key facts and texts. Teachers and pupils at most primary and high schools enjoy at least some freedom from penultimate end-of-year examinations, and there are provisions for teachers to tailor lessons to the interests and standard of their pupils with continuous assessments and assignments that build toward a final ranking for each pupil.

However, the heat is on after six years of high school, with great pressure in the final year to perform well in exams and assessments. The academic hurdle at the end of the high school years is known as **matriculation** and the pupil's score determines whether the pupil gains the university and course of their choice. The system of exams and assessments in Australia is covered in more detail later in this chapter.

Teachers are trained by the government through the university system. Their pay rates are generally on a par with the national average but the length of school holidays is a great bonus, especially for more junior teachers with fewer administrative duties. More senior staff members have shorter holidays (more like the four-week national average), depending on workloads and responsibilities.

Government assistance

To help families pay for uniforms, exercise books, textbooks, writing equipment, calculators and so on there is a small 'back to school' allowance from some state governments. As mentioned, some private schools offer scholarships to children from needy backgrounds or those who are deemed to be outstanding in a field relevant to the school.

Parents of pupils in the final two years before matriculation to university or further education may apply for means-tested grants administered by the federal government (see the end of this chapter for more information). There are a number of special allowances for children from low-income families. Special payments may be made for children who must live away from home or study by correspondence to help counter disadvantages such as geographic isolation, physical or intellectual disabilities. Government financial aid and subsidies for textbooks and equipment are increased now and then, to maintain their value in the face of rising living costs.

PRE-SCHOOL TO HIGH SCHOOL

Pre-school and child care
Local, state and federal governments have comprehensive child care programmes. They help finance the activities of both for-profit and not-for-profit private child care centres in many areas. The private pre-school and long day care sector is booming due to demand by single parents, career issues and financial stresses. Australia has relatively ungenerous maternity leave laws and tax incentives so parents often go back to work before children are of school age. Many working mothers effectively work for very little because they spend so much of their pay on child care. Their hope is that being at work even part time will cement their prospects for career advancement in the future.

Finding a suitable child care centre is a critical issue for working parents and there are shortages of places in crowded urban centres. Even government establishments charge fees though low-income families may be exempt. It can cost $A50 a day for a baby in a child centre and around $A35 for toddlers and pre-schoolers. A cheaper option is family day care, whereby an accredited carer looks after a small number of children in her own home.

Pre-schools are child care centres with programmes specifically to prepare children for school. A group of four or five year olds will receive some foretaste of primary school with a gentle introduction to structured activities like singing and drawing as well as the rudiments of reading and counting.

Pre-schools run by a religious group will include some relevant activities in their programmes. Many private schools have created pre-schools so that young children make a smoother transition to the school and its programmes.

Primary school

In most states and territories primary school years begin in Year K, a kindergarten year, then advance through years 1 to 6. Some states have an extra year in pre-school or another year before high school. These differences exist because each state and territory has the ability to tailor its school education arrangements as it sees fit.

It is not compulsory to send a child to primary school until they are six; though often children start in the year they turn five. Most states enrol new pupils in late January-early February, the start of the school year. Only South Australia offers enrolment to children at the start of any of the year's four school terms, once children have turned five.

Most children in Australia commence their education in government primary schools, but there is a trend to an entirely private education in more affluent areas, among some ethnic or religious communities with their own schools, or in places where government schools have a poor reputation. Class sizes average about 25 to 30 and boys and girls attend lessons together.

Generally one teacher will be in charge of a class for a year in primary school, though specialist teachers may take the class for sport, art, music, dance and so on. The class teacher guides pupils through a wide range of subjects, which include reading, writing, mathematics, elementary science and biology, human society, Australian history and health. There are continuous assessments and reports to parents in person and in writing about each child's intellectual and social progress during the early school years.

Sex education, dental assessments and programmes designed to make children aware of the health risks of drug and alcohol abuse are usually offered provided the parents give their permission. Parental permission also is required in public schools for subjects like religion (scripture classes are run at government schools by visiting representatives of church groups) and for excursions and entertainments for the children that take children away from the school grounds or are provided at a cost to the parents.

Swimming lessons are a feature of Aussie suburban life for young children and may begin in private centres before a child can walk. At primary school basic water safety and swimming classes are taught during supervised classes at public swimming pools. Wealthier private schools and even some government schools have their own swimming pools.

Beyond the school system

Many young children go to Saturday or Sunday schools to receive specialised language, cultural or religious instruction, according to their parents' background. So there are Chinese schools, Japanese schools, German schools, Greek schools and other mother-tongue based establishments in major cities or where there is a concentration of families from a particular ethnic or language group. These lessons are organised by local communities that seek to impart their cultural values and help children to remain conversant in their parents' language.

At private schools it may be mandatory for children to join the school at weekend sport and weekday training, and some require primary students to learn an instrument and play in a school band or ensemble group. Many public schools may also offer private drama, music, sport or lessons in tennis during or after school on a voluntary basis, with parents assisting. Interschool sporting, debating, and music competitions are organised by both private and public schools and can be time-consuming but rewarding for all concerned.

After-school or weekend activities available to children from their first years at school and throughout high school usually include participation in local sports teams, with football increasingly popular among girls as well as boys. Community and sporting groups offer club membership to children of all ages, so weekend matches and weekday training sessions in soccer, cricket, rugby, netball and basketball are part of the family ritual in many Australian communities. Parents volunteer to help with training and managing teams and clubs for children, so this is another venue for newcomers to Aussie to meet people and become involved in the lifestyle.

Moving on

If the child's family moves from one district to another, they are usually expected to move the child to a school closer to the new home. In the middle primary years, when the children are around nine, parents start to move them to private schools, if concerned about securing a place in a desirable high school where existing pupils of a private school generally have priority.

ATTENDING SECONDARY SCHOOLS

In New South Wales, Victoria, Tasmania and the Australian Capital Territory, secondary education begins when a pupil is aged about 12 and is in year 7. In other states the starting point is year 8. All the state school systems end with the pupil attaining a Higher School Certificate at year 12. In private schools the terminology may be slightly different, many referring to class levels as 'forms'. For example, first form is equivalent to year 7 (age 12 or 13) while final year students may be known as 'sixth formers'. Private schools may also offer access to foreign examinations that may qualify the young person to attend colleges or universities in other countries.

On the whole, the curriculum at secondary schools caters for a variety of personal and employment aspirations though some states also have certain high schools which specialise in agricultural or commercial subjects not generally available at government or even private schools.

Pupils entering government high schools are not subject to streaming in most places in Australia. Some states offer a choice between university-orientated academic schools and technical high schools, slanted towards preparing young people for skilled trades or sub-professional courses. As mentioned, there are many shortages in qualified people so it can be expected that new educational programmes will appear in the near future to channel students into trades and technical skills where demand is strong.

Selective high schools

In certain states of Australia, government high schools may be academically 'selective'. Selective high schools tend to receive better funding from the government and have a reputation for superior teaching standards. They cost just a few hundred dollars a year to attend so are an extremely cost-effective solution to the dilemma of how to provide excellent *and* affordable education for children.

It all depends on the secondary education strategy of the particular state or territory government. Selective schools, where they exist, are highly focused on academic achievement and the demand for places is so high that prospective pupils train for months or even years to pass competitive entry tests.

Some selective high schools offer a comparatively narrow range of subjects and activities, in the bid to further focus students and teachers on the serious business of excelling in their results and gaining entry to university courses, where places in Australia are increasingly limited.

EXAMINATIONS AND ASSESSMENTS

In secondary schools, the teachers are more highly qualified academically and specialise in one or a handful of subjects. In recent years, emphasis has been removed from final examinations. Instead, most states have phased in a system of continuous assessments which may or may not be supplemented by examinations. The problem is finding a common denominator to compare students of all types of schools in competing for places in universities, colleges and technical courses to fit them for a career. Each state has a slightly different system, though the crunch comes at the end of the first four years of secondary education, with the need for a qualification which a pupil can take with them into the workplace from the age of 15 or 16 if they intend to leave school at that stage. Allocation of places in tertiary education courses from the age of 17 or 18, after completing two further optional years at secondary school, makes some form of assessment even more necessary. Examinations have been substantially phased out and schools provide a final 'aggregate' drawn from the pupil's performance in various subjects via continuous assessments over the final year at school. This is fairer to pupils who may not respond well to do-or-die examinations and cramming.

EDUCATION IN ISOLATED AREAS

Apart from private schools, the only state-run institutions with facilities for school children living away from home are the agricultural high schools of New South Wales and Western Australia. There may be subsidies paid by a state government for transport costs in bringing children living far from the nearest school. However, some country schools in Western Australian and Tasmania have hostels attached to them for the benefit of those who would otherwise have to travel vast distances to school – or not go at all.

> **Australia has developed a novel system for bringing education to children with no access to boarding schools or hostels, and whose families prefer to have them live at home anyway.**

There are **schools of the air**, which link a teacher with a number of pupils studying at home via radio, as well as correspondence schools. Both government and private schools in isolated areas participate in such programmes, and all schools in declared 'isolated' areas are expected to pool resources provided through government programmes to encourage participation and a higher standard of education for the children involved.

Correspondence lessons

These are usually supervised by a member of the pupil's family. Lessons cater for pupils from primary age to matriculation. Each capital city in Australia has a correspondence school to administer the system. Computer programs, video and audio tapes and electronic devices are distributed, helping to improve such services in recent years and the Special Programmes assist with video recorders, television monitors and videotaped education materials. Some states require payment of tuition fees in secondary school years.

Schools of the air

These provide a radio classroom for children of the outback, and also require the participation and encouragement of a supervisor at home. Two-way radio equipment was first developed by the Flying Doctor Service to homes hundreds of kilometres apart in rural or desert Australia. Pupils and teacher talk directly to each other or use computers, and satellite links as well as other advanced communications are used in schools of the air.

LEAVING SCHOOL AND FINDING JOBS

Australia has a general school-leaving age of 15, when a teenager can legally leave formal education and enter the workforce. However, this is easier said than done. Whether the opportunity of formal education is taken or not, a high level of youth unemployment stares first job-hunters in the face. Unemployment of Australians aged 16 to 25 is well over 15%, higher than in many other developed countries.

Yet many Australian school-leavers are not breaking their necks to improve their education or chances of employment. The allure of beach and 'dole' are commonly blamed. On the other hand, the number of suitable jobs has decreased. There is no compulsory military service nor even a large defence employment sector in Australia. Successive state and federal governments have tried a variety of programmes and incentives in the past decade to avoid the embarrassment of persistently high youth unemployment figures and the drain on the public purse. Mainly, employers and school-leavers are encouraged to find one another through training and apprenticeship schemes. School-leavers electing to learn a trade or meet their career goals through non-university courses often pay relatively lower fees and have a better chance of getting into the courses of their choice, as mentioned in the sections on Technical and Further Education (TAFE) colleges later in this chapter.

Australia has one of the lowest rates of university entry, with only 20% of school-leavers at matriculation level (aged 17 to 19, depending on when they started school) choosing to continue their education at university level. Facilities and opportunities at university are expensive and must be paid for by the student (or their families) before, during and after their studies are complete. The amount paid for tertiary or university education depends on when the bill is to be met and so favours applicants from better off families because a student can buy a place in a course ahead of students with higher marks but less money to spend on fees. This is explained in the following sections.

ENTERING TERTIARY EDUCATION

More money, money, money

The number of higher education places in Australia is tight and, as you will see below, the trend is towards having the full cost of courses met by students. The system of assessing and ranking pupils in year 12 for tertiary places, then favouring people who are prepared to pay full fees, is a complex and emotional issue for the community.

It is argued that, by forcing most university students to go into debt to fund their degrees, academic standards will be higher and unemployment rates lower. Only truly committed young people would be prepared to borrow money to invest in their careers. The counter argument is that rising costs make tertiary education and, therefore, careers in the most prestigious fields, unavailable to people from less wealthy backgrounds. The financial divide in education will lead to long-term social and economic problems for Australia, argue the opponents of the current university funding system.

Training for professions and vocational trades

Australia has two types of tertiary education establishments:

◆ Universities, which offer courses at undergraduate bachelor degree level, postgraduate diploma, master's degrees and doctorate standards. There are over 40 universities around Australia, including a handful of non-government establishments. University courses are at a premium, both cost-wise and in terms of availability. Most degree courses take three years or up to six years for double degrees with honours and are desirable for people seeking careers in white collar professions or as academic experts;

◆ Technical and Further Education (TAFE) colleges and other
  similar institutions at sub-university level or with a trade or
  commercial focus. These offer diplomas and certificates to
  successful graduates in their course of study and some also offer
  year 11 and 12 matriculation studies for people who left school
  early or wanting to improve their results from previous attempts
  at university entry. Most TAFE colleges are government run and
  vocation-oriented. The length of courses varies greatly, reflecting
  the wide range of course choices within the TAFE system.

It is usually cheaper and easier to gain entry to TAFE courses
than to university, though government loans (see section on HECS
below) are not available for TAFE studies. This may motivate
many to aim for a university degree instead. Australia certainly
has greater demand than supply for young people in certain
trades and technical fields, so TAFE colleges are encouraged via
funding incentives to attract more students into areas of shortage
(and the immigration programme does not meet the shortfall of
quality tradespeople). However, around Australia TAFE fees –
like university fees – are rising. In NSW, for example, a TAFE
graduate diploma cost $A1,650 in fees in 2004, double the charge
of the previous year. In Victoria TAFE fees will rise 25% in 2005.

Slightly different from schools, the academic year for colleges and
universities begins in February and ends in December. The
tertiary calendar is usually divided into semesters, broken by a
long holiday over the summer months.

In Britain, America and many other places tertiary students
commonly leave their families to go to study in another city, state
or country (via student exchange programmes) and have the

experience of living away from home while furthering their education. In Australia the opposite is true. Only around 1% of Australian students do any part of their undergraduate degree overseas, with Australian students aiming to attend courses near their homes and living under the parental roof if they can. This helps keep costs down. However, there is a wide range of student accommodation available at most campuses, should living at home prove inappropriate and student or parents can afford the rent.

Higher Education Contribution Scheme (HECS)

Australian students can either pay full fees for a course at TAFE or go to university where the HECS system applies. Under HECS, students pay a smaller fee and borrow the money from the federal government. From 2005 a small number of Commonwealth Learning Scholarships were available for the first time, specifically targeting the most needy of students with little or no personal income or parental support, to help meet rising accommodation and living costs.

Full fees versus HECS

By paying **full fees** Australian students will usually gain a few points to help them secure a place in the course of choice. Foreign students (see Chapter 6) must pay full fees to attend Australian universities, though there are some scholarship programmes. Meanwhile, many Australians are still getting used to the idea that free or relatively cost-effective university courses no longer exist and places are limited. This is because federal government funding of some 38 government universities in Australia is relatively low while demand from local and overseas students for the limited places available is high.

By paying HECS, students take out a low cost loan from the federal government and pay a smaller course fee than if they had elected to pay full fees. Due to lower fees under HECS there is more competition for places. Assuming a student does gain entry to a desired university course under HECS, the debt must be repaid when they graduate and start paid employment. If some or all of the debt is paid up front on behalf of the student, the student receives a 20% discount on a corresponding proportion of their HECS fee.

If students defer all or part of their HECS repayment, 6% of their income will be deducted for the repayment of the loan after they reach the repayment earnings threshold, which is around $A33,000 a year. When the graduate's earnings exceed $A60,000 a year they will pay their debt at the maximum rate of 8% a year until the debt is repaid. The debt accrued rises with the Consumer Price Index (1 or 2% annually in recent years) over the life of the loan. In 2005 a typical new graduate starting his or her first job had a HECS debt of around $A25,000, but could owe much more depending on their course of studies. Income tax and the Medicare levy are deducted from HECS graduates' pay, in addition to the loan repayments.

In a new twist, which along with the influx of foreign full fee-paying students may put even greater upward pressure on the price of the most desirable courses, universities may offer up to 35% of their places to full-fee Australian paying students. Furthermore students **may borrow from the government to pay full fees up to $A50,000 towards undergraduate or post graduate courses**. The repayment rates for the full-fees HECS loan is relatively steep, with the amount borrowed indexed to the Consumer Price Index (CPI) plus 3% on top of the regular HECS repayment rates as explained above. The plan is for graduates to repay at this higher rate for a maximum of ten years before the repayment rates revert to indexation in line with the CPI only.

Paying full fees with the help of a loan means more students with borderline entry points can study their university degree course of choice. A $A50,000 full fee HECS loan is not enough to pay full fees for the most expensive university courses but should be sufficient to pay for most three to four year arts and engineering courses. From 2005 there is a new fee scale with some course fees jumping by up to 30%. Now each university is free to set their own fees based on actual course costs and funding considerations. Some courses to which universities want to attract more students, or which the government wants to promote due to employment demand, may be fee-free or quite inexpensive. For instance, teacher training and nursing are relatively low cost for students due to professional shortages leading to better federal funding of relevant university faculties.

From 2005 typical single-degree students under HECS will pay $A3,800 to $A8,355 annually for their courses. A medium-priced degree, such as computing, engineering or science, may cost around $A21,500 for the four years of study. Arts/law or veterinary science may cost up $A150,000 in fees to complete.

University life

Universities were first established in Australia in the 1850s. Most are newer establishments and may offer better courses than the older 'sandstone' institutions of the large capital cities. The older universities tend to offer a broader range of studies than the newer ones, covering agriculture, architecture, arts, dentistry, education, law, medicine, music, science and veterinary science, often over a number of sprawling campuses. Some universities grew from regional technical colleges. Eventually these technical colleges developed as excellent universities and post-graduate research establishments with a focus on a smaller number of core subjects.

Certainly, universities are no longer a hotbed of extremist politics or ivory towers of learning. The investment and financial sacrifices now required to take a degree in Australia are simply too great for most students to consider student activism and experimental lifestyles just for the fun of it. These days the skills most relevant to success at university include financial acumen to help make ends meet while studying and the determination to get a great job on graduation.

Union fees of several hundred dollars annually are part of the basic cost of attendance, along with the tuition fees already mentioned. Books are another expense, though most places have good second-hand bookshops on campus or nearby. Scholarships are few and far between and while there is some means-tested financial assistance available (see Applying for Financial Assistance on page 285) the number of students receiving welfare support and studying full time is low – most students, whatever their personal or family financial situation, work part time or during the holidays.

Income sources for university research and teaching

Universities undertake research as well as offering degree courses in the academic and professional disciplines. Little research is government funded, with business and private sponsors paying an estimated 90% of universities' research budgets. There are growing links with the business community for funding and sponsorship of courses and teaching positions as well as research. Universities attempt an arms-length relationship with business, but the financial pressures to raise funds for their work are clearly reflected in Australian academic life and can be a controversial matter for the governing bodies of many universities. They need to satisfy the institution's financial imperatives while fostering love of learning within a very vocationally focused community. Another important source of income for universities is fees from foreign students, as mentioned.

Most Australian universities follow British or American traditions in terms of how they are governed and structured, with a series of boards and committees known as university councils and senates responsible for academic matters in most cases. In the more old-fashioned universities, or 'unis' as they are commonly referred to in Australia, the senior academic board remains the professional board comprising professors and non-professional deans and heads of department. Many members may be elected by their peers on the university's academic staff.

The states are responsible for tertiary education, but they are reliant on the federal government for funding. Australian students are required to pay an administration fee of a few hundred dollars. This fee is waived for low income earners, who may have access to other financial help from the government (see section later in this chapter).

Student assessment

Methods of assessing students' progress differ from university to university. Students are expected to participate in tutorials, in particular, and it is not necessarily a disadvantage to express an opinion different from that of the lecturer or tutor. Continuous assessment, as in high school, is a trend for some courses and in some places this assessment is even made by the students themselves. But mid-year and final examinations are still standard at university to master's degree level in many fields.

All establishments offer research programmes at undergraduate, master's and PhD levels and a limited amount of coursework may be offered to complement a postgraduate research programme. However, the award of a research degree is still based on the quality of a final thesis. Postgraduate diploma courses are usually shorter in duration and narrower in subject matter than master's courses. In all universities, teaching and research are inseparable. Academic staff are selected through world-wide advertisements and, certainly, universities enjoy rare freedom in Australia to recruit from abroad and so obtain temporary entry permits for foreign academics, in order to improve local education standards. There is a growing nexus between universities and the business community for funding and academic direction, especially in research.

Technical and Further Education (TAFE)

Technical and Further Education (TAFE) colleges provide tertiary education at sub-trade, trade and technical level. Some states, like Victoria, have a well-developed TAFE support system at secondary school level, the so-called 'technical schools'. Such schools or others offering relevant subjects provide an education base in certain skills which could be needed in vocational studies at a TAFE college. Throughout Australia, TAFE courses are used to supplement apprenticeships or on-the-job training. They provide theoretical or practical back-up on a part-time basis, in combination with the paid apprenticeship or job.

Many people wishing to become skilled tradesmen (often very well paid jobs in Australia) leave high school about Year 4 (aged 15 or 16) to begin TAFE studies. Others complete the full six years at high school before starting the trade course, culminating in an award or certificate.

The cost of TAFE courses is substantially lower than for universities, reflecting a less intense academic environment, shorter courses and more vocational orientation of staff. TAFE staff often teach part-time and make a living by applying their area of expertise in a commercial environment.

Other institutions of higher education
In addition to government-funded tertiary education institutions, there are a number of other options for higher education which are run by the private sector, including the Bond University in Queensland. In addition, there are some non-government teacher training colleges and a number of colleges providing theological and other courses.

Student life
Life on campus of tertiary institutions tends to revolve around clubs, bars, canteens and entertainments. Foreign students, often from South East Asia or the Southern Pacific where Australia is keen to provide education as part of its international aid

programme, are highly visible at universities around Australia. They often have their own social clubs alongside other minority ethnic, religious and political groups which thrive and mix in the university environment.

Most campuses have student counselling services to help them meet the requirements of their lifestyle, while lecturers and tutors are also expected to be available to advise on problems relating to a student's studies.

Institutions often provide housing for eligible students, usually those from remote areas or overseas, in rooms on campus or near the university. Otherwise, as mentioned, it is not taken for granted that undergraduates will go to another city to study, as in Europe or America, and most students remain in the family home.

Applying for financial assistance

Austudy is the federal government's major programme of assistance to students in secondary and tertiary education. Living allowances are available on a non-competitive basis to some full-time students who are enrolled at approved courses at universities, colleges of technical and further education, secondary schools and some private business colleges. Allowances are based on a test of a student's **personal** income and assets. They are payable at different rates depending on age and family circumstances.

Full-time students may also receive the Youth Allowance of about $A175 to $A420 a fortnight, depending on other income and assets available to them directly or *via their families*. (See Chapter 11 for more information.) The **Commonwealth Learning**

Scholarship programme is also newly available, to help poorer students cover living and accommodation expenses while they study. This will help up to 2,500 students by giving them $A2,000 a year for up to four years of study. NSW Department of Education statistics indicated only 5% of students will receive some assistance through this programme.

Other benefits available to certain categories of eligible students include dependent spouse allowance, fares allowance for students living away from home, child care subsidy for sole parents and education supplement (replacing the living allowance) for students who receive certain pensions.

Student Financial Supplement Scheme

There is also a loan scheme which allows students to trade $A1 of their Austudy or Youth Allowance payment for a $A2 loan, up to a total loan limit of $A7,000. The loan is also available to some students who do not qualify for the Youth Allowance or Austudy, up to a loan limit of $A2,000. Like HECS, these loans are repaid when the student graduates and obtains paid employment once their income exceeds $A33,000 per annum at the time of writing.

The Assistance for Isolated Children (AIC) Scheme provides a boarding allowance to help parents of younger children who cannot attend an appropriate school because their home is geographically isolated, or who suffer from physical or intellectual disabilities which prevent them from living at home and attending school daily. It also provides an allowance for children who study by correspondence or where a second home has been established so that the children can attend school daily.

13

Working for a Living Around Australia

BUSINESS MIGRATION INCENTIVES

Each state and territory of Australia wants new people who can contribute commercial know-how and invest capital. Conversely, would-be settlers in every migration category are wise to assess the prospects in each of Australia's eight states and territories with the greatest care.

Apart from the desire to join friends or family or your other reasons for wanting to settle in a particular part of the country, consideration of the lifestyle, climate and landscape of each location will help you make the most of Australia.

An ill-advised choice of location will compound the usual traumas of settling into a new society. Though there is a certain sameness about the buildings, food, standard of living and casual atmosphere of coastal towns and cities where most people live and work in Australia, there are also some marked differences that vary from region to region and coast to coast. Furthermore, government at every level is keen to take the population pressure off the bigger metropolitan areas like Melbourne, Sydney, south-east Queensland and Perth to encourage or even stipulate that residency visas are given, in some cases, only to professionals or business people who agree to settle in more out of the way places.

Friends, relatives or governments are free with advice about where to put down your roots and making the right decision is often a complicated juggling act, balancing your longer term financial and business needs against preferences to do with day-to-day lifestyle.

If you are thinking of going into business in Australia, immigration officials can put you in touch with Australian trade officials as well as non-government contacts if they think these contacts may be useful. Australia's major banks are represented throughout Europe, America and Asia, while the larger accountancy firms and financial services institutions may also be able to provide advice and assistance to people who want to know more about doing business in Australia and investing there.

The eight state and territory governments have detailed websites and occasionally offices in key international cities. A category of the national migration policy has been designed to help states and territories sponsor newcomers with sound business credentials.

This is called the **State/Territory Specific Migration Scheme**
(Regional Sponsorship Migration Scheme). You may win
sponsorship in the Business Owner, Senior Executive or Investor
categories of the Business Skills Sponsorship programme.

Such sponsorship will greatly ease your application and be a great
start to your journey to become a happy, successful new
Australian – but remember your visa can be cancelled if you
immigrate then fail to meet the undertakings you made to
sponsoring governments.

GRANTS AND OTHER GOVERNMENT ASSISTANCE

The federal government has many programmes and incentives to
assist new and established businesses in Australia. State and
territory authorities also offer programmes and incentives for
business, though some will be more active than others in
partnering or otherwise helping local enterprises.

A summary of assistance offered by governments around Australia
is provided at the end of this chapter. Broadly, this assistance
includes:

- tax rebates;
- free counselling, help with business plans, application forms, etc;
- loan guarantees or even cash grants for priority industries.

The states and territories may choose to vigorously push
applications on behalf of Business Skill migrants they consider a
potential asset if the federal immigration department needs

convincing. Each place has its own criteria for desirable business skills though at the time of writing the kind of people and skills they are looking for appeared generally similar. However, the amount of energy with which each government approaches the issue of developing its economy through migration certainly varies, as reflected in the amount of information and support they inject into promoting these activities and the share of migrants they actually receive or manage to attract away from other locations.

So your business plan and location decisions for Australia may require a flexible attitude and could change according to supply of and demand for newcomers with your skills and capital.

Some state governments will help you through the red tape, issue checklists of precise information necessary for a successful application and really hold your hand through the entire bureaucratic process if they think you are worth it. Some will even help you decide which industry to invest in, if that is your intention, but remember that offering to take up such an opportunity may not be enough if other parts of your permanent residency application do not stack up.

Apart from exploring the government websites, your research and planning for the move to Australia can be assisted by contacting local chambers of commerce, professional associations and trade unions. You'll need to know about relevant research and education establishments, potential competitors, cost of living, disposable income, pay and conditions and so on. At least a couple of business trips to Australia to observe some of these factors for yourself should be on your 'to do' list once you get serious.

DEMOGRAPHIC TRENDS

From a colony that started life 220 years ago as a business opportunity for farmers, retired soldiers and ex-convicts with the skills to exploit the land's riches – a society where anyone who was anyone resided on large rural estates – Australia has become a nation of city-dwellers. The drift from countryside to cities continues apace. However, government policy is to encourage new residents from overseas to settle in and provide their services and skills to build smaller communities if possible.

Most business migrants have historically headed for New South Wales and its beautiful, bustling capital city, Sydney. Melbourne, the capital of the state of Victoria, is the other traditional focal point for business people attracted to working in Australia, simply because these places are Australia's economic hub. But there is a trend to change. Since the 1990s the lifestyle, climate and booming economy of southeast Queensland has attracted increasing numbers of new residents from other states as well as from overseas. Encouraged by business-friendly local and state governments, Queensland seems set to become a magnet for people seeking a younger economic setting and (slightly) lower cost of living. If the current demographic shift to this part of Australia continues, in 25 years Queensland could be the most populous state in Australia, overtaking Victoria and New South Wales.

A recent worldwide study by a leading accountancy firm found Sydney was less competitive as a location to do business in – across a range of manufacturing and high-tech industries – than some of its neighbouring state capitals. Yet the same survey found Australia was the second most competitive country in the developed world in which to set up shop, in terms of business costs (Canada came first).

As for the state and territory capital cities, there is no doubt that each has something more to offer in its own way than Sydney. A recent survey by a UK magazine, *The Economist*, rated the world's cities on living conditions. Melbourne (with Vancouver in Canada) was ranked the world's best city for quality of life, with Perth in third place and Sydney sharing eighth position with Brisbane and Adelaide.

For now, Australia's population is most dense around the coast within commuting distance of Sydney. Sydney's sprawling metropolitan area accommodates approximately 4,000 people per square kilometre, Melbourne is the next most dense area with around 3,000 people per square kilometre. Brisbane, Adelaide and Darwin have only 600–700 people per square kilometre, Canberra 400 while Perth and Hobart are Australia's most spacious cities in terms of the distance between people, with fewer than 400 inhabitants per square kilometre.

BUSINESS MIGRATION AGENTS

If you hope to enter Australia under its Business Migration Programme, it may pay to engage a migration agent for guidance on how to maximise your chances of acceptance and for introductions to people or organisations that may help your case.

However, in Australia there have been many vexatious appeals regarding migration matters via shady or ill-informed migration agents touting for business. So controls have been imposed on this relatively unregulated profession in the hope of saving time and money for would-be migrants. Watch out for similar problems if engaging a migration agent in your country of origin.

Fees charged by migration agents vary depending on where you are living and working when you apply. Reputable and experienced agents will not proceed with an application on your behalf if it seems you have little chance of success in gaining permanent residency approval from Australia's federal government, which is the final decision-maker in all cases. The fees should reflect this assessment: if you have little or no chance of getting a visa, there should be little or no charge by the migration agent.

Although Australia is becoming stricter about defining and enforcing a code of conduct for migration agents operating within its borders, check the industry regulations and any other client safeguards that may exist in the country where your migration agent is based. Internationally, there are plenty of cases of self-serving advice from migration agents to people desperate to reach Australia, and thousand of sad rip-offs. It is sensible to contact Australian migration authorities personally whenever possible for guidance through the major hurdles of business skills migration. State governments and local business and professional organisations should also be on your personal contact list, as you decide where you would like to settle and start work in Australia. A reputable migration agent can be a valuable advisor and resource in the red tape and settlement process and they may be helpful in lodging appeals should your application or some person you hope to bring with you to live in Australia be rejected initially.

STATES AND TERRITORIES

As you will see from the rest of this chapter, there is some energetic activity by Australia's six state and two territory governments to attract foreign investors, business people and highly qualified migrants who can add to the prosperity of their region. Each prides itself on 'flexibility' to consider every proposal – no matter how modest – and can advise individuals on where and whether they would have a good chance of success. Yet prospective migrants can also expect frank advice if local authorities think another part of the country is better suited to their business plans and requirements, or if their chances of getting approval are going to be slim.

SOUTH AUSTRALIA

South Australia promotes itself as offering its people the ideal combination of leisure and culture. You may well agree with this assessment if you establish yourself in or near Adelaide, the state capital with just over one million people. Certainly, living and working in suburban South Australia is a fine lifestyle for many migrants since Adelaide and the larger towns offer much of the sophistication of Australia's larger cities without their wretched excesses in terms of living costs and traffic jams. South Australia's coastal regions, where most people live in Australia's driest state (due to the vast desert areas in the centre and north of the state), are mainly temperate in climate, but prone to heat waves.

Adelaide has a thriving artistic and musical life, with its Arts Festival and world music festival (Womadelaide) attracting the cream of international and Australian talent. Despite a reputation for innovation in cultural areas, Adelaide has a conservative atmosphere largely due to the fact it was originally a colony for free settlers rather than a prison-away-from-home for British convicts.

However, Adelaide and its surrounding semi-rural towns have plenty of stylish restaurants, pubs and wineries. The emphasis is on gourmet food and wine tourism, and many Australians know South Australia best for this reason. There is also a flashy nightlife in Adelaide, which is a minor gay capital. It has spawned a series of progressive governments that have led the way in Australian politics with social justice reforms since the 1970s.

The towns and estates around Adelaide feature graceful historic buildings that are often English or German in style. Its people are proud of their history as free settlers and the famous bluestone buildings and low-rise streetscapes make this city one of the most orderly and best-preserved examples of colonial architecture in the country.

Leisure
Holiday attractions for locals and tourist resorts are varied: from

the mysterious 'blue lake' of Mount Gambier, the extensive bird and wildlife reserves, to the magnificent rocky coast from the Victorian border, and some of the best restaurants in the country, many in lovely winegrowing settings where some of Australia's most famous wines are produced. There is also plenty of orange and ochre desert, including the driest area of Australia, rugged mountain ranges and extensive national parks, as well as many unspoilt beaches near the main urban centres. As mentioned, performing arts and music of all styles feature in urban life with regular international class festivals to further develop South Australia's vibrant cultural life.

Trade

South Australia has 1.5 million people and a strong export economy based on wine and wheat as well as manufactured goods, especially motor vehicles. It is the hub of transport activity for Australia's export of farm goods and is the nation's biggest producer of wine and barley. Would-be immigrants planning to start export-oriented projects will soon see it is, as state government advisers point out, a 'cost-effective' location for sea transport of primary produce to Australian or foreign customers. This is already big business for the state, as South Australia is a major supplier of live sheep and beef abroad. It is ideally placed for domestic trade routes, halfway between Australia's main coastal population centres to the east and to the west.

International shipping facilities at Whyalla, Port Augusta, Port Pirie and Port Lincoln are well-located for serving established markets in the Pacific Basin region as well as customers in the Middle East, the USA and Europe. Portland, another major Australian deep-sea port, is just 100 km over the border in

Victoria, putting South Australia comfortably within range of further transport opportunities.

South Australia boasts the best industrial relations in the nation (that is, the lowest number of strikes of any state) while wages are estimated to be around 10% lower than in other places. It has the world's largest uranium and copper mine at Roxby Downs and the biggest lead smelting plant, as well as substantial reserves of oil and gas – all encouraging for development of manufacturing and high technology ventures.

Australia's first technology park was established in Adelaide in 1982 while a new science park is sited in the state capital's southern suburbs, linked to Flinders University.

Historically, the state is a base for heavy industries in Australia, such as car building and white-goods manufacturing. Again, it is well sited and set up for exports and imports. The government and private sector are co-operating in an effort to market its products even more professionally and aggressively in future.

South Australia has also become a hub for back office processing operations for major local and international companies, as a result of the state government's overtures to larger organisations seeking cheaper alternatives to Sydney, Melbourne or elsewhere in South East Asia. Financial service companies, household names in airlines and in telecommunications call South Australia 'home' due to government concessions, lower rents and employment costs, university facilities, a well-educated pool of potential employees in a pleasant, secure environment. These same qualities are naturally attractive to individuals thinking about relocating to Australia, looking for that elusive balance between commercial and lifestyle advantages.

State policy

The state government has a coherent approach to encouraging enterprises of all sizes to locate themselves within its borders. Like the other states and territories, South Australia is keen to attract skilled migrants and those with considerable capital and the expertise to start new ventures or buy existing enterprises in order to run them even better.

There are a range of programmes providing incentives to skilled migrants and permanent residents. Business and skilled migrants may qualify for state assistance with visa applications, help in business matters and in settling into their new homes. The South Australian government can provide the following assistance to any newcomers they want to encourage:

◆ meet and greet services;
◆ accommodation on arrival;
◆ migration employment consultancy services;
◆ migrant loan referral;
◆ overseas qualification assessment service;
◆ settlement orientation service;
◆ state government concessions;
◆ home ownership information.

For businesspeople the state may also provide:

◆ exploratory visit support (before a permanent resident visa and financial investment by a would-be migrant are required);

- networking and referral services;
- relocation services;
- business orientation support;
- industry consultancy subsidy;
- business mentor programme;
- job creation incentives.

Though prime office rents are far cheaper in Adelaide or other large South Australian centres than in Melbourne or Sydney, South Australians are keen to move their population, consumption and industrial centres away from the state capital and the nearby port cities into more sparsely populated areas if possible. Yet even in desirable rural locations an hour's drive from Adelaide, like the nearby winegrowing and south coast districts, there may be extra assistance for incoming business and professional people with serious plans to settle. Each proposal made to the local authorities in the hope of qualifying for various concessions is assessed on individual merits. State and local governments are prepared to tailor their offers and incentives to specific needs of an applicant in the drive to develop the state's economy and markets.

The state government maintains a **register of industrial land and premises** available from both the private and public sectors for lease and sale in the Adelaide area. Specific details on zoning, location, land size, buildings size, general description and real estate agents for these properties are included in the service. Site studies may assess suitable industrial locations for projects in South Australia – in terms of access to raw materials and energy, markets, infrastructure, services and transport.

There are other financial arrangements available through the government, to encourage those who could offer new jobs and investment by starting a commercial venture or expanding an old one.

At the other end of the scale, the state has facilities to help small ventures get off the ground. Many applicants approved as business migrants go to South Australia to start modest consultancy services of various types, based on relatively small amounts of finance but impressive personal expertise.

Further information
Immigration South Australia
GPO Box 1264
Adelaide 5001
South Australia.
Tel: 618 8303 2252.
Email: immigration.sa@state.sa.gov.au
Website: www.immigration.sa.gov.au.

Department for Business, Manufacturing and Trade
Level 10, 178 North Terrace
Adelaide 5000
South Australia
Tel: 618 83032400
Website (includes overseas offices): www.southaustralia.biz

QUEENSLAND

Queensland is one of the most wonderful holiday locations in the world, so it follows that actually living there should be a pleasure too. Every year, thousands of Australians relocate for lifestyle reasons or retire to tropical resorts. The big attractions are the lush natural environment and year-round summery weather. The aim of many newcomers is to live near a coastal resort and enjoy a relaxed outdoor life of beach and sunshine all year round. Therefore most of Queensland's three million inhabitants live in the south-east corner of the state and this region has experienced a huge economic boom and strain on resources due to the influx of people. Over-development is one of south-east Queensland's most serious problems. While the state government and local authorities bask in the glory of commercial success and cultural development, they also struggle to maintain the natural environment. At the Gold Coast and in Surfers Paradise (the most developed section of Queensland's south-east coastline) the number of theme park holiday visitors, casino hotels and high-rise beachside apartments are repellent to light green eco-tourists or those seeking a more back-to-basics way of life. Public transport is largely absent with much focus on freeway and road development, since most tourists and residents squeezed into this small region at any one time, travel by car.

Flash versus conservatism

Brisbane is the capital city, situated beside a river inland from the tourist towns of the south coast. Brisbane has some stunning Victorian architecture in a tropical setting and a profusion of expressways. One of Australia's best-known architects, Philip Cox, once summed it up as 'more Dallas than any other city in Australia' and as such Brisbane is a mildly conservative older sister to the even more flashy Las Vegas-like environment of the Gold Coast. Certainly, this popular part of Queensland has come a long way since it was dubbed 'God's waiting room' for all the retired elderly Australians who moved there from cooler parts of the country.

Coastal Queensland sure has an attractive lifestyle: most days promise sunshine perhaps interrupted by a few hours of hard 'yakka' (work) before getting back to the pub for a cold one or to the beach (if netted – see page 194) for a wet one. However, you may find life in the rugged interior to be backward although huge efforts by the state government and major mining and agriculture industries have started the process of change in places that have been sleepy backwaters for decades.

Slow-talking Queenslanders from far-flung farms or mining towns have been the traditional butt of jokes for many other Australians. For nearly 50 years from the end of the Second World War Queensland was governed mainly by slow-talking rural types with Christian values, but very questionable business morals. Government-sanctioned racist attitudes were evident in the circumstances of large, downtrodden Aboriginal and Islander populations. They were denied many human rights for decades in Queensland, long after the right to vote and a more honest attempt to improve circumstances were offered in other parts of Australia.

Then in the 1990s came a succession of more progressive and less corrupt Queensland governments which went a long way to cleaning up its image. And *then* came a local political bombshell, Pauline Hanson, who set the perception of progress back a decade or more with her narrow conservative views, electorally-appealing frankness and excruciating delivery of said views in the nasal tones and simplistic terms expected of 'hick' Queenslanders by those Australians who think themselves sophisticated.

Pauline Hanson's views were taken seriously because so many Queenslanders and other Australians initially supported her One Nation party. There was a foreign policy mini-crisis as Australia's profile among south-east Asian countries plummeted and the politically conservative federal government went into damage control mode in order to counter Hanson's comments about unworthy Aboriginals, Asian immigrants and the lazy unemployed. Hanson's political career soon failed and she was in and out of jail over allegations of electoral fraud, lately repudiating some of those radical views since her experience behind bars. So far, Pauline Hanson has eschewed political life though the One Nation party still has (a far more low-key) parliamentary presence.

Despite the history, Queensland's current political leaders have fulfilled much of the economic promise of this state, with its rich mining resources, vast agricultural areas and booming tourist market. The challenge is to temper so much 'progress' with sensitive planning to protect the lush, leisurely environment that made Queensland's coast uniquely attractive in the first place.

The Queensland economy

Though Queensland is one of Australia's most welcoming governments with the lowest tax regimes to attract business investment and skilled immigrants, the average weekly income is relatively low due to fewer people with tertiary and post-graduate education among the population. In 2004 a study by the Queensland Treasury found that the state needed to increase the rate of high-school completion in order to boost the state's productivity. Immigrants with skills and business ideas are welcome in order to meet this shortfall in skills. More investment in technology is also required to counter the local economy's strong reliance on a few big primary industries. Queensland dependence on exports of raw materials remains high, with coal remaining its most important export (it is the fifth largest producer in the world). Tourism is the state's major employer and the number of jobs is growing, though much of the work provided by tourism is part time.

Nevertheless the state's economy is bounding along even compared with the rest of Australia's high growth rates and even though its per capita productivity remains lower. This annual economic growth rate of around 5% since 1999 is driven by the population influx from elsewhere in Australia and overseas, at around 1% annually.

Tourism
This is Queensland's second largest industry (after coal mining and exports) and the state is banking on its continued position as Australia's top tourist destination. Billions of dollars are invested in new projects, representing half the total investment in tourism in Australia.

Mostly, the boom is concentrated on the coast, especially close to the Great Barrier Reef. Meanwhile, high-rise apartments, casinos, and hotels lining the so-called Gold and Sunshine Coasts of the south-east cast afternoon shadows along miles of beaches, as the visitors swarm in all year round. Tropical islands are fast being developed into luxury tourist resorts, while visits to the outback and tropical jungles north of Cairns are also great attractions for Australians and foreigners alike, who want a scenically rich and novel experience.

Industry

Queensland is a leading exporter of Australian raw foodstuffs and minerals. Coal is the biggest export commodity, then meat. Copper, crude lead, bauxite as well as sugar, wool, cereal, tropical fruits and other agricultural products pour out of the state's 19 ports for consumption and processing in Australia and elsewhere. But the state government is keen to broaden this economic base – which is where suitable applicants for business or skilled migration enter the picture. Its strategy relies on combining processing, manufacturing and design industries with the huge deposits of minerals and high rate of agricultural production. International price pressures in the past decade have led to rationalisation by some of Queensland's agricultural and mineral exporters – particularly sugar cane products, due to the world price drop in sugar.

There are programmes to aid commercial ventures of all sizes through the Department of State Development. Help to business and skilled migrants and sponsorship for visa applicants may be available through the Department's Skilled Migration Unit. Assistance may include:

♦ information on migration eligibility including the sought-after business skills, training, living and investing;

♦ help identifying suitable industrial sites;

♦ details of Australia's foreign investment policies;

- referrals to other government and private sector agencies that can help you apply and put down roots in Queensland.

Further information
Skilled Migration Unit
Department of State Development
PO Box 168
Albert Street Brisbane
Queensland 4002
Tel: 617 32248576
Email: skilled.migration@sd.qld.gov.au
Website: www.sd.qld.gov.au/migration

VICTORIA

Victoria is the smallest mainland state, containing only 3% of Australia's land mass. Nevertheless, it is the size of Great Britain and, as one of Australia's oldest and wealthiest regions, is home to more than one in four Australians. Melbourne is the state capital, a sprawling metropolis of 3.5 million people and the second largest city in Australia after Sydney. From this springs some sibling rivalry – with most Victorians claiming that their capital is superior to 'Sinney' in terms of the quality of life. A survey published in *The Economist* magazine recently confirmed this view, announcing Melbourne as the best place in the world if quality of life rather than razzle are what you want from a city.

Certainly, comparing Melbourne with Sydney is like trying to find something in common between a gentleman's club and a strip joint – or so they'll tell you in Victoria. Local newspapers and chat shows reveal that people from Sydney sometimes sneer at the awful flatness of the suburban wasteland and its dull brown river (in Sydney the Yarra is said to be the only river in the world that flows upside down). How can it compare with Sydney's leafy harbour frontages? The Victorians snipe back about brassy Sydney's high crime rate, dirty waterways and rip-offs in food and entertainment. Melbourne people tend to boast about their cultural and intellectual leadership in many fields, consistently good coffee, excellent restaurants and a better cocktail party conversation. Not to mention better football and horse racing.

The rolling rural landscape and well-preserved British colonial architecture are the pride and joy of those who barrack for Victoria. People who love living in Australia are generally thrilled by the stunning mountains, beautiful bush and farmland scenery, quirky communities, secluded beaches and some of the most exciting coastal rock formations to be seen anywhere. Victoria is also home to Australia's best skiing country as well as deserts and excellent wine-growing districts. Most of these attractions are within a long day's drive from one another or even shorter distances from Melbourne.

Upper crust Victoria

The wealthy 'squatocracy' in and around the state capital's city are something of a breeding ground for the nation's political and business leaders and have produced many prime ministers. Victoria's top private schools are certainly prestigious locally and if Australians can be accused of snobbery and fostering a class system based on family background, Melbourne and some sectors of Victorian society are places to point the finger.

Multicultural Melbourne

On the other hand, Melbourne is one of the most diverse and proudly multicultural societies in Australia. Some 35,000 people migrate to Victoria (mostly to Melbourne) a year, making it the second most popular destination for newcomers after New South Wales (and Sydney).

Melbourne has some old ethnic communities with deep social, sporting and cultural roots. It boasts some of the best Italian food outside Italy and one of Australia's largest Italian communities. Melbourne is home to almost as many Greeks as the largest Greek cities, and inner suburbs of Melbourne are full of shops, sports centres, community organisations and, of course, restaurants proudly proclaiming their ethnicity.

The Chinese community is well established, and the excellent inner-city Chinatown rivals those of larger capitals around the world. There is also a large Jewish community and much central and eastern European influence in the grocery shops and restaurants of particular neighbourhoods where these groups have flourished over the past century.

The Italian, Greek, Chinese, Vietnamese and other ethnic influences are evident in many of Victoria's country towns as well, for this is an area of Australia well used to integrating communities of diverse backgrounds and customs.

Finance and economics

Melbourne is home to some of Australia's biggest corporations. The headquarters to around 20% of the multinational companies represented in Australia are in Melbourne, as are the national offices of two of the nation's four major retail banks. In the early days of the colony Melbourne was the financial powerhouse of the region. It has experienced stiff competition from other cities since that time, and in the past few decades there has been a gradual shift in focus by many businesses and industries away from Melbourne and Victorian markets to other parts of Australia. This has been an issue for Melbourne's business and political establishment, which has had to work hard to reassert its importance in Australian business in order to stop the drift.

After an economic boom reflected by growth in the state's economy of up to 8% a year since 2000, Victoria is clipping along at an annual expected rate of growth in its economy of around half that, which puts it on par with most of the rest of the country. However, Victoria also has the second highest proportion of business investment per capita in Australia.

In recent years the Victorian economy has been led by climbing property prices and consumer spending. The recent downswing in property prices around Australia has hit Victoria particularly hard, with an oversupply of Melbourne apartments. For newcomers hoping to buy or rent a home this could be good news.

Though Victoria has not the bonanza atmosphere of, say, Western Australia or Queensland, industrial and resource developments are significant – with some major projects underway including fast rail links to rural Victoria, important public works projects in Melbourne city centre, expansion of the motor vehicle industry, rejuvenation of Melbourne docklands and a massive oil and gas project in the Bass Strait, where some 75% of the nation's known oil reserves are located. Victoria is also a leader in financial services, medical research, tourism, the performing arts and entertainment industries.

About 30% of Australia's manufacturing output is from Victoria. The state is an important centre for high tech manufacturing as well as being the leading processor of dairy foods, canned meat and fruit. As a result of its manufacturing base and central location, the nation's most intensively trafficked and best served domestic trade routes run through Victoria – rail, road and sea – and it is also a focal point for international trade transport. Melbourne's road freight tonnage is a third bigger than that of Sydney, indicating the significance of its location as a crossroads for commercial production moving through, in and out of the country. Port Melbourne is the largest general cargo port in Australia and the biggest container terminal in the southern hemisphere. Sydney's airports handle half the level of domestic traffic moving through Melbourne's three airports – Tullamarine International, Essendon and Moorabin. Tullamarine is Australia's only 24-hour-a-day airport.

Favoured projects in Victoria

The Victorian government appears to be among the most focused in Australia when it comes to attracting business migrants. The state government is clear about the types of projects it considers favourable to its economy and its website promoting and proclaiming the kind of assistance and information that newcomers may expect from Victoria was second to none at the time of writing.

Experts in the following industry categories were actively sought by the state government through skilled and business migration programmes.

- automotive
- advanced science
- furniture making
- health
- horticulture
- hospitality
- metal machinery
- tool making
- urban and regional planning
- welding
- teaching.

Assistance to migrants

As in most Australian states and territories, Victoria claims business-friendly legal and taxation structures to encourage migrants and will also sponsor or help employers to sponsor individuals with skills in demand on a viable business proposition. Some of the other assistance Victoria may proffer include:

- priority visa processing;

- exemption from work experience requirements for eligible international students who have recently graduated from an Australian university or TAFE;

- referral of the individual's CV to Victorian employers who have registered their job opportunities;

- information about job opportunities in Victoria's regional areas;

- references to qualification assessment services;

- nomination to migrate to Victoria if you have a skill in demand in that state;

- references to specialist industry and professional organisations.

Further information
Skilled Migration Unit
Level 8, 1 Spring Street
Melbourne
Victoria 3000
Tel: 613 92083334
Email: info@liveinvictoria.vic.gov.au
Website: www.liveinvictoria.vic.gov.au

Business Migration Unit
Level 15, 1 Spring Street
Melbourne
Victoria 3000
Tel: 613 92083319
Email/website: as above.

NEW SOUTH WALES

New South Wales (NSW) is the richest, mostly highly developed and heavily populated area of Australia. This is where the first British colonies were established. It now accounts for around 35% of the nation's gross domestic product (GDP) and the state's economy is larger by value than all the South East Asian countries (excluding Indonesia) combined. New South Wales' population is six million, and three quarters of its residents live on the coast.

Sydney

Older than San Francisco, Washington DC, Los Angeles, Singapore or Johannesburg, Sydney is home to four million people. Covering 50 kilometres to the north, south and west of its central business district and main harbour, this is one of the biggest cities in the world in terms of area. Nearby cities, Wollongong to the south, Gosford to the north and the towns of the Blue Mountains in the west, are virtually satellite cities and many people commute long distances to work.

Sydney has been described as the world's most beautiful city and many of the water-bound stretches along rivers and harbours are splendid indeed. There are also many bushland reserves across the Sydney landscape, often adjoining people's backyards. The outlook is breathtaking from the various waterways over lush, semi-tropical vegetation. Neo-Tuscan mansions and suave minimalist apartments ogle at glittering waterways of many shapes and sizes and well-appointed beaches.

Yet top Australian architect, Philip Cox, has likened Sydney to 'an untidy child – vulgar and unruly'. It is part holiday resort, part business centre and part disorderly suburban sprawl for all is not ideal in this suburban Garden of Eden. Away from the waterfronts and high-rise glitter, Sydney's suburbs can be hot, monotonous miles of brick bungalows. From some locations it can be an hour's drive often through heavy traffic to a reasonable picnic spot. Some swimming areas are health hazards due to water pollution and many local beaches are regularly closed to swimmers mainly due to inadequate storm water arrangements when it rains...if it rains. For Sydney like much of the east coast has been in the grip of drought since the early 2000s and there is a $A220 fine for hosing gardens in daytime hours or on certain days of the week. Hosing hard surfaces or cars attracts the same fine. There has been a recent clampdown in building codes and inducements by governments and authorities at all levels to dissuade builders and homeowners from wasting power and to encourage them to save water. Many have called for a slowdown in the rate of Sydney's growth and a halt to the building of high-density suburban palaces known as MacMansions (a pun on the international burger chain of a similar name). However, the return to smaller houses which leave plenty of unpaved garden on their sites is going to be a sacrifice for many Sydney people who have more ambitious plans for their dream homes.

In the meantime, Sydney-siders are being obliged to replant their once lush semi-tropical gardens with less thirsty bush and desert species as the enduring suburban drought establishes itself into the climatic norm. Reduced rainfall is the outcome of mismanaged environmental resources by generations of Australians in the cities and on the land and aging stormwater and sewerage infrastructure has failed to cope with a population boom.

However, most people migrating to Australia seriously consider living in Sydney. It has thriving ethnic communities, good infrastructure, excellent consumer choices and cultural pastimes, strong local and international business activity and, while the cost of living may be relatively high compared with elsewhere, so are the rates of pay.

Out and about in NSW
Beyond Sydney, New South Wales is a large, rugged state with green belts along the coast and major rivers as well as many

historic, colonial towns which live – or have died – with local booms in farming or mining. Like Victoria, climates of New South Wales have the variety of a whole continent. There are the Snowy Mountains (and Australia's highest peak, Mt Koscuisko, 2,228 metres above sea level) for skiing in winter, as well as semi-tropical lakes, rivers, subtropical rain forests and palm-ringed coastlines in the north, desert in the far west, plus millions of acres of flat farmland and bushland. Despite being Australia's most populated region, the landscape can be surprisingly empty away from the Sydney and central coast area.

A financial capital

Sydney joins Hong Kong and Singapore as one of the most important financial growth centres in the southern hemisphere. The Reserve Bank of Australia is headquartered in Sydney, as are 60% of Australia's top 100 companies, according to the way the statistics have been interpreted (conflicting with a similar claim on behalf of Melbourne by the Victorian government). Sydney's impressive modern stock exchange building has more companies listed on it than the exchanges of Melbourne or Perth, with half the total share turnover and the only local exchange in Australia maintaining a market in call options. Sydney's nearby Futures Exchange is the only one where dealings include gold, wool, meat, export beef and interest rates. There is also a foreign exchange hedge market covering market risks. Its state government, like the other mostly Labour and nominally left-leaning governments of Australia's states and territories, works hard to accommodate business interests. Legal structures are generally transparent and stable. Governments at all levels seem to have close relationships with the financial community – the leading lights of the political stage typically coming from and/or returning to careers in banking, law and industry when they leave politics.

Business in NSW

In terms of exports, NSW and Sydney are the hub of big and medium sized business in Australia. The state provides close to half of the nation's services exports. It also provides about 35% of the nation's total employment and 20% of its manufacturing exports. It manufactures food, beverages, tobacco, textiles, footwear and clothing through to fabricated metals. It has three oil refineries and more than 30 petrochemical plants.

New South Wales is the biggest steel producer in the country – some 80% of the national annual output – as well as being Australia's leading producer of wool and poultry goods and ranking second to Queensland in terms of beef production.

Coal is the state's main mineral resource. It also has significant reserves of silver, copper, zinc, lead, tin, titanium and rutile. Government policy has aimed at building up the state's electricity supply for industrial purposes. Coal, natural gas as well as hydro-electric schemes provide its present power supply for domestic and commercial purposes.

However, the state has experienced a swing away from manufacturing and mining activities to investment in services and high technology for both local and export markets. At the start of the decade, this sector accounted for only 15% of all investment but now represents more than two-thirds of all new projects. Mining and manufacturing have declined from a 40% share of investment activity to 15%. Local authorities encourage siting for **advanced technology** parks (where such enterprises share industrial or office sites) and service industries. Sydney is now a centre for a highly competitive computer industry.

Over a third of Australia's skilled business migrants settle in New South Wales, mainly in Sydney. They come mostly from south and north-east Asia, Britain, North America, the Middle East, and Africa. The success of Asian settlers is reflected by the size and influence of Sydney's Oriental community which is the largest in Australia and represents about 10% of the population, many more if you add Sydney siders who were born in Australia of north and south-east Asian migrant parents.

Business incentives

The state provides a range of business programmes and incentives to newcomers and established residents, to help them with investment or business expansion plans. These are generally administered by the **NSW Department of State and Regional Development**. Specific private or public sector proposals are considered for assistance on the basis of likely contribution to employment and economic development. At its international offices in London and Tokyo, the state government maintains investment and trade advisory services to help organisations and would-be immigrants to research business opportunities, set up joint ventures, arrange licensing agreements, and the exchange or sale of technology as well as the establishment of operations in Australia. The state provides individual counselling and step-by-step guides through the morass of red tape that a suitable business migrant will encounter in seeking permission to set up in New South Wales.

The Department of State and Regional Development aims to help business migrants to NSW set up and become established. Most of its assistance is in the form of advice, and areas of expertise that may prove helpful include guidance on:

* business start-up;
* business expansion;
* marketing of innovative ideas for services and products;
* new technology and e-commerce;
* retail leasing including advice on mediation with landlords and retail tenants of commercial properties.

The Department will also co-ordinate and provide intermediary support for newcomers with providers of telecommunications services, energy, property agents, legal and financial organisation.

Further information
Government Department of State and Regional Development
Level 35, Governor Phillip Tower
1 Farrer Place, Sydney
PO Box N818
Grosvenor Place,
Sydney NSW 1220
Tel: 612 92283111
Email: businessweb@business.nsw.gov.au
London: invest@nsw.co.uk
Tokyo: nswtokyo@gol.com

TASMANIA

Known as 'Tassy' to Australians, Tasmania is an island that is often left off the national map altogether. Yet it is a real jewel: green, mountainous and relatively unpolluted. The island state of the island continent actually comprises 334 islands to the south east of Australia's mainland, though most of the action is in the heart-shaped main island, also known as the Apple Isle, which most people think of as Tasmania.

The health freaks, conservationists, farmers and suburbanites who live in Tasmania declare it to be the finest place for a healthy lifestyle, safe from the horrifying effects of nuclear accident or war. 'I am always building veritable castles in the air about emigrating and Tasmania has been my headquarters of late,' wrote Charles Darwin back in 1854 – and today's nature lovers may also do well to consider a move there. However, it is isolated from the mainland by the Bass Strait which, despite considerable transport subsidies to help the island's trade and commerce, is said to be the major drawback from a business point of view.

A tiny population – fewer than half a million people – means that the state has limited domestic markets. However, with the recent tourism and economic boom of the 90s and 00s, there are now three car ferries a day from Victorian ports to the north of Tasmania. For decades until transport links and economic activity became more vigorous, Tasmania's population was static and even started falling in the mid 1990s. Back then, Tasmania's economy and society seemed immune from the cultural activity and growing commercialism of the rest of the nation. Australians from the mainland to its north joke about in-breeding due to a shortage of people but, jokes aside, the main cities of Hobart and Launceston are quite cosmopolitan. As well as the British, who settled what was for its first 70 years a notoriously barbaric prison colony known as Van Diemen's Land, Tasmania's larger ethnic groups are of Mediterranean, East European and Dutch origin.

The big news of recent years is that Tasmania has a progressive state government which is notionally Labor, but in Tasmania more than in most other places the main parties, Labor and

Liberal, have been traditionally close in terms of their policies and good relationship with the business community. Tasmania seems to have come a long way towards encouraging a business boom and it is especially welcoming to migrants sponsored by local enterprises. There are acute job shortages in some areas of industry and professions due to the state's tiny population, and the fact that many would-be skilled or business migrants are attracted to settle in other parts of Australia. By the mid 2000s economic growth was around 3.4% which is as strong as anywhere in Australia, and being a big fish in a small pond may be worth considering if you are thinking of places to invest and build a new life in Australia.

The average income in Tasmania is lower than most other parts of Australia but so are the prices of goods and services which make up the cost of living. Property is easier and cheaper to rent and buy than in the more crowded locations in the mainland. Not surprisingly, fans of Tasmania speak highly of the possibility of working and building a career in a place which is closer to the natural environment than most other urban areas, and the verdant, rolling landscape around the towns is highly reminiscent of England's pretty countryside.

Even in Hobart's peak hour traffic it takes just half an hour to traverse the capital by car from its farthest suburb to the centre. The locals go down to the docks to buy seafood fresh from trawlers, whereas in the mainland cities people rarely see a fresh fish, unless it has been scaled, gutted, filleted and presented under supermarket lighting in plastic wrapping.

Boat ownership is far more common among workaday Tasmanians than elsewhere in Australia and relatively low property prices mean that many more suburbanites also own a 'shack' by the beach or near a fishing stream. In fact, Tasmania has been referred to as the sanatorium of tropical Australia. Detractors maintain it is a teensy bit dull and that even the capital, Hobart, is not a true city since it has only a couple of thousand inhabitants. However, if you favour a spacious, relaxed environment of forests and lakes, without extremes in temperature, and if you prefer sailing and outdoor activities to organised entertainments and indoor culture, Tasmania could be perfect.

Ecology and business
In Tasmania perhaps more than elsewhere the two main political parties battle it out to claim the middle ground as their own. The biggest threat to Tasmania's comparative peace and safety is the fight over the logging of old-growth forests. Forestry is a vital plank of the Tasmanian economy and many Tasmanians want the right to harvest the logs as they see fit. Passions have run high over the years and the government has promised to halt logging of the ancient forests by 2010 this is a 'compromise' which has angered conservationists around the world who fear that irreparable damage will be done as trees continue to be felled in sensitive wilderness.

The state has a history of clashing with federal government policy over environment. Flooding of the Franklin River and other hydro-electric projects were eventually halted after a High Court battle that amounted to a political civil war in the 1980s, with Tasmanians arguing they need to harness their environmental riches to provide power on an industrial scale. In 1989 a controversial plan to build a pulp mill on the Bass Strait coastline was also stalled after another political arm-wrestle between governments in Canberra and Hobart. Hardwood-chipping has been a political hot potato for decades and it seems that in Tasmania a theme for local business and industry is the degree to which economic progress is stymied by 'greenies' from interstate or overseas.

Certainly, the problem of ecology versus economics weights heavily on the minds of many Tasmanians. The state is famous for its bushland and big rivers, boasting the last temperate wilderness on earth with 40% of the state locked up in national parks and other conservation areas. Exploitation of available land for the timber industry and waters to generate power are certainly vital to the state's economy – though tourism has become increasingly profitable as, ironically, people come from far and wide to see what the fuss is all about.

Tourism

These fights over environment have helped put Tasmania on the 'must-see' list for eco-tourists from around the world. Rafting down the Franklin and other wild rivers of Tasmania, bushwalking or driving to see the famous wilderness from more accessible vantage points is a popular holiday among middle-class mainlanders.

There are also many fascinating and grisly reminders of Australia's colonial past, with a range of historic settlements and prisons still standing as a reminder that Tasmania's original purpose was as a penal colony for the most hardened felons.

The genocide of Tasmania's Aboriginals is another, even less glorious if interesting, historical fact and a great point of interest for many visitors who seek to better understand Australia's origins and to dig deeper into the whitewashed history of the British colonies around Australia.

By 2005, Tasmania was attracting up to 700,000 tourists a year and both temporary and permanent migrants to work in hospitality industries are in demand. The potential for tourism to boost the Tasmanian economy is acknowledged through the introduction of Australia's first hospitality and tourist-industry courses at the state's tertiary education centres.

Industrial development

Zinc and aluminium smelting are major industries, as well as the above mentioned forestry and wood products industries. The effort to attract heavy industry to Tasmania through subsidised transport costs to compensate for distances from major markets and mainland ports has resulted in the opening of Australia's first silicon factory, north of Hobart. Aquaculture ventures like oyster, trout, abalone, scallop and Atlantic salmon farming have started up, helping to increase employment opportunities.

Tasmania is considered so pristine that it is one of the few places in the world from which live oysters can be imported by Japan. Agriculture is also a strong contributor to growth due to a temperate climate, clean air and reliable rainfall. Boutique wines and foods from Tasmania have a great reputation around Australia, representing opportunities for outsiders with relevant skills or experience.

Innovative industries such as those that extract and export natural chemical and essential oils of plants such as boronia, peppermint, spearmint and caraway have sprung up and there are many other smaller-scale industries based in Tasmania. Cheeses for Japan, sporting rifles for the United States, catamarans and computer software for Europe and even prefabricated igloos are sold to Iceland.

Like other parts of Australia, Tasmania specifies 'economic diversification', 'high tech' and 'manufacturing' sectors as the keys to continued prosperity and economic expansion. Tasmania is keen to develop processing and manufacturing ventures based on its sea and land farming. The presence of a large available workforce with a low incidence of strikes and other union disruption is emphasised in making the case for relocating in Tasmania. Prospective business migrants and foreign investors are invited to approach the Investment, Trade and Development arm of the Department of State Development.

There is a range of services available by contacting Multicultural Tasmania, another state government body dedicated to helping suitable sponsored, skilled and business migration applicants.

Further information
Investment, Trade and Development Department of the
Tasmanian Department of State Development
22 Elizabeth Street
Hobart 7000
Tasmania
Tel: 6136 2335790
Website: www.dsd.tas.gov.au

Multicultural Tasmania
Tel: 6136 2333439
Email: MULTITAS@dpac.tas.gov.au
Website: www.dpac.tas.gov.au/divisions/multitas

CANBERRA AND THE AUSTRALIAN CAPITAL TERRITORY (ACT)

Canberra is the main city in the smallest of Australia's states and territories, the Australian Capital Territory (ACT). Its permanent population is under 350,000 and it is known as the 'bush capital' – however, Canberra is the business base of many of the most powerful people and organisations in the land. This is a city of Australian politicians, public servants, government lobbyists, academics, military chiefs, as well as diplomats and journalists from around the globe. Unsurprisingly, its main industry is said to be the production of hot air but as a political hub it can also be one of the most invigorating places in the nation to live and work.

Canberra is headquarters to the federal parliament, its government departments and military academies. Canberra is also a mecca for academics from arts and sciences for it is home to the Australian National University which is perhaps the most highly rated internationally of all the nation's universities. The Commonwealth Scientific and Industrial Research Organisation (CSIRO), as well as that training ground for aspiring athletes, the Australian Institute of Sport, are also in Canberra.

A capital lifestyle
Rising from a desert of dusty green bush somewhere in the 'middle of nowhere' between Australia's two largest cities, Sydney

and Melbourne, Canberra is a vast low-rise oasis of local and European flora, of showy public architecture, and of seasonal colour in autumn and springtime. It is planted with 12 million trees, many of them imported from Europe to meet the needs of Canberra's first generation of homemakers, public servants, and keen gardeners who came early in the 20th century to civilise the place and make it a showpiece for Australia. Its three main mini-city centres are separated by bush and parkland picnic areas. There is a vast artificial and very manicured lake in the middle of a cityscape that is also adorned with many public buildings for government, law, museums, ambassadors, the arts and higher education experts of many fields. These days ordinary citizens can windsurf and sail on the lake, fish or swim in nearby rivers or drive two hours in one direction to the gorgeous wild beaches of the NSW south coast or drive in another direction to ski or walk (depending on the season) in the Snowy Mountains. Many people with jobs or businesses in Canberra live in hamlets or on properties and farms outside the city proper and excellent roads mean commuting to work is no trouble.

Its population may be a sparse, yet Canberra's cultural life is relatively rich due to the number of important visitors, the high education level of its residents and their diverse and often sophisticated interests. The close proximity to Sydney (just 20 minutes away by air, an hour or two by train and about three hours by road) also encourages most big name stars and arts productions to include Canberra on their itinerary.

Canberra's social life has neither the hedonism of Sydney's nor the cultural richness of Melbourne's, say the detractors. On the embassy and parliament house cocktail circuit, people you meet the first time may seem far too keen to discover who you work for, and therefore what potential power or network you possess in the realms of politics and policy-making.

The presence of Australian national parliament makes Canberra what it is: a privileged showpiece for government, Australia's Geneva or Washington DC for Down Under. The billion-dollar Parliament House was officially opened in 1988. The building has attracted as much criticism as admiration. Detractors argue the luxurious facilities are too good for the 'pollies' (politicians) and not good enough for everyone else using the building. Nevertheless, its distinctive and excruciatingly expensive flagpole ($A10 million) has pride of place as the symbol of the city.

Canberra's origins

Canberra was founded in 1911, ten years after the various colonies of Australia amalgamated under a single federal government. There was a dispute between Sydney and Melbourne over which should be Australia's capital city and an area some 911 square miles (2,359 square kilometres, about the size of Luxembourg) was granted by the state of NSW for the new Capital Territory. The area was roughly halfway between the two major cities and was a sheep station known for nearly a century as Canberry, a name derived from an Aboriginal word which, by chance, means 'meeting place'.

In 1912 a Chicago architect, Walter Burley Griffin, won a competition to design the model city. His concept included the aforementioned artificial lake at the centre and a number of widely separate satellite towns on roads radiating from the monumental and parliamentary heartland of the new capital.

After major bushfires swept through Canberra in 2003, there was a rethink in the layout of this unusually decentralised and carefully planned city-state. Its reputation as a wonderful way for suburbanites to live and work close to bush and corridors that separate Canberra's satellite centres of business and industry, has been blackened literally and metaphorically by the threat of fire. The enduring drought in eastern Australia and the tinder dry climatic conditions are probably there to stay, transforming that lovely bushland fringe around most of Canberra's residential streets into a serious threat to public safety. So the suburban 'bushland capital' idea will not be extended as Canberra's population grows and alternative town planning solutions will be found to minimise the bushfire hazard.

Light industry is strictly confined to three areas of the city. Industry associations, pressure groups and lobbyists tend to have their offices around Parliament House and, unlike elsewhere in Australia, land in Canberra cannot be purchased outright but bought subject to a 100-year lease.

After nearly 80 years of federal administration, Canberra finally achieved self-government in 1989. An election of the ACT House of Assembly replaced the government minister (who usually lived elsewhere in Australia). The push for full statehood is not as strong as in the Northern Territory due to the tangled interests of the ACT and federal government, a fact also reflected in the slowness of the territory administration to build an economy independent of the public service and government.

Canberra's economy
Since the mid 2000s the ACT's own government has been

implementing a plan to create a radical shift in the economy. Known as **the Canberra Plan**, the idea is to boost the contribution of private sector jobs and earnings, thus overcoming the ebbs and flows in wealth and populations cause by occasional funding changes to the federal public service. Attracting more people with suitable skills is an important part of the Canberra Plan to insulate the economy from periodic cuts and expansions in government departments. At the start of the 1990s the ACT was plunged into a major recession from which it took decades to emerge due to cuts in the bureaucracy and an exodus of talented and employable people who left for jobs in other places.

It is hoped that by attracting more private businesses and non-government enterprises to the ACT future fluctuations of this sort can be avoided. In 2004 the sectors targeted for support by the ACT government in developing a more balanced business environment and selecting skilled and business migrants include:

◆ information and communication technology;
◆ public administration;
◆ education;
◆ space sciences;
◆ biotechnology;
◆ environmental industries;
◆ defence industries.

Tourism
Canberra and its environs, including the large New South Wales town of Queenbeyan on its border, is home away from home – often for years – to many powerful people. Many 'temporary residents' buy homes or apartments in Canberra in addition to

their real homes in other parts of Australia. Canberra is also host to the gabfests and conferences associated with its political life and the infrastructure to support these events is a major driver of its economy and associated tourist industry.

Three million tourists a year come to the ACT, and while many are there for a conference or on a study mission, the architectural and cultural allure of many stunning public buildings also put Canberra on the map. Outstanding places of interest include the Australian Museum, National Library, National Science Centre, the High Court, National Gallery, Australian War Memorial and of course the new and old Parliament House buildings.

In order to feed the source of all that hot air emanating from Capital Hill, restaurant catering and eateries of all kinds are vital to local economic and social life. On a busy night its up-market clubs and international hotels are crammed with more grey suits than a bankers' convention – which is probably where everyone was before they hit the town. There are a number of staid, elite clubs with excellent restaurant and entertainment facilities as well as the obligatory leagues and football clubs both in the ACT and across the border in the NSW town of Queenbeyan, offering vast 'halls of culture' (poker machines and casinos) to the masses.

Employment

Canberra can be one of the most one-dimensional places in Australia to live and work. It all depends on whether you have a job and what job you do. The Commonwealth Public Service employs nearly half the territory's workers and its citizens are the best paid and most highly educated in Australia. Government primary and secondary schools have top-rate facilities and staff compared with elsewhere in Australia. However, youth unemployment is consistently high. The young are often forced to move elsewhere if they cannot get work – especially in one of those periods when the public service is being pruned, which has happened regularly over the decades by successive governments keen to show they have what it takes to cut public spending.

After the public service, the tourism industry is Canberra's next biggest employer and the Canberra Plan aims to boost the contribution of the many small businesses that dominate the ACT's non-government sector. In fact 50% of the territory's industry is represented by small business, higher than for any other Australian state or territory. This number is growing rapidly and small enterprises are active in delivering a wide range of sophisticated and broadly-based service industries to support local clients. Research and science in both public and private sectors are important employers in the ACT with demand for expertise from government departments, the Australian National University and other scientific establishments, Canberra's many museums, libraries and so on.

Immigration and the Canberra Plan

The Canberra Pan is a strategic approach to the need to build a strong private sector in the ACT. The Plan makes it a priority to attract new people from overseas and elsewhere in Australia to live and work in the ACT, in order to stimulate and diversify the ACT's business life away from government-linked activities.

The Plan needs around 2,000 newcomers a year to help fulfil the ACT's economic promise and, ultimately, to raise its now stagnant population by about 100,000 people. The Business Migration section of the ACT Chief Minister's Department has an office of business and tourism that administers matters related to business migration and sponsorship of skilled migrants.

Each applicant must show evidence of their:

* financial capacity and commitment to run a business or investment in the ACT;

* business skills, expertise and related capabilities; and

* research to demonstrate their business idea is viable.

They are also required to demonstrate how the ACT will benefit economically from the applicant's business proposition. These benefits may include the fact the new venture will generate jobs, introduce new skills, expertise and technologies and/or help to develop export markets or replace imports.

Compared with other state and territory governments, the ACT's push to attract foreign migrants is low key. There is little in the way of offers of support with applications or other inducements to would-be new arrivals to choose the ACT as their home. Perhaps the assumption is that the high standard of living and quality government services for people living in the national capital should speak for themselves.

Further information
Business Migration, Office of Business and Tourism, Chief Minister's Department
PO Box 243
Civic Square

Canberra
ACT 2608
Tel: 612 62050725
Website: www.business.act.gov.au

NORTHERN TERRITORY

'The Northern Territory is more than a land of contrasts...It's a
spiritual experience.'

Well, it's hard to resist a giggle at such overblown sentiment in
the territory government's official literature about the attractions
of Australia's least populated and most rugged of terrains. Until
you go there. Compare the promotional blurb with the reaction of
people who've actually experienced the Northern Territory's
staggering beauty and mystical qualities for the first time. Visit
Uluru (Ayers Rock), in the orange heart of Australia, strangers
have likened the experienced to feeling 'as if my head has been
lifted off and changed for a new one'.

Locals may cackle that the speaker has consumed too many
Darwin stubbies (litre bottles of beer), but this reaction is not so
unusual among newcomers to the heady mix of tropical and
desert environments that make the Northern Territory unique.

Aboriginals and the environment
Those too young for beer feel the impact of the natural
environment in other ways, even if they are of non-Aboriginal
origin. At a mixed race school in the outback, the story goes that
a teacher asked children to draw self-portraits. Many handed in

landscapes with trees, rocks, rivers and gullies – no human faces. It is no coincidence that the Northern Territory is the home of and inspiration for so much Australian Aboriginal art which epitomises the role of landscape in the Australian psyche.

Despite new wealth that land rights, mining royalties and artistic fame have brought to many communities, Aboriginals remain the poor relations of the rest of the population. They frequently slip through government welfare and education safety nets. Migrants of many origins who come to live and work in the Northern Territory often dismiss the Aboriginals (who constitute about a third of the territory's population of 200,000) as a bunch of lazy drunks and no-hopers. They can't understand why the native blacks have not responded more positively to the funding and 'civilizing' facilities now available to their communities. While this is a question that niggles at Australian society in general, nowhere is the gap between the Aboriginal population and people of other racial origins more apparent than in this part of Australia.

Strenuous efforts have been made by local authorities to address this social imbalance, with some success. Now some 50% of the land in the Northern Territory officially belongs to Aboriginal groups through various forms of native title and there appears to be an important cultural shift to genuinely include and manage the interests and cultural heritage of this largely youthful indigenous population.

After all, tourism (though not the Territory's biggest earner) makes an important contribution to the economy by providing employment and facilities for national and international tourists – many of whom come to wonder at the Aboriginal sacred sites and related environmental wonders.

Informality rules

The Northern Territory's overall style is informal to say the least. It's a place where the vast distances between the few townships are measured by the amount of beer you'll need for the journey. Drink-driving rules notwithstanding, the joke is that you'll need a sixpack to make it from Tennant Creek, the main town at the centre of the Northern Territory, to Alice Springs in the south – about 500 kilometres (300 miles) away.

As in most mining areas, the going is rough, tough and macho. The richest mines extract natural gas, oil, uranium, gold, copper, tin, tantalite, wolfram, manganese and bauxite. After mining comes tourism, then agriculture and fisheries in the Territory's list of prominent employers and wealth-producing activities. Not surprisingly, the movers and shakers in many towns and communities are generally earthy, straight shooting types without a suit in their wardrobe.

Climate and population

If you can't stand hot climates, then the Northern Territory is probably not the best place to settle in the long term. However, if you enjoy the heat then the advantages in terms of lifestyle are tremendous – a lifestyle based on year-round warmth both inland (the Centre) and on the tropical coast (the Top End). Nor should you throw away your jeans and blankets, for in many places nights are chilly or a cooler daytime temperature may at times apply.

Darwin is the capital, and it has been flattened by three major cyclones in its short history, the most recent being Cyclone Tracey in 1974. Each time Darwin has risen from the rubble into a low-rise sprawl. Darwin has the hottest average temperature of any city in Australia for both summer and winter. Expect about 31°C on average in high summer (January) – and a whole half a degree cooler in mid winter (July) at 30.4°C. Forget about four seasons when living on the far north coast of Australia. Instead, think of weather patterns in terms of wet and dry seasons. Wet or dry, Darwin has a higher average number of hours of sunshine than anywhere else on the continent at 8.5 hours per day. It also has the smallest number of people, at around 100,000, or half the Northern Territory's population, less than for any other state or territory in Australia. People are strikingly young – on average the age is just 24 years with 80% of the population under 40.

Younger people are clearly leaving the Territory by the time they reach maturity, which can be a problem, though there are now more facilities and lifestyle choices to encourage residents to stay on due to strong economic growth in recent years. The government has gone to some lengths to foster the cultural heritages of its diverse population. Apart from the large proportion of Aboriginals and local Islander peoples, Darwin in particular is a melting pot city even compared with Australia's many other multicultural population centres. It is home to people from 120 countries speaking 60 different languages, many from the Asian region. To outsiders and newcomers, the tropical Top End has a colourful frontier atmosphere where racial harmony is the norm due to the non-Caucasian background of many influential inhabitants. Attitudes of youthful exuberance and a raw enthusiasm for development and financial opportunism abound.

The presence of large numbers of armed forces personnel, posted
to monitor the important regional border of neighbouring lands
and trading partners, adds to the buzz in coastal centres where
soldiers, sailors and airforce staff mix with backpackers, miners
and locals in daily life and in bars and restaurants at night.

Public policy and environmental issues

The Northern Territory became self-governed with the Federation of
Australia in 1974. It has a Chief Minister rather than a Premier (the
top political position in the states) and an Administrator not a
Governor (who represents the British monarchy in the states).
Eagerly, this region is moving towards full statehood as its economy
develops. For now, the mood politically is savvy with a touch of
cowboy and governments of recent years have been progressive and
open to new ideas for business and financial growth.

Naturally, there are many political arguments over the interests of
business versus the protection of the environment. Ironically, the
conservationist case is often put by non-Territorians who want to
stop uranium mining and protect landscape and wildlife in areas
like the Kakadu National Park, which is a must-see for eco-tourists
and already has World Heritage Listing. As in many places around
Australia, it seems that fast tourism development is taking place in a
race against mining and agricultural interest groups that want to
secure and develop tracts of desirable land without new constraints.
Over-development by either mining or tourism interests is a real risk
– but for the moment it seems the tourism industry has gained
ground, with the opening of the new rail link to Adeline, safari-style
holidays, cruise ship visits, casinos in Darwin and Alice Springs, and
construction of large luxury 'villages' to accommodate well over a
million visitors a year. These major developments are sited near

fragile attractions such as the Olgas (Kata Tidja), huge stone remains of a long-buried mountain range and of course the biggest boulder in Australia, Ayers Rock (Uluru).

Business and industry

More than anywhere in Australia, the Deep North needs businesspeople and skilled workers with ideas and capital to invest. Land is concentrated in relatively few hands while a number of public mining companies have traditionally been the largest employers in a lop-sided economy. In the past decade, construction of defence facilities and related measures to protect Australia's northern border has led to an influx of new residents to the Northern Territory and an injection of Federal government funds for the local infrastructure.

But many people who come to this part of Australia do so on a temporary basis, as their career demands. For the Territory government and long-term residents, the challenge is to foster a larger, more permanent community to provide a robust local market for goods and services. This will lead to smaller employers – not just a few large groups – sharing in economic power.

Certainly there are many opportunities for business located so close to the capital cities and large markets of South East Asia, with Darwin and its port far better sited for trade than capitals like Sydney and Melbourne. In fact Darwin is Australia's largest port and constantly being upgraded. The airport has also been redeveloped to meet the needs of a larger, more sophisticated clientele. There is also a programme to seal more outback roads to improve road transport since air fares and freight charges internally are high. The freight and passenger rail link from

Adelaide in South Australia to Darwin 3,000 kilometres to the north was finally opened in 2004 and has been a huge success. Much of the Territory's future prosperity appears to hinge on this rail link, even more than a bitumen-sealed highway covering the same inland stretch.

Due to plentiful mineral resources and natural power, the NT can now cater for medium-scale steel fabrication, earth moving and electrical and engineering projects which could be useful in developing the region's infrastructure for trade and industry in future.

The downside for the Territory's economy, dependent as it currently is on exports of gas, minerals and primary produce, is the impact of rollercoaster prices for commodities and international exchange rates.

Incentives for business

Since the economy is a baby compared with the rest of Australia, the Northern Territory's economic planners can be more open-minded about the areas eligible for planning permission and government incentives. The government aims to encourage growth in private sector investment generally. Not surprisingly, mining, the processing and export of livestock and fish, and of course the tourism industry are defined as desirable areas to encourage. Economic diversification through manufacturing or business services is also sought after. If you have professional skills like medicine, dentistry, pharmacy, teaching or if you are a tradesperson in an area of defined shortage, the Northern Territory could be very welcoming to your application for residency and you can expect considerable help with your migration application.

Government incentives for new investments depend on the project and are decided in each case by the Territory's industry experts. The government has established the Department of Business, Industry and Resource Development (DBIRD) to create investment opportunities, strengthen economic development in partnership with business and industry – and to balance these against the need for sustainable management of natural resources. Sales tax, customs and excise duty incentives and exemptions are available to eligible applicants.

Further information
Department of Business, Industry and Resource Development
Development House
76 The Esplanade
GPO Box 3000
Darwin NT
Tel: 618 89244280
Email: info@dbird.nt.gov.au
Website: www.dbird.nt.gov.au

Migration Services
(Part of DBIRD contacts as above)
Email: migration@dbird.nt.gov.au

WESTERN AUSTRALIA

The so-called 'wild west' of Australia is said to be the best place in the country for people to make their first million dollars. The people of Perth in the prosperous, buzzing, south-west corner of Western Australia have made a name for decades in international business and within Australia with their aggressive approach to business and a touch of showmanship that astounds the brashest Easterners. The international tourist trade and wine industry has also helped focus attention on Western Australia's talented and innovative population as well as this vast state's natural beauty.

Perth

Perth, the capital of a state which comprises more than half Australia's land mass, is a beautiful city inland from the coastal port of Fremantle. Its natural vistas and the high quality of low-rise suburbs along the Swan River are a breath of fresh air for those who have lived in the bigger cities of the world – for Perth still has many of the advantages of a small town plus the facilities and choices of a major regional centre. Like Sydney at the opposite side of Australia, Perth has a sunny climate and relaxed lifestyle featuring water sports and beach-living. Also like Sydney, Perth suffers from water shortages and so has water restrictions which look like being here to stay, after centuries of mismanagement of the environment and water catchment systems.

Perth is a place where newer residents have quickly put down roots. It is home to a host of business, political and mining industry stars as well as those maverick socialite types. Leading lights (and perhaps the most embarrassing big names who are linked to Perth) are former jailbird businessman Allan Bond, a Pommy 'moygrant' who is once again making a new life for himself having made and lost millions of his own and other people's money. Bond is a classic rags to riches story perhaps best loved for leading the team that won the America's Cup in the early 1980s for Australia, an international sailing prize that made the rest of sports-mad Australia and the world sit up and take notice. The other person more famous for being nouveau riche than anything else (but quite adept at clinging to her squillions) is Rose Porteous, the beautiful Filipina housekeeper who married her elderly mining magnate boss and inherited a chunk of his fortune. The glamorous Rose has led a most public life ever since, being in and out of the social pages as well as in the courts because the late magnate's enraged daughter has battled for decades to regain what she argues is her rightful inheritance. But enough gossip – the irony is that most of the Australians of the eastern seaboard have never actually been to Perth except perhaps in transit on their way to an Asian or European holiday. Consequently, there is certainly a sense of independence from the rest of the nation due to Western Australia's geography.

The 'real' WA
There are about two million people living in this state, but only a quarter live outside Perth and the south-west. Links with South East Asia are strong in cosmopolitan Perth and a few other places on the coast, like the old pearling port city of Broome in the north. The hub cities of eastern Australia are relatively distant while Asian communities and markets beckon. The proximity to Asia, has led to growing economic and trade links of recent years.

Even Australians, including those from Perth and WA coastal towns, may be shocked at the culture of cowboys and miners of Western Australia's outback and into isolated mining-based communities.

As one young Easterner, freshly graduated from a university course in Melbourne, wrote back to his family during his first holiday job in a remote WA mining centre: 'Meekatharra is a typical outback Australian town. I think some of the people I have seen in its Royal

Mail hotel were extras in (Paul Hogan's movie) *Crocodile Dundee*. Out of the three times I have been in the pub, I have witnessed two brawls. It is totally different from the East. The pub which the Aborigines frequent is referred to as the "coon pub"...I have spent most days out with the drilling rigs taking soil samples, etc. It is quite interesting as we are working around a lot of old sites – mine shafts that were in operation around the turn of the century. To be a driller I think you must have to pass a word speed test. If you can say "f..." ten times within the space of sixty seconds of normal conversation, it must help.'

However, those heavy drinking, hard swearing blokes at work extracting various ores from the ground are highly paid to compensate for their isolation from women, children and the comforts of the suburbs thousands of kilometres distant.

Mining industries

Mining, gas, oil and sales of minerals as well as export of agricultural goods are the foundations of the state's wealth. The Western Australian economy is heavily influenced by external factors, such as commodity prices, exchange rates and the timing of large resource investments. In addition to new mineral developments and downstream processing, huge investments have been made in the North-West Shelf gas project. Major export commodities include iron ore, gold, diamonds, nickel, mineral sands, salt, alumina, meat, wool and wheat. The state's port, road and energy infrastructures are well established and crucial to stoking the demand of key customers – the biggest being Japan and the United States.

Fluctuating demand, see-sawing exchange rates and prices offered for raw materials and foodstuffs by its big customers in Asia and the USA have forced both government and business to look to technology, financial services, processing and manufacturing to generate WA's future wealth. Much of Western Australia's business activity still flows from huge farming, mining and export efforts so commercial and manufacturing sectors remain another kind of gold mine for people in WA. As ever, the emphasis for success, given a relatively small and concentrated local market, is on export.

Business buzz

Western Australia's main commercial centres are enjoying a burst of activity because of rapid population growth, due to foreign migration and some large local infrastructure projects. After the big cities of the east (Sydney, Melbourne and Brisbane) Perth is the next most popular migrant destination. Isolation from the better established consumer markets across the continent also presents many opportunities for newcomers with skills and ideas. Expertise in mining, dry land farming and the prevention of soil erosion are 'exported' to clients around the world by entrepreneurs from Western Australia. Consumer goods, such as beer and machinery for mining and farming, are made and marketed by Western Australians for customers at home and overseas. The thriving south-west region is also popular among wine tourists, keen to taste and holiday at the surfing beaches, forests, vineyards, cafés and vinery restaurants just a day or two's driving holiday from Perth.

The downside of all this business buzz and success at exporting its commodities is the fact that Western Australia's taxpayers effectively subsidise more populated regions across the continent. In Australia the wealthy, less populated areas with vast export earnings, including Queensland as well as the Northern Territory and Western Australia, help pay for schools, roads, hospitals and other infrastructure and services around the nation. Criticising federal bureaucrats is a blood sport in Australia, but no more so than in Western Australia where a secessionist movement has been spluttering away for years about the inequities of a federal system. In 2004 the state's treasurer – the aptly named Eric Ripper – reportedly declared that the state had a booming economy, healthy budget surplus and a tax contribution that were being 'savaged by the commonwealth'.

Investment opportunities

People who might be tempted to reside in WA could spend a week reading about its economic potential and the progress of its industrial and commercial sectors. The government produces impressive statistics showing that growth in employment, production and trade are well ahead of averages for the rest of the country. It also identifies perceived areas of growth and opportunities for migrants, right down to the cost of office space and lists of the categories of businesses they would like to develop.

Investment incentives are available to selected immigrants on application to the state's Small Business Development Corporation. There are loans and advances to help submit plans for new investments, consultancy services on how to set up in WA, detailed guidelines for writing business plans and a wealth of information about travel, climate and the regions within the state where you might like to settle.

The Small Business Development Corporation has been established to offer information and advice to existing and new small and medium-sized businesses. It holds training seminars and workshops in both city and selected country areas for both newcomers to WA and long-term residents.

The following business sectors were being promoted to would-be permanent residents interested in starting or taking over a business in Western Australia at the time of writing:

◆ Services such as health care, recreation and building;

◆ Tourism-related services and activities, since this sector is benefiting from five-hour flight times from major Asian centres such as Singapore and the perception that Australia is a relatively safe travel destination;

◆ Boat building – WA leads the world in building commercial vessels and particularly in the construction of high-speed craft;

◆ Information and communication technology is a strongly growing and internationally competitive sector with a particular reputation for providing communications solutions in remote areas;

◆ Environmental management, waste water recycling, solar and wind energy are areas the state government wants to foster;

◆ Food and beverage industries, mining, franchising, aquaculture, transport and storage are other areas the Western Australian government wants to promote with the injection of capital and skills from new residents of the state.

Further information
Small Business Development Corporation
553 Hay Street

Perth

Western Australia 6000

Tel: 618 92200222

Email: info@sbdc.com.au

Websites: www.sbdc.au

www.businessmigration.sbdc.com.au

GRANTS AND FINANCIAL ASSISTANCE TO BUSINESSES IN AUSTRALIA

Grants, funding programmes and industry assistance are available from the federal and state and territory governments. Grants and other assistance available in 2004 for starting and expanding your small business, research and development, innovation and exporting enterprise are summarised below. This information is continuously updated – for the latest version of the summary pages below go to: www.business.gov.au.

FEDERAL GOVERNMENT

Starting and expanding a business

Agriculture Advancing Australia (AAA)
AAA is a package of programmes designed to help primary producers in agriculture, fishing, forestry and processed food industries become more competitive, sustainable and profitable.

Australia China Agricultural Cooperation Agreement (ACACA)
ACACA provides funding for agricultural oriented exchange projects between Australia and China. ACACA enables project

teams to visit locations within China and make contacts that would otherwise not be possible.

Automotive Competitiveness & Investment Scheme (ACIS)
ACIS is open to motor vehicle producers, automotive component producers, automotive machine tool or automotive tooling producers and automotive service providers. Registered participants receive a quarterly issue of import duty credits which may be used to offset customs duty payable on eligible automotive imports. AusIndustry provides industry assistance to business.

Australian Tourism Development Program
The ATDP provides funding to businesses for the development of tourism attractions, facilities, special interest markets, cultural and heritage attractions that will develop regional tourism.

Business Development Program (BDP)
BDP promotes indigenous economic development by enabling indigenous people and communities to acquire or develop commercially successful enterprises. Business finance is available as loans, grants, guarantees or a combination of these.

Certain Inputs to Manufacture (CIM)
The CIM programme provides import duty concessions on certain imported raw materials and goods to improve the competitiveness of Australian industry both in terms of import replacement and export enhancement. AusIndustry provides industry assistance to business.

Fisheries under the second phase of the Natural Heritage Trust
Fisheries Action Program provides funding to help Australia's commercial and recreational fisheries rebuild to more productive

and sustainable levels. The Program will fund projects on a matching dollar for dollar basis.

Enhanced Printing Industry Competitiveness Scheme (EPICS)
EPICS grants are designed to assist firms involved in book production by encouraging the use of innovative technologies, improved business practices, training and skills development.

Enhanced Project By-Laws Scheme (EPBS)
This scheme provides tariff duty concessions on eligible capital goods of significant sized projects in the mining, resource processing, food processing, food packaging, manufacturing, agriculture and gas supply industry sectors.

Fuel Sales Grants Scheme (FSGS)
FSGS, administered by the Australian Taxation Office, allows different grant amounts to be made depending on the different regions where the fuel is sold. Amounts are paid for each litre of petrol oil diesel sold by a registered retailer to final consumers. Phone the Diesel Fuel Infoline on 1300 657 162.

GrantsLINK
GrantsLINK is an online database to help you find sources of federal government funding and assists you to complete application forms. Alternatively you can phone the GrantsAssist line on 1800 026 222.

Information Technology Online (ITOL) Program
ITOL is a grants programme administered by the Department of Communications, Information Technology and the Arts designed to accelerate the national adoption of business-to-business (B2B) e-commerce solutions, especially by small to medium enterprises

(SMEs), across a broad range of industry sectors and geographic regions.

New Apprenticeship Scheme
New Apprenticeships offers financial assistance for eligible employers to help reduce the real cost of training. Incentives and subsidies from $A1,375 are available. For information on how to access these incentives and subsidies and the full range of incentives employers may be eligible for, contact a New Apprenticeships Centre in your region.

New Industries Development Program (NIDP)
NIDP provides competitive-based funding assistance for 'pilot commercialisation' of new innovative agribusiness products, technologies and services. The maximum NIDP contribution is $A100,000.

Petroleum Products Freight Subsidy Scheme (PPFSS)
PPFSS is operated to subsidise the freight cost of delivering eligible petroleum products to remote Australian areas. AusIndustry provides industry assistance to business.

Shipbuilding Innovation Scheme (SIS)
SIS provides financial assistance for registered shipbuilders who undertake eligible R&D activities related to the construction or modification of a bountiable vessel. AusIndustry provides industry assistance to business.

Shipbuilding Bounty
The Shipbuilding Bounty provides financial assistance to registered shipbuilders for eligible costs incurred in the construction or modification of a bountiable vessel. AusIndustry provides industry assistance to business.

Small Business Answers Program

Small Business Answers is a competitive grants programme providing financial grants to organisations to deliver advisory services to small business owners, particularly in regional areas. Locate your nearest Small Business Answers Officer (SBAO) from the list of service providers, available from the AusIndustry website. www.ausindustry.gov.au.

Small Business Enterprise Culture Program (SBECP)

The Small Business Enterprise Culture Program aims to develop and enhance the business skills of small business owner-managers and demonstrate the contribution that such skills can make to business viability and growth. AusIndustry provides industry assistance to business.

Small Business Interest Rate Relief

The Interest Rate Relief is a taxable payment to eligible small businesses in Exceptional Circumstances (EC) declared areas. Businesses are entitled to assistance of up $A10,000. Read the fact sheet to find out more or go to the Centrelink website www.centrelink.gov.au.

Textiles, Clothing & Footwear Corporatewear Register

The Corporatewear Register allows employers to register noncompulsory occupational clothing, thereby avoiding liability for FBT and allowing employees to claim the cost of such clothing as a tax deduction.

TCF Expanded Overseas Assembly Provisions Scheme (EOAP)

The TCF EOAP provides duty concessions to firms who assemble garments and footwear overseas from predominantly Australian fabric and/or leather and then import them back into Australia for local consumption.

Textile, Clothing and Footwear Strategic Investment Program (TCF SIP)
SIP is an entitlement programme which provides incentives in the
form of reimbursement grants to promote investment, innovation
and value adding in Australia's textiles, clothing, footwear and
leather industries. AusIndustry provides industry assistance to
business.

Wage Assistance
Wage Assistance provides subsidies to Australian employers who
give ongoing jobs to eligible indigenous job seekers. Please note
that jobs must meet certain criteria. Go to the Wage Assistance
website (www.wageassistance.gov.au) to find out how to apply for
Wage Assistance online and to download an application form.

Exporting

Export Market Development Grants Scheme
EMDG, administered by Austrade, provides assistance to small
and medium Australian businesses to develop export markets by
reimbursing part of their export promotional expenses. Applicants
may qualify for up to 50% reimbursement of eligible export
marketing expenses above $A15,000 pa to a maximum of seven
grants. Up to $A150,000 pa may be reimbursed.

Food into Asia
Food into Asia is a CSIRO-government initiative which aims to
increase the level of Australian food exports into Asia by
providing an $8.4 million subsidy for research conducted with
CSIRO. CSIRO will match every dollar your company spends on
research with CSIRO to improve your exports into Asia.

Tradex Scheme
Tradex provides relief to individuals or organisations via an up-front exemption from Customs duty and GST on imported goods intended for re-export or to be used as inputs to exports. AusIndustry provides industry assistance to business.

Research & Development and Innovation

Building on IT Strengths (BITS)
BITS is a $A158M initiative with three core elements: Incubator Centres to assist IT&T small to medium enterprises ($A78M), Advanced networks and Test-beds ($A40M); and Developing Tasmania as an 'Intelligent Island' ($A40M).

Commercialising Emerging Technologies (COMET)
COMET is a federal government programme focusing on innovation and its commercialisation. AusIndustry provides industry assistance to business.

Food Innovation Grants
The National Food Industry Strategy's Food Innovation Grants Program provides funding of $A34.7 million over five years to significantly improve levels of innovation by the food industry in Australia. Information, guidelines and forms are available from www.nfis.com.au or by phoning 1300 130 360.

Forest and Wood Products Research and Development Corporation Projects
The FWPRDC invests in a range of research and development projects for the benefit of the Australian forest and forest products industry.

Grape and Wine Research and Development Corporation Projects
Provides funding for six research projects on innovation and technology adoption, wine grape production, wine grape and

wine quality and specification, wine production, industry information and R&D management.

Horticulture Australia's R&D Program
This programme provides funding, on a dollar for dollar basis, for projects which focus on experimentation, analysis and the application of knowledge in the fields of science and technology, marketing and economics.

Innovation Access Program (IAccP) — Industry
The Innovation Access Program (IAccP) – Industry is a competitive programme designed to foster innovation by increasing the take up of leading edge technologies and best practice processes by Australian firms. Applications are accepted for industry led proposals from private sector companies and industry organisations, or consortia which can include additional organisations such as Cooperative Research Centres, training institutions and federal scientific organisations.

Innovation Investment Fund (IIF)
The Innovation Investment Fund is a venture capital programme that invests in nine private sector venture capital funds to assist small companies in the early stages of development to commercialise the outcomes of Australia's strong research and development capability.

Land and Water Australia
Land and Water Australia's primary aim is to identify and fund R&D that will help maintain the natural resource base vital to Australia. It provides funding for research projects, postgraduate scholarships and conference support.

Pharmaceuticals Partnerships Program
The Pharmaceuticals Partnerships Program (P3) is a competitive grants programme through which successful applicants will receive 30 cents for each additional dollar they spend on eligible pharmaceutical R&D in Australia.

Pooled Development Funds Program (PDF)
PDF is designed to increase the supply of equity capital for growing Australian small and medium-sized enterprises (SMEs). PDFs are private sector investment companies established under the PDF Act which raise capital from investors and use it to invest in Australian companies. AusIndustry provides industry assistance to business.

R & D Start
R & D Start is a competitive, merit based grants and loans programme that supports businesses to undertake research and development and its commercialisation.

R & D Tax Concession
R & D Tax Concession is a broad-based, market driven tax concession which allows companies to deduct up to 125% of qualifying expenditure incurred on R & D activities when lodging their corporate tax return. A 175% Premium (Incremental) Tax Concession and R & D Tax Offset is also available in certain circumstances. AusIndustry provides industry assistance to business.

Renewable Energy Equity Fund (REEF)
REEF is a specialist renewable energy fund based on the existing Innovation Investment Fund (IIF) model. It provides venture capital (equity) to assist small companies to commercialise R&D

in renewable energy technologies. AusIndustry provides industry assistance to business.

Research and development programmes for rural and regional Australia
The programmes' objectives are to improve the availability and application of research and data on rural social and economic issues, to foster community development activities and to enhance community understanding to development techniques and processes.

Rural Industries Research and Development Corporation Research Programs (RIRDC)
RIRDC works closely with Australian rural industries to fund programmes relating to prospective new industries, emerging new industries, established industries and future agricultural systems.

STATE AND TERRITORY GOVERNMENTS

Australian Capital Territory

ACT Business Incentive Fund
Provides incentives to businesses in return for major investment and/or employment growth.

ACT Export Growth Program
Through the Export Growth Program ACT companies can apply for assistance to enter new offshore markets, to engage market development managers and to tailor products or services to suit an identified offshore market. Visit the BusinessACT website www.business.act. gov.au to download the guidelines and an expression of interest form.

Canberra Business Development Fund (CBDF)
Does your business have high growth potential? The CBDF
invests in early stage companies that require capital to expand
their business operations.

Knowledge Fund
Assists business with research and development, especially that
which has significant commercial application or provides
significant social benefit.

Business Acceleration Program
Provides a flexible approach to supporting developing companies
from start up to expansion activities through three assistance
programmes that provide ACT business development assistance.

New South Wales

High Growth Business Program
Provides limited financial assistance to eligible companies. This
assistance is intended to stimulate company growth,
competitiveness and profitability.

NSW Government Business
Provides a list of grants available to small businesses, such as
cultural grants, funding for community projects, information
technology grants and petroleum subsidies. Alternatively you can
contact a Small Business Advisory Centre in your area.

Small Business Expansion Program
Assist clients with a subsidy to offset the cost of employing private
sector consultants to establish a growth path for your firm.

Technology Diusion Program
Supports NSW small and medium firms in NSW to accelerate
their adoption of appropriate new technologies by organising and
funding the activities.

Northern Territory

Trade Support Scheme (TSS)
Under TSS, companies and business entities may apply for
financial assistance to offset the international marketing costs of
specific trade projects which will deliver identified trade outcomes.

Queensland

Grants and subsidies
The Department of Innovation and Information Economy
administers a number of grants and subsidies that offer support to
Queensland businesses and communities.

Ideas 2 Market
The Ideas 2 Market website www.ideas2market.qld.gov.au provides
innovators and entrepreneurs with advice, ideas and links that can
assist them in commercialising their ideas.

International Trade Show Assistance Progam (ITSAP)
ITSAP can help approved ICT or biotechnology companies to
exhibit at an international trade show or participate in a trade
mission outside of Australia and New Zealand by providing up to
$A5,000 to assist with direct expenses incurred.

Queensland Investment Incentive Scheme (QIIS)
The Queensland Investment Incentive Scheme (QIIS) allows the
government to provide targeted financial support, if and when

required, to influence the location of important projects and the attraction of leading companies to the state.

Queensland Industry Development Scheme
Aims to help companies to innovate, expand and employ more people. Assistance is provided on a dollar for dollar basis. A minimum of $A5,000 and maximum of $A50,000 is available per project.

Regional Business Development Scheme
Assists companies and regional groups to identify opportunities for economic development. Financial assistance is generally provided for up to 50% of the total project costs.

South Australia

Business & Community Grants, FarmBis
Grants available for individual business, community support and FarmBis in South Australia.

Regional Funding and Grants Register
This website is a registry of funding and grant solutions for your business and community initiative.

Trainee Wage Pay-roll Tax Rebate Scheme
Employers can claim a rebate of 80% of the pay-roll tax paid in respect of wages paid to eligible trainees and apprentices engaged in an approved Contract of Training. Group Training Companies supplying small businesses with trainees and apprentices are eligible for a pay-roll tax rebate of 98%.

Tasmania

Small Business Employment Initiative
The Tasmanian Government provides a payment to employers
who create jobs for new apprentices. Up to $A2,000 is available
for each new apprentice. For further information phone 1800 804
687.

Tasmanian Government Oce Federal Funding Database
This database contains summary information on approximately
400 federal funding programmes and assistance for businesses.
Hotlinks and signposts to programmes accompany each summary.
For further information phone 02 6209 2150.

Tasmanian Innovations Program
This grants programme assists small businesses by providing up to
$A150,000 to help commercialise innovative new products and
services. Up to $A20,000 is available to employ a mentor to
provide guidance and advice. Visit the Department of Economic
Development website www.development.tas.gov.au to download
the programme guidelines.

Victoria

Business in Victoria
Business in Victoria is a comprehensive online resource designed
to help you start, run and grow your business.

Business programmes and industry assistance
Business in Victoria can help you find out about financial support,
advice, education and training programmes available to help you
improve your business.

Grow Your Business
Through the Grow Your Business programme eligible businesses can apply for a grant to employ an independent specialist to conduct a strategic review of their business or to develop a business plan.

Western Australia

Grants Directory
The Grants Directory is a compilation of grants and other assistance programmes available to regional and metropolitan communities, businesses and local governments.

14

The Taxation System

This section is a simple overview of systems and terminology that constitutes Australian tax law. Obviously, if you are serious about earning a living in Australia, one of the most important people you'll want on your team is a good local accountant and some personal understanding of tax basics that apply to your situation and business.

Tax law and accountancy are booming industries Down Under, hardly surprising since this is a well-regulated and relatively highly taxed country. There are many layers of government keen to extract their revenue entitlements while balancing their taxation intake against the electoral need not to be perceived as greedy and to keep the whole process as user-friendly as possible. So allow yourself plenty of time on this topic if you are going into business or taking up employment – you can't assume that an accountant will do all the thinking for you!

TAX BASICS

The main categories of tax-payer in Australia are companies, trusts, partnerships, superannuation funds and individuals. Any entity earning income must file an annual tax return to the Australian Taxation Office (ATO), the national body that administers the tax system. Tax-payers in Australia pay duties, rates or taxes at three levels corresponding to the tiers of government: federal (national), state and local government. There are possible tax deductions, rebates, offsets and so forth at each of these three levels of government taxation. However, the greatest interaction between tax-payer and government is at federal government level via the ATO. Most of the money paid in tax in Australia ends up in the federal government coffers and is then redistributed back to the states and territories using a system of Commonwealth Grants.

In Australia the tax year runs from 1 July to 30 June rather than with the calendar year. State, territory and federal budgets – and any changes in taxation – are usually announced in May or June. Mini-budgets at other times may be used for urgent alterations to taxation.

The three main rates of taxation in Australia are:

◆ tiered tax rates, paid by individuals and sole traders. The top rate is 45%;

- ◆ flat 30% rate, paid by companies and trusts;

- ◆ a concessional rate of 15% for complying superannuation funds, to encourage long-term retirement savings.

There is also a capital gains tax (CGT) levied at tax-payers' marginal (highest) rate of income tax on profits from sale of assets like property and shares – though some CGT discounts apply to encourage investment by certain categories of tax-payer, as noted later in this chapter.

In addition, there is a Goods and Services Tax (GST). This is a consumption tax of 10% applied at the point of sale. A few categories of consumer goods and services are exempt from GST. There is a range of other taxes that employers must levy on their employees in particular circumstances including the Fringe Benefits Tax (FBT), HECS tax and taxes to do with superannuation contributions and employment termination payments. Payroll tax is also levied by the states and territories on larger employers.

These taxes are the focus of most of this chapter.

TAX FILE NUMBER (TFN)

Australian residents and people earning a living on a temporary or permanent basis must have a Tax File Number (TFN). This is a unique number issued to each tax-paying entity and is shown on notices of assessment and correspondence sent by the ATO. The number identifies the taxpayer to whom income is paid and helps distinguish between taxpayers of the same name.

You should apply for your TFN as soon as you arrive in the country, if it is your plan to work or reside in Australia. Without a TFN employees are taxed at a much higher rate. In Australia you can telephone the ATO on 132861 and have the relevant application form mailed to you, or you can apply by internet (www.ato.gov.au). Proof of your identity will be required, similar to the rules for issuing a passport, so you may need the original or certified copy of your birth certificate handy.

It is compulsory for anyone starting a job to quote their TFN to prospective employers. If you do not have a TFN your paycheck will be reduced because withholding tax will be paid at a higher rate, plus the 1.5% Medicare levy. Individuals also need a TFN for:

◆ claiming employment and sickness benefits;

◆ opening and managing bank accounts and other investments;

◆ education, as students attending universities or colleges;

◆ share trading;

◆ superannuation contributions and investment.

PAYE, PAYG AND INCOME TAX

Income tax is an almost universal form of taxation in Australia because it is levied on earnings streams and pay packets before they reach employees. Income tax is levied by the Australian Taxation Office (ATO) on behalf of the federal government under the **Pay As You Earn (PAYE)** system whereby the tax is deducted directly from pensions and pay packets. Self-employed people,

those with private incomes and companies are obligated under the
Pay As You Go (PAYG) system whereby their tax is calculated
based on previous years' earnings and paid quarterly or annually,
then checked against actual income after the close of the tax year
when they file a return.

If you employ other people you will need to register for **PAYG
Withholding**, which means you are permitted (and obligated) to
deduct and pass on tax owed to the ATO by your employees, as
well as the PAYG instalments owed by your own business.

ACTIVITY STATEMENTS

All tax-paying 'enterprises' (which means businesses of all types
but **excluding** employees and individual tax-payers in most cases)
must submit their PAYG, GST and other tax payments using an
Activity Statement. This is a single page document issued by the
ATO on a monthly or quarterly basis. The financial controller of
the businesses follows its specific format to provide dollar amounts
and totals for the income earned and tax collected by the
enterprise. From the totals tax refunds, if any, are subtracted
along with overpayments and other amounts claimed in refunds.
The enterprise then submits payment or claims a refund,
whichever is appropriate after the sums are done. At the end of
the tax year the Activity Statement is reconciled against the
enterprise's tax return and any errors, overpayments or
underpayments must be reported. Although there are fines for late
lodgment and considerable administrative and accountancy time
expended in filling in the Activity Statement, it is not as onerous
as it sounds and usually there is no need for a small business to

engage an accountant to undertake this responsibility. The ATO's telephone help service is very accessible and not at all intimidating for business people with limited accountancy skills who need to be talked through the process from time to time.

INCOME TAX RATES

Some 40% of federal government's revenue comes from income tax payers. Income tax revenue is rising, despite a series of cuts by the government to personal tax rates. This is due to the fact that lower tax rates do not compensate for wages inflation caused by a buoyant economy, helping most people on the steady march towards a higher income – and corresponding higher tax brackets.

Below is a guide to the tax rates and the 'tax brackets' which refer to how much you need to earn to pay each level of income tax applied in Australia in 2004 and 2005. Details of the current Australian tax rates can be obtained from Australian high commissions and trade representatives or from the extensive ATO website (www.ato.go.au).

Income tax bracket (A$) from July 2005–6	Rate %	Income tax bracket (A$) from July 2006–7	Rate %
0 – 6,000	0	0 – 6,000	0
6,001 – 21,600	15	6,001 – 25,000	15
21,601 – 63,000	30	25,001 – 75,000	30
63,001 – 95,000	30	75,001 – 150,000	40
95,000 +	47	150,001 +	45

ABNs AND INVOICING

If you run a business which employs people and therefore withholds income tax regularly on behalf of the ATO, you will need to register for an **Australian Business Number (ABN)** for taxation purposes and for invoicing. If you run your business through a company you will need an **Australian Company Number (ACN)** for taxation purposes and for invoicing. (Your company won't need an ABN if it has an ACN). If you set up as a sole trader (see definitions later in this chapter) and are not withholding tax on behalf of employees, your TFN is all you will need at the top of your invoices. The ATO has many explanatory tax booklets and internet information pages to help newcomers to efficiently meet these kinds of taxation requirements. The ATO has helpful telephone services to answer technical questions – and to cut the amount of time and money you spend with an accountant on the basic tax requirements for your enterprise.

Broadly speaking, if you do not include the ABN, ACN or TFN on your invoices, customers are obliged to withhold a percentage of income tax (at the top personal or company rate of tax) and pass this on to the ATO. However, you can reclaim such amounts at the end of the financial year in your tax return if you show that an overpayment has been made.

SELF-ASSESSMENT

Australia's taxation system relies on 'self-assessment' whereby you, perhaps via your accountants, calculate and lodge tax returns, claim tax deductions and work out what net tax is to be paid. Failure to lodge a return is subject to financial penalties. Lodging a fraudulent return will result in fines that rise with the degree of the fraud. Just because a self-assessment is accepted by the ATO and a tax refund is made, this is not necessarily the end of the matter. You may be audited by the ATO at a later date.

TAX AUDITS AND APPEALS

An audit means your recent tax returns will be studied. Any receipts and other proof of your financial claims must be produced to check if items have been omitted or wrongly claimed. You will be required to repay amounts owing, plus interest, and there are stiff fines and even jail terms for business and taxation fraud as well as possible referral to other authorities if anything outside the ATO's jurisdiction looks suspicious to the auditors. In the worst cases the ATO may check the taxpayer's entire tax history. If, on the other hand, you convince the ATO's auditors that you were genuinely ignorant or confused by all the tax requirements, they may demand you repay them with interest and that will be the end of the matter.

Lately the emphasis has been on checking for tax cheating by investment property owners, superannuation funds, fraudulent work-related expenses and that old enemy of tax authorities everywhere, the 'black market' or cash economy. If you are audited in one of the ATO's random checks this does **not** mean they are suspicious of you, since certain categories of tax-payers are audited regularly. If you are audited, you can expect crosschecking of your tax records nationally and internationally, data matching reviews and field visits to your premises by ATO staff.

As in many countries where tax evasion is a persistent problem, Australia has boosted the staff levels and technology available for investigation of suspected evaders but also has many educational and information opportunities for those stumped by the system. All tax-payers have the right to object to an assessment made of their tax liabilities. An inexpensive system of appeals is provided.

YOUR TAX RECORDS

Given the vague possibility of a random tax audit, good record keeping is vital. As an employee or sole trader, you will need to retain all records of your taxation and earnings for at least five years, even longer if you are claiming depreciation on assets claimed as a tax deduction that have a depreciable life over five years. Companies, partnerships and trusts should keep their records for at least seven years.

NON-RESIDENTS TAXATION
Non-residents in Australia are subject to particular rates of income tax (see the International Double Taxation Agreements section on page 391). Keep your records carefully for verification of the taxes or refunds that may be due in Australia or in your country of origin.

MEDICARE LEVY

Australia's individual tax-payers pay for the Medicare system of basic public medical and hospital care through a levy on their income of 1.5% at the time of writing. You may be eligible for a reduction in this rate if on a low income. There are additional tax penalties for high-income earners who choose not to take out (tax deductible) private hospital insurance (see Chapter 11).

WHAT INCOME IS TAXABLE

Residents who are permanent or temporary, whether paid via companies, trusts, partnerships or as individual employees, are required to pay tax on their worldwide income. Except for special exemptions for pensioners and low-income earners when the tax-free level is more generous, after the $A6,000 tax-free threshold, tax applies to all income you declare. The tax is applied on the 'taxable income' of an individual, which means your **assessable income** less **allowable deductions**. A similar system applies for companies paying taxes at their flat 30% rate (though there is no $A6,000 threshold, relevant only to people paying income tax).

Assessable income includes ordinary tax trading receipts and investment income as well as salaries and wages.

Assessable income also includes:

◆ nominal capital gains, after adjustments to account for the impact of inflation, made on the sale of assets with some key exemptions as defined by capital gains tax guidelines given later in this chapter;

◆ realised capital losses may be offset against capital gains;

◆ superannuation and retirement lump sum payments, though these may be subject to lower tax rates depending upon the individual's circumstances – except for that part of the lump sum payment rolled over into an Approved Deposit Fund, complying superannuation fund or annuity (see section on Superannuation on page 374).

◆ allowances, gratuities, compensation, benefits or bonuses related to services rendered;

◆ royalties, bounties and subsidies relating to a business, fees or commissions for procuring a loan and certain bonuses relating to life insurance policies;

◆ insurance and indemnity payments for loss of trading stock or loss of profit.

'Gifts' such as lottery wins and legacies when someone dies (there are no death duties on deceased estates) are not included in assessable income.

BUSINESS TAX DEDUCTIONS

Some tax deductions can be offset against the income mentioned above. Broadly, the law allows deductions for expenses incurred in gaining or producing assessable income. For individuals claiming more than $A300 a year in tax deductions, records of receipts to prove these expenses to the ATO auditors need to be kept. If you claim up to $A200 a year in deductions the ATO recommends you make a note of what you purchased, when you purchased it and the price you paid but you don't need to retain the receipts or invoices as proof.

A deduction for depreciation is allowed for industrial plant and other commercial equipment owned and used in the process of earning at the rate determined by its effective life, plus a loading of 20%.

In addition to annual deductions, a system of balancing adjustments applies when the tax-deductible plant or equipment is sold or destroyed. There are also tax deductions available as incentives to Australian companies in business to plan and start eligible projects seen as helpful to the Australian economy, to reduce non-renewable energy emissions or to aid environmental planning.

Tax deductions that can be claimed by an individual taxpayer include:

◆ trade union or professional dues;
◆ tools of the trade;
◆ allowances for certain reading or study materials;
◆ protective clothing;
◆ travelling to and from work.

INCOME TAX OFFSETS AND REBATES

While tax deductions help reduce assessable income, there is also a range of potentially valuable tax offsets and rebates that come off the bottom of your tax bill after income and deductions have been calculated.

There are a range of tax rebates and offsets for:

◆ dependent spouses and children;

- live-in helpers caring for disabled and disadvantaged dependants;

- parents and parents-in-law and children over 16 who are financially dependent on the taxpayer;

- pensioners, who may take advantage of a range of Pensioner Tax Offsets thresholds that reduce their tax if they are on lower incomes. However, this offset is unavailable to people of pensionable age earning approximately $A40,000 (singles) and $A60,000 (couples) or more a year;

- higher medical expenses. A 20% tax rebate applies to the families of tax-payers who have paid over $A1,500 during the financial year (at the time of writing) for medical costs that have not been provided free by government services or reimbursed by private health insurance. It is important to keep records of medical expenses to help calculate and substantiate a claim for this rebate.

SUPERANNUATION TAX

Contributions to complying superannuation funds and eligible termination payments are **taxable at a concessional rate of 15%**.

The concessional 15% superannuation tax rate also applies to income derived from investments held by the superannuation fund, as well as to capital gains and income streams – though income streams are tax-free in some situations for self-managed funds. A 30% discount on capital gains tax is available to superannuation funds as an additional incentive to Australian tax-payers to save for retirement (see section on Capital Gains Tax on page 383).

Contributions by employers to employee superannuation are allowable tax deductions for the employer providing these contributions are made to complying funds and are no higher than each employee's **aged-based limit**. For employees making additional pre-tax (salary sacrifice) contributions to their fund from wages, leave entitlements and bonuses, the age-based limits also mean they will pay just the 15% tax on contributions up to the relevant amount for their age.

Salary sacrifice

Salary sacrifice arrangements rely on the employer agreeing to organise their accounting systems to accommodate this tax-effective contribution for their paid staff – but employers are not obliged to make salary sacrifice arrangements. Also, salary sacrifice contributions to superannuation must be from *future* entitlements to wages, leave and bonuses – the tax breaks do not apply if these have already been earned by employees who decide at the last minute to increase their superannuation contributions.

If employees want to contribute more than the age-based amount to superannuation at any time, they are free to do so after they have paid the regular amount of income tax on their earnings.

Employers are obliged under a system known as 'superannuation guarantee' to contribute at least 9% of an employee's pre-tax earnings to their superannuation fund, and this contribution is taxed at 15% when paid to the fund. Self-employed people, employees, retirees up to certain age limits and even children (via their parents or grandparents) may also make contributions up to the amount allowed according to their age under a flexible but complicated system to encourage superannuation savings and take the pressure off the public purse to meet the costs of age pensions and other living expenses for the elderly. Chapters 3 and 11 also cover this area.

The introduction of **government co-contributions** is an incentive to assist lower income earners to save more money for retirement. The government supplements contributions to superannuation by an individual (in addition to the Superannuation Guarantee contribution made by his or her employer) up to certain limits. At the time of writing a person earning $A28,000 or less will have $A1.50 added for each $A1 they add to their superannuation fund, up to a $A1,500 maximum from the government. There is a smaller government co-contribution for employees earning up to $A58,000 a year (close to the average wage) and a further indicator of the urgency with which the government is trying to boost Australia's relatively inadequate level of retirement savings.

Another inducement to convince more people to plan and save for their retirement includes tax benefits in paying for life insurance through a superannuation fund.

From 2005 all employees were free to choose their own superannuation fund (rather than invest in company or industry funds) and employers adjusted and expanded their payment systems because they became obliged to pass on contributions, minus tax owed to the ATO, to any complying fund that is chosen by the individual.

Many business people in Australia are members of **self-managed superannuation funds**. These can be time consuming for members, who must make their own investment decisions, and such funds are strictly regulated to ensure they are not exploited for the tax breaks. Self-managed superannuation funds have many tax planning advantages compared with the mainstream public offer funds. Public offer funds are open to any member of the public or industry member but give each contributor little opportunity to influence investment decisions and manage any tax implications.

Self-managed superannuation funds (also known as DIY funds) must have four or fewer members who are usually trustees as well as beneficiaries of the fund. They are an appealing superannuation vehicle for small businesses with a few partners or family members not only because of the tax benefits of superannuation saving, but also due to the control that they provide to fund members. As long as they are within the laws that govern compliance for self-managed funds, members can decide how the money is invested and have the freedom to select the most tax-effective way to pay members as they reach pensionable age and want to draw an income.

However, penalties are tough for people found by the Tax Office to have exploited concessions in order to use their fund for purposes other than retirement savings. Strict separation of fund investments from investments belonging to companies, trusts, partnerships and individuals is essential and you will need expert advice on setting up and running a self-managed superannuation fund.

EMPLOYER OBLIGATIONS – PAYG WITHHOLDING

As already mentioned, the ATO depends heavily on employers to withhold and pass on a range of taxes from employees, as well as taxes due on the earnings of their own business. This is part of the PAYG system, and covers the Medicare levy, superannuation guarantee, income tax, non-residents withholding tax or amounts withheld from employees or creditors without tax file numbers (TFNs), Australian Business Members (ABNs) and so forth.

There are also PAYG obligations on employers to collect repayments to the government for higher education through the HECS loan scheme and obligations to withhold the correct amount of tax when making employee termination payments, as outlined below.

GRADUATE TAX (HECS)

The Graduate Tax, commonly known as the 'Higher Education Contribution Scheme', is an arrangement with the federal government and the ATO whereby a former student can repay a student loan when they become employed. As mentioned in Chapter 12 outlining the education system in Australia, HECS debts are paid via the tax system according to a formula based on the graduate's wages. If students take such a loan from the government to cover their university or TAFE fees, the annual course fees will accumulate, subject to various interest rate charges depending on the type of loan. Employers must deduct the HECS repayment from the former student's earnings when that person's wage reaches around $A33,000 annually. The former student's TFN or Withholding Declaration will notify the employer of the HECS obligation for that individual and the ATO supplies the information required by the employer about how much to deduct from wages and pass on through the PAYG Withholding tax system.

ELIGIBLE TERMINATION PAYMENTS

When an employee's position is terminated an **Eligible Termination Payment (ETP)** needs to be made to that person. A concessional tax rate usually applies to at least some of the money.

If the person is resigning from their job then payment terms may depend on their contract with their employer. Any unused leave (holiday) payment will be among their financial entitlements.

BUSINESS STRUCTURES

There are four main categories of business structures for taxation purposes in Australia:

1. sole trader;
2. companies;
3. trusts (including superannuation funds);
4. partnerships.

You will need to decide which structure is best for your enterprise when you set up Down Under.

Sole traders

A sole trader is an individual trading on their own who controls and manages a business. The income of the business is treated as the individual tax-payer's income and they are solely responsible for any tax payable by the business. A sole trader may apply for an ABN and use this for all business dealings to do with invoicing and payments. Otherwise the sole trader uses their TFN when lodging income tax returns relating to their business.

Companies

For taxation purposes, a company includes all bodies and associations, incorporated or unincorporated but not including partnerships. There is a flat rate of income tax payable by companies at 30%. After lodging its first tax return, the company will be notified by the ATO about the PAYG instalments that must be paid, based on that first year of trading. Each year the instalment rate may be varied depending on the amount of tax paid in the previous year.

Companies cannot claim many of the allowances available to individual tax-payers but they can claim tax deductions for previous years' losses. Some tax deductions for business-related expenses may be readily available to companies although such deductions are unavailable to sole traders, which is one of the attractions of the company structure.

However, efforts have been made to stop businesspeople, some contractors and employees from setting up companies simply to benefit from the more flexible tax deduction arrangements and the lower income tax rate of 30%, which used to be a tempting strategy given that the highest personal taxation rate is 47%. Now a person seeking to be paid by clients or customers as employee or director of a company must satisfy the ATO that they are genuinely conducting a business and are not merely contractors working for a short time for one employer at a time.

New companies need to apply for an Australian Business Number (ABN) and a Tax File Number (TFN) and are regulated by the Australian Securities and Investment Commission.

Dividends

When company dividends are moved from a parent company to an Australian resident subsidiary, the recipient company will usually qualify for a full or partial rebate for the Australian tax attributable to those dividends. Dividends received by an Australian company from a non-resident company which is resident in a 'comparable tax country' are exempt from income tax at the corporate level. If you are thinking of deriving income under Australia's foreign taxation provisions you should seek advice from an international accountancy firm.

Company directors

If you use a company to operate your business in Australia, you will probably be paid as a director or employee. In either case, the company will need to withhold amounts for payment of tax, superannuation, the Medicare levy from your income under the PAYG system and you will nccd a TFN to receive the same taxation rates as other Australian residents.

Trusts and superannuation funds

A trust is defined by tax authorities as an obligation imposed on a person to hold property or income for the benefit of others. Trusts are subject to a flat 30% rate of tax and have many of the taxation features of a company in terms of income and expenses.

Trusts are not liable to pay tax under the PAYG instalment system though trust beneficiaries or trustees may be required to do so under the PAYG system.

Rules in relation to trusts are regularly under the microscope of legislators and occasionally tweaked to avoid giving the beneficiaries an unfair tax advantage. Family or discretionary trusts are sometimes used by wealthy families in Australia to distribute income and assets in a tax effective manner. For instance, the lower-income earning beneficiaries of a trust in the same household may receive a greater distribution because they pay a lower rate of personal income tax compared with the family's main bread-winner, whose income may be taxed at the top 47% rate.

A trust's Tax File Number is used in lodging tax returns and the entity (often a company) that is trustee will need to register for an Australian Business Number (ABN).

Superannuation funds are a category of trust subject to a lower 15% of tax, as outlined earlier in this chapter.

Partnerships

In Australia income tax returns by partnerships should be lodged whenever two or more people conduct a joint business or joint income-producing activity (but not as a company). The profit and loss is distributed to each partner's taxable income (rather than retained in a company). Partnership agreements are not compulsory but unless there is an agreement stating otherwise, all partners are regarded as having an equal share and will be taxed on that basis.

As with trusts, there have been recent efforts by government and tax authorities to ensure partnership structures are not used for tax avoidance and that the people involved do not have an unfair advantage over other taxpayers. Partners may apply for an ABN and use this in their business dealings. The partnership also needs its own TFN, which must be used when lodging tax returns. Partnerships do not have to pay tax instalments under the PAYG system though individual partners may be required to do so.

CAPITAL GAINS TAX (CGT)

Broadly, Australia's Capital Gains Tax (CGT) is levied at the taxpayer's highest ordinary rate of income tax. If the asset has been bought after 21 September 1999 and owned for more than a year, a 50% discount on the assessable capital gain may be applied *if* the owner is an individual tax-payer or a superannuation fund (see below).

A Capital Gains Tax applies to Australian companies, trusts and individuals. For individuals, Australia's Capital Gains Tax top rate is levied at 23.25% on assets held more than a year when the person's income and the capital gain together exceed $150,000. Companies and trusts generally pay tax on capital gains at their normal tax rate.

The law also allows an individual, company, trust or partnership to offset realised capital losses against capital gains.

Your principal place of residence is usually exempt from CGT, though investment properties are not (see below). There are no

> **death duties, so if an asset is willed to a beneficiary no CGT is due until that asset is disposed of by the new owner or the administrator of the estate.**

If an asset is made as a gift, the donor is generally liable to pay CGT as if the asset had been sold at the prevailing commercial value. The new owner is deemed to have received the asset at its market value at the time of acquisition. However, various tax breaks apply for donations to charities.

CGT discount method

For individual tax-payers and for complying superannuation funds, there is a 50% CGT discount if the asset has been in the hands of that owner for at least a year, provided it was acquired after 21 September 1999. This method aims to encourage investment savings because the final tax paid is half that due under the alternative method whereby tax is paid on the full capital gain (less costs) by short-term investments.

For individuals, their top rate of income tax – up to 47% – will apply to that 50% of the capital gain that is taxable. In the case of superannuation funds the tax rate is 15% and 30% of the capital gain is exempt from tax. This discount method is not available to companies, which must pay tax at 30% on the entire profit, after expenses, made by the sale of the asset.

Exemptions from CGT

These include:

♦ the taxpayer's principal place of residence and a 'reasonable' (2 hectare) tract of land around it. However, no exemptions apply to houses owned by a family trust or private company and lived in by a trust beneficiary or shareholder;

♦ superannuation or life insurance policies in the hands of the original beneficial owner;

♦ sale of motor vehicles and most types of personal use assets (like furniture) with a disposable value below certain limits;

♦ debentures, bonds and other loans that do not have a defined interest element (including shares with fixed dividends);

♦ any asset acquired before 20 September 1985.

Nor does the tax apply to 'rollovers' (arrangements to reinvest and so defer a capital gains liability), compensation payments for stolen or destroyed property and asset ownership changes associated with certain types of business organisations. Expenditure in buying, improving or selling an asset are all part of the CGT assessment of the value of the property and the amount of profit made in selling it. However, as a general rule, annual expenses such as repairs and interest payments on financing the asset, whether for business or non-business purposes, can be deducted from income while the asset is owned to reduce the amount of tax to be paid.

FRINGE BENEFITS TAX (FBT) AND SALARY SACRIFICE

Fringe Benefits Tax (FBT) at 47% is paid by employers on certain employment extras or benefits that they provide to employees. Typically a company will pass on the cost of the fringe benefit, less any tax deductions that company may be getting for these items as business expenses, and the employee will experience a corresponding cut in their pay. Certainly, there may be some advantages in having the item paid for by the employer in a remuneration packaging approach known as 'salary sacrifice'. This means that the employer pays in pre-tax dollars for certain goods or services on behalf of the employee, who gives up part of their future pay packet to repay the company. Income tax may have been avoided – but a FBT liability usually cancels out the advantages of having the item pre-paid because the FBT rate is equal to the top income tax rate. Some goods and services are FBT-free, as mentioned later in this section and may be worth considering as part of your salary package. Yet the purchase or lease by the company of valuable items, like cars, remains an appealing option for employees who do not want to save or borrow to pay for these themselves.

FBT will probably be part of the employment implications for, say, a temporary resident coming from overseas to work in Australia. Foreign consultants, for instance, may have relocation expenses, cars, rent, occupational health and counselling, holiday travel and children's education fees built into their job offer in Australia. However, depending on the employer, this may not be a tax burden for the temporary employee from overseas.

The FBT applies to almost every potential company pre-paid job perk. Nevertheless, cars and work vehicles are the biggest fringe benefit that may be provided because employees don't have to find large amounts of money to buy these from their own resources. But gloss certainly has gone from 'the company car', now that FBT is part of the cost.

There are a series of formulas for calculating FBT on motor vehicles which provide employees with some flexibility about the car payment scheme and tax implications to suit their circumstances. Distance travelled on company business is the key factor. There are also some car leasing alternatives that will avoid or minimise the implications of FBT.

The taxable value of company cars using the statutory formula method is based on how many kilometres the car travels during the tax year. The greater the distance travelled on company business, the lower the taxable value. The maximum taxable value of a company car for FBT purposes was 26% when acquired (at the time of writing) falling to 20% if it travels more than 15,000 but less than 24,999 kilometres annually, then to 11% for 25,000 to 39,999 and 7% if the business travel is greater than 40,000 kilometres annually.

Apart from the tiered rates for company cars, fringe benefits tax also applies to:

◆ car parking;

◆ free or low-interest loans;

◆ free or subsidised accommodation or board;

◆ goods and services sold at a reduced rate or provided free (above certain limits in value);

◆ expenses paid on behalf of an employee;

◆ entertainment expenses (except for staff canteens and some forms of in-house dining);

◆ airline transport provided free or at a discount to employees in the travel industry;

◆ living away from home subsidies to employees, though 'reasonable' costs for food and accommodation during business travel are not subject to the tax.

FBT exemption

Salary sacrifice for employee superannuation payments and employee share schemes are FBT-exempt, along with lap top computers (one per employee), mobile phones primarily used for work, minor benefits valued at less than $A100, some taxi travel and in-house health care facilities. As mentioned above, there is a possible tax concession if 'packaging' an employee's car using salary sacrifice, depending on how much it is used for company business.

GOODS AND SERVICES TAX (GST) AND OTHER CONSUMER TAXES

In mid 2000 the retail and wholesale sales tax systems were replaced with a point of sale **Goods and Services Tax (GST)**. It was applied at 10% on most consumer goods and business services. Amazingly, the rate of this tax has not yet been raised – despite claims by cynics that Australia would follow in the footsteps of countries like Britain and its Valued Added Tax (VAT) system and gradually increase the GST rate. Don't get too excited, for if the Australian government ends its current run of budget surpluses and needs new sources of tax revenue, the GST could well be increased.

Businesses, including sole traders, trusts, companies and partnerships with an annual turnover over $A100,000 must register for and pass on GST collected through their invoices using their monthly or quarterly Activity Statements. GST paid to providers of business equipment and services can also be reclaimed for the same period.

Smaller enterprises, which usually do not have the turnover that obliges them to register for GST, can volunteer for GST registration if that suits them – usually for cash flow purposes, if they are regularly purchasing goods or services on which they have paid GST and want the tax refunded to them as soon as possible. Alternatively, the GST charged by the smaller business to clients or customers can be paid annually when the tax return is lodged.

From the start, the GST proved administratively difficult for many businesses. Its introduction is part of an important revamp of the Australian tax system and the PAYG concept. Many businesses of all sizes have had to invest in new computer systems, taxation education and financial advice as well as other human and financial costs of meeting their own tax obligations while calculating, collecting and passing on to the ATO a range of taxes from employees and customers. The plus side is that the new tax system, featuring the GST, forces businesses and sole traders to be scrupulous in daily, quarterly and annual record keeping and to keep a studious eye on the actual cash flows of their business in order to meet these continual tax obligations. There are plenty of computer-based solutions that will doubtless reduce accountancy time for many businesses in years to come.

Some sectors of the economy are GST-exempt, such as share transfers (but not brokerage), education and charities. There is a range of other consumer taxes on petroleum products, alcohol and cigarettes. These also include import taxes and duties that aim to protect Australian-manufactured and other local products from the competition of imported alternatives.

In addition, car owners must consider the luxury car tax of 25% on the sale value – including GST – of vehicles over $A60,000 at the time of writing. This tax has little impact on average car prices which are well below this threshold (see Chapter 10 Driving in Australia).

IMPUTATION OF COMPANY DIVIDENDS

Under the imputation system of company taxation, dividends paid by Australian resident companies carry imputation credits for the amount of tax that has been paid at the corporate level. Dividends with imputation credits attached are known as 'franked' dividends.

Australian resident shareholders are taxed on the sum of franked dividends received and attached imputation credits. However, the amount of the imputation credit is allowable as a tax rebate in the assessment for the year of income during which the dividend was derived. Any excess of the rebate over the tax assessed is also refundable, so at times the ATO will owe trusts, companies and individuals for excessive payment of company tax on their dividends.

The amount of the imputation credit is based on the company tax rate for the financial year during which the dividend was paid.

Non-resident shareholders are not entitled to imputation credits. However, franked dividends paid to non-residents are exempt from dividend withholding tax. The excess of the imputation credit over the dividend withholding tax that would otherwise be payable is not refundable.

Unfranked dividends, or the unfranked part of partially franked dividends derived from non-residents, continue to be subject to dividend withholding tax at the general rate (30%) or, in the case of residents of countries with which Australia has a tax treaty, at the reduced rate (15%) applicable under the treaty. Non-residents carrying on business in Australia through a permanent establishment are subject to dividend withholding tax on the same basis as other non-residents.

INTERNATIONAL DOUBLE-TAXATION AGREEMENTS

People from, or with investments in, countries sharing a double-taxation agreement with Australia are protected from having to pay tax in both their country of residence and the country of source for a certain income.

However, if your country of origin has no such agreement on taxation with Australia, it is best to consult authorities for both Australia and your own country before you leave to discover how much money you may be required to pay while earning income in Australia. Extra tax liabilities may also arise when you try to move your money from one country to another, especially if a tax haven is involved.

Australia has *comprehensive double-taxation agreements* with Britain, the USA, Canada, New Zealand, Singapore, Japan, France,

Belgium, the Netherlands, Malaysia, Korea, Ireland, Norway, Italy, Denmark, Sweden, Finland, Malta, the Philippines, Switzerland, Austria, and Germany as well as limited agreements with India, China and Greece.

These agreements usually mean that the country where people have been contracted to work temporarily has the primary right to tax their income. The other contracting country, the worker's country of residence, also has a right to claim taxes due but, if it does so, must allow credit for the amount already paid in the place where the income originated.

For example, you may be undertaking a temporary job in Australia paid at a rate which puts you in the 47% tax bracket. In the meantime, you could normally be paying income tax at a 60% rate for that amount of income in your country of residence. So the first 47% of income tax will be levied by Australia, and the other 13% is paid in tax to the country where you normally live.

Exemptions

However, in some cases the agreement may provide a reduction or even an exemption from tax imposed by the country where the income originated. For instance, the Australian tax on non-residents' income from dividends in Australian companies is generally limited to 15% of the gross amount of the dividends.

Salary and wages

As is commonly the case in Australia's double-taxation agreements, payment by British-based employers to employees working in Australia, but resident in Britain, are subject to British – *not* Australian – taxes in the following circumstances:

◆ if the time spent in Australia is not more than 183 days in the income year, *and/or*

◆ the salary is paid by an employer who is not an Australian resident, *and*

◆ the salary is not deductible in determining the taxable profits of a permanent establishment of the employer in Australia.

A would-be immigrant laying the groundwork for living and working in Australia permanently at a later stage would be subject to Australian taxation.

If the working visit by a British resident is longer than 183 days, the fees or wages paid are subject to Australian tax, and a credit will be given against tax paid in Britain. If the services are performed in Australia at a 'fixed base' readily available to a British resident, tax may be levied in Australia.

Paying tax on foreign source income

Resident taxpayers of Australia have their income tax assessed on their world-wide income on a country-by-country basis. Income from each company is further categorised into 'interest income' and 'other income'. As you can see below, this is a jargon-laden area of tax-law and an expert's advice is usually essential to ensure you do not do the wrong thing. Here is a brief rundown.

Allowable deductions for foreign sourced income must be allocated, firstly, to the country to which they relate, then to the category of income (i.e. 'interest' or 'other'). Tax losses (when allowable deductions exceed assessable and exempt income) are quarantined to the income category and country of source. They may be recouped no later than the seventh year after the year in which the losses were incurred. Australian sourced tax losses may, at the tax-payer's election, be offset against foreign sourced taxable income – though this can have an adverse result on the foreign tax credit entitlement.

Credits for foreign (ex-Australian) taxes paid may be claimed but these are limited to the lesser of the following:

1. **Foreign tax** paid (converted to Australian dollars at the exchange rate prevailing on date of payment and substantiated by documentary evidence), *or*

2. **The Australian tax** payable on the foreign sourced income.

There has been some fine tuning in the taxation of foreign sources to stop people dodging tax through use of tax shelter countries. Regulations now include the following:

◆ Since 1 July 1990 most income sheltered in 'listed low tax countries' by Australian taxpayers, whether in foreign companies, trusts or other structures, is subject to Australian income tax as it is earned (commonly called 'as accruals taxation') rather than when, if ever, the income is credited to the tax-payer in Australia.

◆ Most income by Australian companies derived from substantial interest in companies resident in 'listed comparable-tax countries' will be exempt both from the accruals tax and from company tax when the income is remitted.

Tax on royalty income

If a person is a resident in a country with a double-taxation agreement with Australia, the Australian tax on most royalties derived by that person is limited to no more than 10 to 15% of the royalties. But this limitation does not apply if the royalties are effectively connected with the permanent establishment of the recipient in Australia.

Royalties included in this provision are:

◆ industrial and copyright royalties;
◆ payment for use of equipment;
◆ know-how payments.

Exceptions are mining and other natural resource royalties and royalties derived from 'permanent establishment of the beneficial owner in the country in which they originate'. If the country of residence also taxes royalties, the tax authorities party to the agreement on royalties will allow a credit for tax paid in the other country.

Pensions and annuities

Pensions and personal annuities other than government pensions payable in respect of government services are exempt from taxation in the country of source, whether or not they are taxable in the country of residence.

STATE GOVERNMENT TAXES

Payroll tax and stamp duty on the sale or purchase of property are the biggest source of tax revenue for Australian state and territory governments. Employers are required to lodge monthly returns, in most cases, at a rate of about 5–6% in most places. Small businesses with only a few people on their payrolls may be exempt from payroll tax, depending on the size of their payroll bill, and need not lodge monthly returns to the state Department of Taxation. All states have abolished death or estate duties.

Stamp duty

Stamp duty, however, is generally payable to the state taxation authorities on a range of documents and transactions as well as on property transactions. These may include transfers of marketable securities, cheques and bills of exchange, registrations and transfers of motor vehicles and trailers, partnership deeds, power and letters of attorney, company documents (in New South Wales), declarations of trusts and instalment purchase agreements. Rates vary according to the transaction's value or, in other cases, at a fixed rate.

Land tax

Land tax is also imposed by all states and territories (except the Northern Territory) of Australia on the value of land at differing rates, depending on the tax law in that state. But land used for certain types of primary production or farming, and residential land which is the site of the owner's home, may be exempt partly or in full, depending on the state's or territory's threshold.

Motorists

Driver licence and car registration fees are also the tax prerogative of Australia's states and territories. These vary and are charged on an annual, renewable basis.

LOCAL GOVERNMENT TAXES

Local governments comprise city councils, boroughs, shires and municipalities elected by the local residents and ratepayers. They levy taxes on land value of private property or on its 'annual' value, on both houses and businesses. Called 'rates', this tax money is used by the locality for building control, health inspection facilities and garbage collection and disposal (though in some places garbage services are covered by a separate levy). Roads, footpaths, town planning, parks and recreational facilities, public libraries as well as community and welfare services are also supported by ratepayers' monies and administered by the local council.

15

The Slanguage – An Introduction to Australian Slang

Australian English has two unique qualities: the accent, and the words. In the past 200 years some 10,000 new words and a host of colourful expressions have become common usage, uttered by everyone from 'pollies' to 'garbos' with that peculiarly nasal clamp-jawed intonation known as the Aussie Accent. There is often a rising inflection at the end of the typical Aussie sentence, so that that 'Nice weather we're having' may sound like a question, not a statement, which can be a worry.

Another verbal feature of Australian English is the deadpan delivery of a jocular comment. Imagine some new Aussie friends offer to pour some chocolate sauce on your curry with no visual or verbal hint they were just 'having you on'. The joke is largely

in your confusion and the po-faced delivery is an essential element
of larrikin humour Down Under. The selection of words and
expressions below gives a brief overview of a rich if crude English
dialect. The evolution of Australian English owes much to the
slang of southern and eastern England, Ireland, and the convict/
criminal terminology of the eighteenth and nineteenth centuries. It
also shows the influence of Aboriginal words and Americanisms.

Abo – Australian Aboriginal, the abbreviation is a term in daily
usage.

apeshit or ape – as in: 'Go apeshit'. Lose your temper or become
wild with joy. Context-specific, eg. 'Craig's footy team won the
Grand Final and he went apeshit!' *or* equally valid if Craig's
team had lost, e.g.: 'Craig's footy team was slaughtered in the
final and he went absolutely apeshit!'

apples – as in: 'She'll be apples, mate'. Everything will be OK.

award – as in: 'The Australian Arbitration Commission yesterday
increased the award for left-legged firemen by 2.25 per cent'.
Refers to the wages and conditions awarded to workers in
particular industries.

barmaid's blush – drink to disguise the taste of alcohol, as in rum
and coke.

bent – morally corrupt, also used in reference to homosexuals.

blotto – drunk.

blue – as in 'having a blue with the missus'. Could mean a row, an
argument, a tiff, even physical violence. See **domestic** below.

bombo, plonk – cheap wine.

bonza – terrific, as in: 'What a bonza sheila!'

boofhead – a dunce, a fool.

Bruce – could be your mate's given name, but a bit of a cliche since
Jasons, Julians and Simons also abound in Australia, as in
other Anglo societies.

brucellosis – a disease which infects cattle and even humans, not to be confused with Brucelene or Brucette, which is what sheilas are supposed to be named when they are not Cheryl, Doreen or Raelene – though once again there is no shortage of Sarahs, Amys or Emilys.

bucket – to embarrass, castigate, or otherwise tip a bucket of abuse and true revelations upon a person.

bust a gut – as in: 'Don't bust a gut over your tax bill'. Reference to the deleterious effects of worry or hard work.

chockablock, chocka – crowded as in: 'Jeez, the pub was chocka block tonight, mate'.

chook – a chicken, as in 'roast chook'.

corroboree – originally an Aboriginal assembly, now a reference to any large and noisy gathering.

dag – first used to describe bits of excrement that cling to the wool of a sheep, nowadays to denote one who is socially embarrassing, perhaps unknowingly nonconformist or unfashionable.

daks – clothes or garments, as in 'underdaks', meaning underpants.

dead set – an oath or promise, as in 'Strewth, mate, course I'll see youse down the pub this arvo (afternoon) . . . DEAD SET!'

digger – a soldier, though before that a term for a worker in the gold rush era in New South Wales and Victoria of the nineteenth century. Now used with 'mate' or 'bobber', the word has been associated with Australian-born media magnate Rupert Murdoch, who was dubbed the 'Dirty Digger' by his competitors in Fleet Street in reference to the style of tabloid journalism he introduced to London's newspaper world.

dinkum – as in fair dinkum, dinky-di. Something or someone true blue and honest-to-goodness.

domestic – as in 'having a domestic'. Can mean a very bad 'blue' (see above). Police jargon for a family argument serious enough for them to be called to the scene, in response to neighbours' complaints or because at least one party has become uncontrollably violent.

drongo, dill – a fool. There is no shortage of disparaging expressions for those thought unintelligent or mentally deficient.

drop off the twig – to die. Other Aussie expressions for death include **cark it, cark out, kick the bucket, peg out** and **pop off.**

dry as a dead dingo – thirsty.

dunny – toilet, WC. Also see **reading room** below.

esky – usually a plastic box for keeping drinks cold in; otherwise known as a chillybin.

five finger discount – shoplifting.

flash as a rat with a gold tooth – overdone, overdressed.

flutter – as in: 'have a flutter'. To bet or gamble, usually on dogs or horses.

Fremantle Doctor – the sea breeze off Perth. Fremantle is Western Australian capital's port town.

frosty, tinny, tube, amber fluid or nectar, neck oil, singing syrup, brewery broth, etc. – beer.

full as a Pommy complaint box – overflowing, reference to Australian stereotype of the 'whingeing Pom' migrant.

ga ga – mindless, childlike simplicity, describing how someone may feel and behave when totally blotto or after being hit on the head.

galah – a noisy bird. Used like 'drongo', 'dill', or 'nong' to denote the object is not only empty-headed, but loud and talkative as well.

garbo – garbage collector.

gigglewater – champagne.

Godzown – God's own country, Australia.

gravel rash – crawlers and sycophants are said to suffer from this condition.

gumsucking – kissing, also 'face sucking'.

hairy leg – feminist.

hard word – as in 'put the hard word on', meaning to make a pass at a bloke or sheila.

having you on – a joke, not to be taken seriously and often delivered with a serious facial expression, e.g. 'What? You won't have pepper in your gigglewater? OK, OK, I was just having you on...'.

hoon – lout, also see yobbo.

in like Flynn – quick to take an opportunity, a reference to the founder of the outback's nationally famous Flying Doctor Service, in which medical teams airlift the sick from remote farms.

Jeez – short for 'Jesus' or perhaps a version of 'gee'.

jumbuck – aboriginal word for sheep (of which Australia has more than 130 million).

kangaroos in the top paddock – crazy, 'top paddock' referring to the brain.

knockback – rejection by one of the opposite sex.

larrikin – a loveable bad boy-type of guy, a prankster with no really mean streak. The larrikin character was famously portrayed in the bush stories of Henry Lawson and other colonial writers, and nowadays by artists of stage and screen in Australia.

lemonhead, surfie – someone who enjoys surf board riding for sport and the beach as a social centre.

lollywater – non-alcoholic drink.

love handles – cellulite, spare tyre, extra flab around the hips.

mad as a cut snake – angry.

mate – term of address for a friend, or someone whose name you've forgotten or do not know. Unlike other English-speaking societies using this word, blokes do not hesitate to address sheilas as 'mate'. Note the reverse does not apply. A woman would not refer to a man as a 'sheila'.

matilda – swagman's swag or pack which he 'waltzes' round the outback.

mole – loose woman.

nipper – child, also known as an **ankle biter**.

nong – a fool or dunce. See also **boofhead** and **dill**.

nuddy – naked, as in: ' in the nuddy'.

oldies, the olds – parents.

on – favourite Australian suffix. As in to 'go ON the grog' (start an alcoholic binge); 'go ON the wagon' (give up alcohol); to 'rave ON' (keep talking), etc.

OS – overseas, abroad.

pissant – small.

pollies – politicians, Members of Parliament.

Pom or Pommy – a Brit or Briton. First noted in Australian usage around 1912 in association with immigrants from England arriving under schemes for assisted passages to the fledgling nation. Theorists say 'Pom' could be an acronym of Prisoner of Mother England (POME) or a reference to pomegranate, and the similarly red, no doubt sunburnt, cheeks of the British arrivals.

pop a joey – to give birth to a child.

poppyshow – show the legs and underwear.

prang – a motor vehicle accident, e.g. 'Me sheila pranged the car'.

prawn – shrimp, shellfish.

prezzie – present, gift. In fact Ausspeak features the suffix -ie, -y, -i applied to many objects and names. Other examples include Aussie, lolly (sweet, candy or money), lippie (lipstick), cardie (cardigan), etc. as well as the abbreviation of names, as in Brucie, Davy and Hughy.

race off – to seduce, as in: 'race off a bonza sheila'.

rack off – get lost, etc. What you might decide to say to one who has put 'the hard word' on you.

rat face – as with the metaphoric usage of 'veggie' below, referring to someone who is rendered incapable after too much of a good (or bad) thing.

rave – to talk, alternatively to party.

raw prawn – deception or joke, as in: 'don't come the raw prawn with me mate'.

reading room - the toilet (see **dunny**).

reffo – refugee, though loosely applied to any European who migrated to Australia after the Second World War. The suffix -o is also a popular way to abbreviate people, objects and place names in frequent use or convey familiarity e.g.: boyo (boy), Johnno (John), rego (car registration), bottle-o (bottle shop).

Reg Grundies, Reginalds, undies – underwear. An example of the Australian addiction to rhyming slang. Reg Grundy was a television producer who came to prominence Down Under in the 1960s and 1970s. His name lives on in this convenient euphemism for bras, vests, slips, singlets and underpants.

rort – something of a con trick, a method of making easy and probably illegal money. It also has political connotations. As the *Sydney Morning Herald* described rort in 1981, it is 'a charmingly flexible term to cover such practices as stacking branch membership, rigging elections, cooking branch records, as a last resort, losing all branch records to frustrate a head office inquiry'.

rough as guts – sleazy, badly done.

rubbidy, watering hole – pub, bar, club, hotel ... anywhere where beer and ever-more popular wine are available.

sheila – the bloke's type of woman.

shirt lifter, horse's hoof, poofter – pejorative terms for male homosexuals. Unfortunately, Australia remains a homophobic society in many ways, and there are plenty of other terms to describe homosexuals.

sickie – a day off work, officially because that person is sick.

slab – 12 bottles or tins of beer, packaged in cardboard and plastic for easy transport. The size and success of a social gathering may be measured by the number of slabs consumed.

sort – as in 'a good sort', meaning an attractive sheila.

stepins – tights or stockings.

stirrer – a troublemaker.

strine – abbreviation of 'ostralian'.

stroppy – to be annoyed, irritated.

tatts – tattoos.

technicolour yawn – to vomit.

uey, lefty, righty – driving terminology, as in an instruction to the person behind the wheel to 'chuck a lefty, mate . . .', advising you to turn left. 'Uey' (rhyming with 'dewy') refers to a U-turn.

vegemite – yeast extract sandwich or biscuit spread. Tastes salty and looks like Marmite.

veggie – could also be a literal reference to vegetables or, metaphorically, to a person's mental and physical condition after heavy drinking or drug-taking, for instance.

wog, wop, boong, etc. – foreigners of various extractions. Included here just in case the term is applied to you, so you know what the yobbos are talking about. Let's hope you never hear these words, anyway.

wouldn't do it to a Jap on ANZAC Day – wouldn't do it to your worst enemy under dire circumstances, a reference to the Japanese enemy during the Second World War. ANZAC Day is a national holiday to commemorate the contribution of Australian war veterans in various campaigns.

yabby – a freshwater crayfish. Also reference to a wicket keeper in cricket.

yakka – work, as in 'doin' lotsa hard yakka'.

yobbo – a lout, see also boon.

Further Reading

General

Fairley, Alan, *The Observer's Book of National Parks of Australia*, Warne.

Golding, Jonathan, *Working Abroad*, International Venture Handbooks/How To Books.

Jones, Roger, *How to Retire Abroad*, How To Books.

Mead, Robin, *Australia*, Batsford.

Notes for Newcomers: Australia, Women's Corona Society.

Peterson, Vicki, *Australia*, Cassell.

Sherington, Geoffrey, *Australia's Immigrants 1788-1978*, Allen & Unwin.

Sharples, Reginald, *Pommy in the Outback*, New Horizon.

Wheeler, Tony, *Australia: Travel Survival Kit*, Lonely Planet.

Background and social life

Campion, Edmund, *Rockhoppers: Growing up Catholic in Australia,* Penguin.

Carter, Paul, *The Road to Botany Bay: Australian Civilisation to 1986*, Faber.

Chapple, S. G., *The Ramblings of an Australian*, Stockwell.

Grant, Bruce, *The Australian Dilemma: A New Kind of Western Society*, Macdonald Futura.

Hansen, Gary, *Australia: Impressions of a Continent*, Angus & Robertson.

Horne, Donald, *The Lucky Country: Australia in the Sixties*, Angus & Robertson.

Keneally, Thomas, *The Outback*, Hodder & Stoughton.

McGregor, Craig, *The Australian People*, Hodder & Stoughton.

McLean, Hazel, *Ladies One Side, Gentlemen the Other*, Carolina (Australian social life 1920 to 1950).

Moore, David & Hall, Rodney, *Australia: Image of a Nation 1850-1950*, Collins.

Tomlinson, Gerry (ed), *Bring Plenty of Pickles: Letters from an Emigrant Family 1842-1902*, Tomlinson.

Terrill, Ross, *The Australians: A Journey to the Heart of a Nation*, Bantam.

The Australian economy

Cost of Living & Housing Survey, Commonwealth Bank of Australia.

Establishing a New Business in Australia: The Legal Implications, Ellison, Hewison & Whitehead, London.

Gruen, F. H., *Surveys of Australian Economies*, Allen & Unwin.

Head, Brian, *Politics and Development*, Allen & Unwin.

Head, Brian, *State and Economy in Australia*, Oxford University Press.

Jobsons Year Book of Public Companies, Dun and Bradstreet (Publications), 24 Albert Street, South Melbourne, Victoria 3205.

Kamm, Herbert & Pepper, Thomas, *Will She Be Right? The Future of Australia*, University of Queensland Press.

Martin, Joseph, *The Management of the Australian Economy*, University of Queensland Press.

Smart Start, Hobsons Press (Australia), 270 Pitt Street, Sydney, NSW 2000.

Telecom National Business Directory, Telecom Australia (available from most large libraries).

Wealth, Poverty & Survival, Allen & Unwin.

Whitwell, Greg, *The Treasury Line*, Allen & Unwin.

Magazines and newspapers

Australian Traveller Magazine, 21 Craven Terrace, London W2
3QTI. Tel: (0171) 706 3594.

Australian News, Outbound Newspapers Limited, 1 Commercial
Road, Eastbourne, East Sussex BN21 3XQ. Tel: (01323) 412001.

Australian Outlook, 1 Buckhurst Road, Town Hall Square, Bexhill-
on-Sea, East Sussex TN40 lQF. Tel: (01424) 223111.

Brisbane Courier-Mail, Campbell Street, Bowen Hills, Brisbane.

The Adelaide Advertiser, 121 King William Street, Adelaide.

The Australian, 2 Holt Street, Surrey Hills, NSW 2007.

The Melbourne Age, 250 Spencer Street, Melbourne.

The Sydney Morning Herald, 235 Jones Street, Broadway, NSW
2007.

The West Australian, 219 St. George's Terrace, Perth 6000.

Useful Addresses and Contacts

AUSTRALIAN GOVERNMENT REPRESENTATIVES

United Kingdom

Agent-General for Queensland, Queensland House, 392–393 The Strand, London WC2R 0LZ. Tel: (020) 7836 1333. Fax: (020) 7240 7667. Web: http://www.qld.gov.au

Agent-General & Trade Commission for South Australia, South Australia House, The Strand, London WC2B 4LG. Tel: (020) 7836 3455. Fax: (020) 7887 5332. Email: info@south-aus.org

Agent-General for Victoria, Victoria House, Melbourne Place, The Strand, London WC2B 4LG. Tel: (020) 7836 2656. Fax: (020) 7240 6025. Email: london@dsd.vic.gov.au

Australian Consulate, Chatsworth House, Lever Street, Manchester M1 2DL. Tel: (0161) 228 1344. Fax: (0161) 236 4074.

Australian High Commission, Australia House, The Strand, London WC2B 4LA. Tel: (020) 7379 4334. Fax: (020) 7240 5333. Web: http://www.australia.org.uk

Australian Visa Information Service. Tel: (0891) 600 333.

Austrade (suggests ringing Australian Visa Service).

Government for Western Australia, 5th Floor, The Australia Centre, Corner of Strand and Melbourne Place, London WC2B 4LG. Tel: (020) 7240 2881. Fax: (020) 7240 6637. Email: agent_general@wago.co.uk

Web: http://www.premier.wa.gov.au/portfolios/ministry/
premoffice2.html#E11E1

Key addresses internationally

Australian Consulate-General, Harbour Centre, 25 Harbour Road
(PO Box 820 Central), Wanchai, Hong Kong. Tel: 2827 8881.
Fax: 2827 6583.

Australian Embassy, 37 Dimitriou Soutsou Street, Ambelokipi,
Athens 11521, Greece. Tel: 1 645 0404. Fax: 1 646 6595.
Web: http://www.ausemb.gr

Australian Embassy, Fitzwilton House, Wilton Terrace, Dublin 2,
Ireland. Tel: 676 1517. Fax: 678 5185. Email:
services@australianembassy.ie Web: http://australianembassy.ie

Australian Embassy, Via Alessandria 215, Rome 00198, Italy.
Tel: (06) 852721. Fax: (06) 8527 2300.
Email: info@australian-embassy.it.
Web: http://www.australian-embassy.it

Australian Embassy, 6 Jalan Yap Kwan Seng, Kuala Lumpur,
Malaysia. Tel: 242 3122. Fax: 241 5773.
Email: pa@austhc.po.my. Web: http://www.australia.org.my

Australian Embassy, 25 Napier Road (Tanglin Post Office, PO Box
470), Singapore 10. Tel: 737 9311. Fax: 733 7134.

Australian Embassy, 1601 Massachusetts Avenue NW, Washington
DC 20036, USA. Tel: (202) 797 3000. Fax: (202) 797 3168.
Web: http://www.austemb.org.

Australian Embassy, 292 Orient Street, Arcadia, Pretoria 0083,
South Africa. Tel: 342 3740. Fax: 342 4222.

Australian High Commission, Riverside Drive, Nairobi, PO Box
39341, Kenya. Tel: 44 5034. Fax: 44 4617.

USEFUL CONTACTS IN THE UNITED KINGDOM

Australia and New Zealand – British Chamber of Commerce, 393
   The Strand, London WC2R 0LT. Tel: (020) 7379 0720.
   Fax: (020) 7379 0721. Email: MurrayC@anzcc.org.uk
   Web: http://www.anzcc.org.uk
Australian and New Zealand Banking Group, Minerva House,
   Montague Close, London SEI 9DH. Tel: (020) 7378 2121.
   Fax: (020) 7378 2378. Web: http://www.anz.com
Australian Broadcasting Corporation, 54 Portland Place, London
   W1N. Tel: (020) 7631 4456. Fax: (020) 7323 1125.
Australian Financial and Migrant Information Service,
   Commonwealth Bank of Australia, Senator House, 85 Queen
   Victoria Street, London EC4 VHA. Tel: (020) 7710 3999.
   Fax: (020) 7710 3939.
Australian Forwarding Agency Ltd, 131 Earls Court Road, London
   SW5 9RH. Tel: 0800 731 4700. Fax: (020) 7244 7888.
   Email: afa@dial.pipex.com
Australian Gift Shop, 26 Henrietta Street, Covent Garden, London
   WC2E 8NA. Tel: (020) 7836 2292.
   Web: http://www.australiashop.co.uk
Australian Studies Centre, 28 Russell Square, London WC1 5DS.
   Tel: (020) 7862 8844 . Fax: (0171) 862 8820.
   Email: ics@sas.ac.uk
Australian Tourist Commission, 1st Floor, Gemini House, 10–18
   Putney Hill, London SW15 6AA. Tel: (020) 8780 2229.
   Fax: (020) 8780 1496. Web: http://www.australia.com
Commonwealth Institute, 230 Kensington High Street, London W8
   6NQ. Tel: (020) 7603 4535. Fax: (020) 7602 7374.
   Email: info@commonwealth.org.uk
   Web: http://www.commonwealth.org.uk
Department of Social Security, Pensions and Overseas Benefits
   Directorate, Tyneview Park, Whitely Road, Benton, Newcastle

upon Tyne NE12 9SJ. Tel: (0191) 213 5000. Fax: (0191) 218 7120.

Qantas Airways Travel Centre, 182 The Strand, London WC2 1ET. Tel: (020) 7497 2571.

Westpac Banking Corporation (formerly the Bank of New South Wales), 63 St Mary Axe, London EC3A 8LE. Tel: (020) 7621 700. Fax: (020) 7623 9428. Web: http:/www.westpac.com.au

USEFUL CONTACTS IN AUSTRALIA

National Office of Overseas Skills Recognition (NOOSR), GPO Box 1407, Canberra ACT 2601, Australia.

Trades Recognition Australia: Department of Employment and Workplace Relations, GPO Box 9879 in the capital city of each of Australia's states and territories.

Website for the Department of Science, Education and Training: www.dest.gov.au/noosr

Trades Recognition Australia, Department of Employment and Workplace Relations, GPO Box 9879 Canberra ACT 2601. Telephone enquiries: +61261217456.

www.anta.gov.au for more on Australian Quality Training Framework.

Occupational English Test (OET), GPO Box 372 F Melbourne, Vic 3001.

International English Language Testing System (IELTS), GPO Box 2006, Canberra 2601 ACT. www. ielts@idp.edu.au

Australian Department of Education, and Science, PO Box 9880, Canberra, ACT 2601, Australia. Tel: (02) 6283 7008. www.dest.gov.au

Immigration South Australia, GPO Box 1264, Adelaide 5001, South Australia. Tel: 618 8303 2252.
Email: immigration.sa@state.sa.gov.au

Website: www.immigration.sa.gov.au.

Department for Business, Manufacturing and Trade, Level 10, 178 North Terrace, Adelaide, South Australia, 5000. Tel: 618 83032400

Website (includes overseas offices): www.southaustralia.biz

Skilled Migration Unit, Department of State Development, PO Box 168, Albert Street Brisbane, Queensland 4002.
Tel: 617 32248576. Email: skilled.migration@sd.qld.gov.au
Website: www.sd.qld.gov.au/migration

Skilled Migration Unit, Level 8, 1 Spring Street, Melbourne, Victoria 3000. Tel: 613 92083334.
Email: info@liveinvictoria.vic.gov.au
Website: www.liveinvictoria.vic.gov.au

Business Migration Unit, Level 15, 1 Spring Street, Melbourne, Victoria 3000. Tel: 613 92083319. Email/website: as above.

Government Department of State and Regional Development, Level 35, Governor Phillip Tower, 1 Farrer Place, Sydney, PO Box N818, Grosvenor Place, Sydney NSW 1220. Tel: 612 92283111.
Email: businessweb@business.nsw.gov.au
London: invest@nsw.co.uk Tokyo: nswtokyo@gol.com

Investment, Trade and Development Department of the Tasmanian Department of State Development, 22 Elizabeth Street, Hobart 7000, Tasmania. Tel: 6136 2335790.
Website: www.dsd.tas.gov.au

Multicultural Tasmania. Tel: 6136 2333439. Email:
MULTITAS@dpac.tas.gov.au
Website: www.dpac.tas.gov.au/divisions/multitas

Business Migration, Office of Business and Tourism, Chief Minister's Department, PO Box 243, Civic Square, ACT 2608.
Tel: 612 62050725. Website: www.business.act.gov.au

Department of Business, Industry and Resource Development, Development House, 76 The Esplanade, GPO Box 3000, Darwin NT. Tel: 618 89244280. Email: info@dbird.nt.gov.au

Website: www.dbird.nt.gov.au

Migration Services (part of DBIRD contacts as above).
Email: migration@dbird.nt.gov.au

Small Business Development Corporation, 553 Hay Street, Perth,
Western Australia 6000. Tel: 618 92200222.
Email: info@sbdc.com.au Websites: www.sbdc.au
www.businessmigration.sbdc.com.au

NEW SOUTH WALES

Immigration

DIMA, 88 Cumberland Street, The Rocks NSW 2000. Tel: 131 881
(general enquiries), 131 880 (for citizenship). Fax: (02) 9258
4599.

DIMA, Level 4, Commonwealth Offices, 2–12 Macquarie Street,
Parramatta NSW 2150. Tel: 131 881 (general enquiries), 131 880
(for citizenship). Fax: (02) 9893 4813.
Email: dimapabc@ozemail.com.au

DIMA, Ground Floor, 81 Railway Street, Rockdale NSW 2216.
Tel: 131 881 (general enquiries), 131 880 (for citizenship).
Email: dimarockd@ozemail.com.au

DIMA Onshore Protection, Level 22, 477 Pitt Street, Sydney, NSW
2000. Tel: (02) 9219 7631. Fax: (02) 9219 7600.
Web: http://www.imii.gov.au

Migrant resource centres

Blacktown MRC, Level 2, 125 Main Street, Blacktown NSW 2148.
Tel: (02) 9621 6633. Fax: (02) 9831 5625.

Botany MRC, Suite 3–4, Level 3, 85 Flushcombe Road, Blacktown
NSW 2148. Tel: (02) 9621 6633. Fax: (02) 9831 5625.

Botany MRC, 3-3A General Bridges Crescent, Daceyville NSW
2032. Tel: (02) 9663 3922. Fax: (02) 9662 7627.
Email: bmrci@qpa.com.au

Cabramatta Community Centre, Ground Floor, Civic Centre, Railway Parade, Cabramatta NSW 2166. Tel: (02) 9727 0477. Fax: (02) 9728 6080. Email: fmrc@fl.net.au

Canterbury MRC, 139 Beamish Street, Campsie NSW 2194. Tel: (02) 9789 3744 or (02) 9718 0236. Fax: (02) 9718 0236.

St George MRC, 554–556 Princes Highway, Rockdale NSW 2216. Tel: (02) 9597 5455. Fax: (02) 9567 3326. Email: sgmrc@qpa.com.au

Illawarra MRC, 70 Kembla Street, Wollongong NSW 2500. Tel: (02) 4229 6855. Fax: (02) 422 6364.

Innerwest (Ashfield) MRC, 6–8 Holden Street, Ashfield, NSW 2131. Tel: (02) 9798 4777. Fax: (02) 9798 4408.

Liverpool Migrant Resource Centre, 1st Floor, 179–183 Northumberland Street, Liverpool NSW 2170. Tel: (02) 9601 3788. Fax: (02) 9601 1398. Email: liv-mrc@tig.com.au

Newcastle MRC, Suite 3–4, Chaucer House, 8 Chaucer Street, Hamilton NSW 2303. Tel: (02) 4969 3399. Fax: (02) 4961 4997. Email: mrcnh@fastlink.com.au Web: http://www.fastlink.com/au/subscrib.mrcnh

Housing

Department of Housing, 23–31 Moore Street, Liverpool 2170. Tel: (02) 9821 6111. Fax: (02) 9821 6900. Web: http://www.housing.nsw.gov.au/

Education

Department Education and Training, 35 Bridge Street, Sydney NSW 2000 (GPO Box 33, Sydney 2001). Tel: (02) 9561 8000. Fax: (02) 9561 8759. Web: http://www.det.nsw.edu.au

Customs

Australian Customs Service, GPO Box 8, 477 Pitt Street, Sydney NSW 2000. Tel: (02) 9213 2000. Fax: (02) 9213 4043.

Web: http://www.customs.gov.au

Skills and qualifications recognition

Industrial Relations, Employment and Education. Information and referral only. Sydney Tel: (02) 229 2929, (02) 288 8600, (02) 287 6111.

Overseas Qualifications Officer, Ground Floor, 255 Elizabeth Street, Sydney, NSW 2000. Tel: (02) 9269 3500.

Skills Assessor, Trades Recognition Australia, Level 7 North Wing, Sydney Central, 477 Pitt Street, Sydney NSW 2000. Tel: (02) 9246 0760. Fax: (02) 9246 0735.

Tourist bureau

Tourism NSW, Head Office, Tourism House, 55 Harrington Street, The Rocks, Sydney 2000. (GPO Box 7050, Sydney 2001). Tel: (02) 9931 1111. Fax: (02) 9931 1490. Web: http://www.tourism.nsw.gov.au

VICTORIA

Immigration

DIMA – Preston, Cnr Bell St and Plenty Road, Preston VIC 3072. Tel: 131 881 (for all Victorian offices), 131 880 (citizenship information). Fax: (03) 9487 3463.

DIMA – Dandenong, 51 Princes Highway, Dandenong VIC 3175. Tel: 131 881 (for all Victorian offices), 131 880 (citizen information). Fax: (03) 9706 7068.

DIMA – Melbourne, Casselden Place, 2 Lonsdale Street, Melbourne VIC 3000. Tel: 131 881 (for all Victorian offices), 131 880 (citizen information). Fax: (03) 9235 3300.

Migrant resource centres

Geelong MRC, 153 Pakington Street, Geelong West VIC 3218. Tel:

(03) 5221 6044. Fax: (03) 5223 2848.

Email: gmrc@geelongmrc.org.

Web: http://www.geelongmrc.org

Gippsland, 100–102 Buckley Street, Morwell 3840. Tel: (03) 5133 7072. Fax: (03) 5134 1031. Email: gmrc@gippsland.net.au

Inner West Region MRC, Head Office, Level 2, 289 Barkly Street, Footscray VIC 3011. Tel: (03) 9689 2888. Fax: (03) 9687 9286. Email: headoffice@iwrmc.org.au

North Eastern Region (Preston/Reservoir) MRC, 251 High Street, Preston VIC 3072. Tel: (03) 9484 7944. Fax: (03) 9484 7942.

Northern Metropolitan MRC, 175 Glenroy Road, Glenroy VIC 3046. Tel: (03) 9306 5611. Fax: (03) 9306 5644.

Email: nmmrc@nmmrc.org.au Web: http://www.nmmrc.org.au/

North West Region MRC, 27 Alfrieda Street, St Albans VIC 3021. Tel: (03) 9367 6044. Fax: (03) 9367 4344.

Email: mrcnw@mrcnorthwest.org.au

South Central Region MRC, 24 Victoria Street, Windsor, VIC 3181. Tel: (03) 9510 5877. Fax: (03) 9510 8971.

Email: mrcprah@vicnet.net.au

South Central Region MRC, Oakleigh Outreach Service, 22A Atherton Road, Oakleigh VIC 3166. Tel: (03) 9563 4130. Fax: (03) 9563 4131.

South Eastern Region MRC, Level 1, 314 Thomas Street, Dandenong VIC 3175. Tel: (03) 9706 8933. Fax: (03) 9706 8830. Email: semrc@vic.net.au

Westgate Region MRC, 78–82 Second Avenue, North Altona VIC 3025. Tel: (03) 9391 3355. Fax: (03) 9399 1796.

Housing

Department of Human Services, Office of Housing, Customer Service Centre, Level 6, 555 Collins Street, Melbourne, VIC 3000. Tel: (03) 9616 7777. Fax: (03) 9616 7792. International code: (61).

Education

Department of Education, Training and Youth Affairs, Victoria
State Office, GPO Box 1820Q, Melbourne, VIC 3001. Casseldon
Place, 12/2 Lonsdale Street, Melbourne 3000. Tel: (03) 9920
4777.

Customs

Australian Customs Service, Ground Floor, Customs House, 414 La
Trobe Street, Melbourne VIC 3000. Tel: (03) 9244 8000.
Fax: (03) 9244 8017. Email: information@customs.gov.au
Web: http://www.customs.gov.au

Skills and qualifications recognition

Overseas Qualifications Unit, Level 27, Naura House, 80 Collins
Street, Melbourne VIC 3000. Tel: (03) 9655 6164. Fax: (03) 9655
6151.

Skills Assessor, Trades Recognition Australia, 8th Floor Customs
House, 414 Latrobe Street, Melbourne VIC 3000. Tel: (03) 9954
2534. Fax: (03) 9954 2688.

Tourist bureau

Tourism Victoria, GPO Box 2219T, Melbourne VIC 3001,
Australia. Tel: (03) 9653 9818. Fax: (03) 9653 9755.
Web: http://www.tourism.vic.gov.au

QUEENSLAND

Immigration

DIMA – Brisbane Office, 313 Adelaide Street, Brisbane QLD 4000.
Tel: 131 881 (general enquiries), 131 880 (citizenship).
Fax: (07) 3360 5006.

DIMA – Cairns, 19 Aplin Street, Cairns QLD 4870. Tel: 131 881
(general enquiries), 131 880 (citizenship). Fax: (07) 4051 0198.

DIMA – Southport, Level 1, 72 Nerang St, Southport QLD 4215.
Tel: 131 881 (general enquiries), 131 880 (citizenship).
Fax: (07) 5591 5402.

DIMA – Thursday Island, Victoria Parade, Thursday Island QLD
4875. Tel: 131 881 (general enquiries), 131 880 (citizenship).
Fax: (07) 4069 1884.

Migrant resource centres

Logan and Beenleigh MRC, 164 Wembley Road, Logan Central
QLD 4114. Tel: (07) 3808 9299. Fax: (07) 3208 9319.
Email: labmrc@lrvnet.org.au

Townsville MRC, T and G Building, 426 Flinders Street, Townsville
QLD 4810. Tel: (07) 4772 4800. Fax: (07) 4772 1840.
Email: mrc@beyond.net.au Web: http://www.beyond.net.au/mrc

Housing

Department of Housing, Brisbane Central, 360 St Paul's Terrace,
Fortitude Valley 4006. Tel: (07) 3872 0320. Fax: (07) 3872 0316.

Education

Department of Education, Level 5, Education House, 30 Mary
Street, Brisbane QLD 4000. Tel: (07) 3237 0111.
Web: http://www.education.qld.gov.au

Customs

Australian Customs Service, Terrica Place, 140 Creek Street,
Brisbane QLD 4000. Tel: (07) 3835 3444.
Web: http://www.customs.gov.au

Skills and qualifications recognition

Skills Assessor, Trades Recognition Australia, 10th Floor, Citibank
Building, 215 Adelaide Street, Brisbane QLD 4000.
Tel: (07) 3223 1425. Fax: (07) 3223 1399.

Skills Recognition Branch, Level 5, Education House, 30 Mary
    Street, Brisbane QLD 4000. Tel: (07) 3237 1900.

Tourist bureau
Queensland Tourist and Travel Corporation, GPO Box 328,
    Brisbane QLD 4001. Tel: (07) 3833 5400. Fax: (07) 3833 5436.
    Email: qldtravel@ozemail.com.au

SOUTH AUSTRALIA

Immigration
DIMA, 4th Floor, Commonwealth Centre, 55 Currie Street,
    Adelaide SA 5000. Tel: 131 881 (general), 131 880 (citizenship).
    Fax: (08) 8237 6699. Web: http://www.immi.gov.au

Migrant resource centre
MRC of South Australia, 53 Flinders Street, Adelaide SA 5000.
    Tel: (08) 8223 3604. Fax: (08) 8223 7947.
    Email: mrc@camtech.net.au

Housing
Department of Human Services, South Australia Housing Trust,
    Riverside Centre, North Terrace, Adelaide SA 5000.
    Tel: (08) 8207 0211. Fax: (08) 8207 0199.

Education
Department of Education, Training and Employment, Wyatt
    House, 115 Grenfell Street, Adelaide SA 5000. Tel: (08) 8306
    8700.

Customs
Australian Customs Service, Customs House, 220 Commerical
    Road, Adelaide SA 5000. Tel: (08) 8447 9211. Fax: (08) 8447

9208. Email: information@customs.gov.au
Web: http://www.customs.gov.au

Skills and qualifications recognition

Economic Development Branch, Office of Multicultural and Ethnic
Affairs, 24 Flinders Street, Adelaide SA 5000. Tel: (08) 8226
1944.

Skills Assessor, Trades Recognition Australia, Level 7 North Wing,
Sydney Central, 477 Pitt Street, Sydney NSW 2000.
Tel: (02) 9246 0760. Fax: (020) 9246 0735.

Tourist bureau

South Australian Tourism Commission, GPO Box 1972, Adelaide
SA 5001. Tel: (08) 303 2222. Fax: (08) 303 2231.

WESTERN AUSTRALIA

Immigration

DIMA – Perth Office, Australian Taxation Office Building, William
and Francis Streets, Northbridge WA 6003. Tel: 131 881
(general), 131 880 (citizenship). Fax: (08) 9228 0444.

Migrant resource centres

South Metropolitan MRC, 241–243 High Street, Freemantle WA
6160. Tel: (08) 9335 9588. Fax: (08) 9430 6352.
Email: kim@fmrc.asn.au Web: http://www.fmrc.asn.au
Northern Suburbs MRC, Unit 1, 14 Chesterfield Road,
Mirrabooka WA 6061. Tel: (08) 9345 5755. Fax: (08) 9345 5036.
Email: nsmrc@q-net.net.au

Education

The Education Department of Western Australia, 151 Royal Street,
East Perth WA 6004. Tel: (061 8) 9264 4111. Fax: (061 8) 9264 5005.

Customs

Australian Customs Service, Customs House, 2 Henry Street,
Freemantle WA 6160. Tel: (08) 9430 1444. Fax: (08) 9430 1391.

Skills and qualifications recognition

Overseas Qualification Unit, 7th Floor, 190 St George's Terrace,
Perth WA 6000. Tel: (08) 9320 3747. Fax: (080) 9320 3766.

Skills Assessor, Trades Recognition Australia, 8th Floor, 215
Adelaide Street, Brisbane, QLD 4000. Tel: (07) 3223 1425.
Fax: (07) 3223 1399.

Tourist bureau

Western Australian Tourism Commission, GPO Box X2261, Perth
WA 6001. Tel: (08) 9220 1700. Fax: (08) 9220 1702.
Web: http://www.wa.gov.au

TASMANIA

Immigration

DIMA – Hobart Office, Level 13, Australian Govt Centre, 188
Collins Street, Hobart TAS 7000. Tel: 131 881 (general), 131 880
(citzenship). Fax: (03) 6223 8247. Web: http://www.immi.gov.au

Migrant resource centres

MRC of Northern Tasmania, 1st Floor, 93 York Street, Launceston
TAS 7250. Tel: (03) 6331 2300. Fax: (03) 6334 2660.
Email: mrcltn@tassie.net.au

MRC of Southern Tasmania, 49 Molle Street, Hobart TAS 7000.
Tel: (03) 6234 9411. Fax: (03) 6231 1264.
Email: imatthews@mrchobart.org.au

Housing

Department of Health and Human Resources, 118 Collins Street,

Hobart TAS 7000. Tel: (03) 6233 3736.
Email: housing.tasmania@dchs.tas.gov.au

Education
Education, 116 Bathurst Street, Hobart TAS 7000.

Customs
Australian Customs Service, 1st Floor, MBF Building, 25 Argyle
Street, Hobart TAS 7000. Tel: (03) 6230 1201.

Skills and qualifications recognition
Overseas Qualifications Unit, Department of Vocational Education
and Training, Level 3, 99 Bathurst Street, Hobart TAS 7000.
Tel: (03) 6234 4358.
Skills Assessor, Trades Recognition Australia, 8th Floor Customs
House, 414 Latrobe Street, Melbourne VIC 3000. Tel: (03) 9954
2534. Fax: (03) 9954 2688.

Tourist Bureau
Tourism Tasmania, GPO Box 399, Hobart TAS 7001. Tel: (002) 308
138 Fax: (002) 308 355.

NORTHERN TERRITORY

Immigration
DIMA – Darwin Office, 40 Cavenagh Street, Darwin NT 0800.
Tel: 131 881 (general), 131 880 (citizenship). Fax: (08) 8981
6245.

Migrant resource centre
MRC of Central Australia, 2nd Floor Belvedere House, Corner
Bath and Parsons Streets, Alice Springs NT 0870. Tel: (08) 8952
8776. Fax: (08) 8952 5176. Email: mrc@dove.net.au

Housing
Department of Housing, RCG House, 83–85 Smith Street, Darwin NT (GPO Box 4621 Darwin NT 0801). Tel: (08) 8999 8814.

Education
Department of Education, GPO Box 4821, 69 Smith Street, Darwin NT 0800. Email: sitemaster.ntde@nt.gov.au
Web: http://www.ntde.nt.gov.au

Customs
Australian Customs Service, Customs House, 21 Lindsay Street, Darwin NT 0800. Fax: (08) 8946 9999.

Skills and qualifications recognition
Office of Ethnic Affairs, Department of the Chief Minister, Ground Floor, Palm Court, 8 Cavanagh Street, Darwin NT 0800. Tel: (08) 8999 7332. Fax: (08) 8999 5482.
Skills Assessor – see Southern Australia.

Tourist bureau
Northern Territory Tourist Commission, GPO Box 1376, Darwin NT 0801. Tel: (08) 8999 3900. Fax: (08) 8999 3888.
Web: http://www.nttc.com.au

AUSTRALIAN CAPITAL TERRITORY

Immigration
DIMA – Act Regional Office, Levels 3 and 4, 1 Farrell Place, Canberra City ACT 2601. Tel: 131 881 (general), 131 880 (citzenship). Fax: (02) 6248 0479.
DIMA – Central Office, Benjamin Offices, Chan Street, Belconnen ACT 2617. Tel: (02) 6264 1111. Fax: (02) 6264 2747.
Web: http://www.immi.gov.au

Migrant resource centre

MRC of Canberra and Queanbeyan, 1st Floor, Griffin Centre,
Bunda Street, Canberra City ACT 2601. Tel: (02) 6248 8577.
Fax: (02) 6257 7655. Email: mrccjpet@spirit.com.au

Education

ACT Department of Education and Training, 186 Reed Street,
Greenway ACT 2900. Tel: (02) 6207. 5111. Fax: (02) 6205 9333.
Web: www.decs.act.gov.au

Housing

ACT Department of Health and Community Care. Tel: (02) 6205
1342. Fax: (02) 6207 5775.

Customs

Australian Customs Service, Customs House, 5 Constitution
Avenue, Canberra City ACT 2601. Tel: (02) 6275 6666.

Skills and qualifications recognition

ACT Vocational Education and Training Authority, 5th Floor, 40
Allara Street, Camberra ACT 2601. Tel: (02) 6205 7777.
Skills Assessor, Trades Recognition Australia, Level 9 North Wing,
Sydney Central, 477 Pitt Street, Sydney NSW 2000. Tel: (02)
9246 0760. Fax: (02) 9246 0735.

Tourist bureau

Canberra Visitor's Centre, 330 Northbourne Avenue, Dickson, ACT.
Tel: (02) 6205 0044. Fax: (02) 6205 0776.
Email: canberra.tourism@act.gov.au
Web: http://www.canberratourism.com.au

Motoring organisations

National Roads and Motorists' Association (NRMA), 92–96
Northbourne Avenue, Canberra City, ACT 2601. Tel: (02) 6243
8888.

National Roads and Motorists' Association (NRMA), 151 Clarence
Street, Sydney, NSW 2000. Tel: (02) 9292 9222. Fax: (02) 9292
9311. Web: http://www.nrma.com.au

Royal Automobile Association of South Australia Inc., 41
Hindmarsh Square, Adelaide, SA 5000. Tel: (08) 8202 4600.

Royal Automobile Club of Victoria (RACV) Ltd, 123 Queen Street,
Melbourne, VIC 3000. Tel: (03) 9607 2211.

Royal Automobile Club of Western Australia Inc., 228 Adelaide
Terrace, Perth, WA 6000. Tel: (08) 9421 4444.

Index

Getting into Australia
The complete immigration guide to gaining a short or long-term visa
Matthew Collins

Whether you want to get temporary work in Australia or take up permanent residence, this informative guide reveals how you go about it as it explains in simple terms how to put your application together. Matthew Collins is Managing Partner of the international visa consultancy, Amber Collins, based in London and has many years of experience in assisting individuals, families and companies to prepare and process successful visa applications for Australia.

'Easy to read and to dip in and out of, for that nuts and bolts information, this book is a must-have for all would-be migrants.'
Australian News

ISBN 978 1 84528 170 0

Going to Live in Australia
Mathew Collins and Mary Neilson

You want to move to Australia, but you're not sure about how to get the right visa, find work and where to live once you've arrived. This up-to-date book tells you everything you'll need to know to settle successfully into your new life 'down under'. It not only covers visas, finding work and where to live, but also deals with health care, education, and such potentially difficult issues as self-employment and retirement.

'... puts together all the information needed to smooth your transition into the country. The authors are experienced in the fields of visa applications, travel and property, so their advice is constantly informative.' *Australia News*

ISBN 978 1 84528 261 5

Going to Live in New Zealand
Mathew Collins and Mary Neilson

Moving to the other side of the world is a huge step, but this new book takes much of the hard work out of relocating to New Zealand. It is full of information on the latest immigration policies to identify what category may work best for you, plus all you need to know about housing, taxes and healthcare. It even covers how best to ship your property and pets to your new home, and the best places to visit once you're there.

ISBN 978 1 84528 274 5

Emigrating to New Zealand
Steve Horrell

This book is an indispensable guide to the roller coaster ride that is the emigration process. It covers all the topics and issues that anyone thinking of emigrating to New Zealand will need to know about, from the discussion phase through to making friends when you're there.

ISBN 978 1 84528 116 8

Living & Working in New Zealand
Joy Muirhead

'The definitive guide to setting up a new life in the other Down Under.' – *Overseas Jobs Express*

'... takes you by the hand and leads you through the confusing maze of immigration categories and visa applications ... And once you're there, the book tells you how to earn a dollar, what gummies, dummies and chooks are and whether you're likely to encounter avalanches (and what to do if you do!).' – *Destination New Zealand*

ISBN 978 1 85703 912 2

A City by City Guide to Living and Working in Australia
Roberta Duman

This book will equip readers with enough information to prepare them for the day-to-day realities of living and working in Australia, as this often turns out to be very different from what was expected. It provides comprehensive information about what to expect from each of the main cities in terms of lifestyle, employment opportunities, recreation, residential options and information on education and childcare for those with families.

ISBN 978 1 84528 089 5

How To Books are available through all good bookshops, or you can order direct from us through Grantham Book Services.
Tel: +44 (0)1476 541080
Fax: +44 (0)1476 541061
Email: orders@gbs.tbs-ltd.co.uk

Or via our website

www.howtobooks.co.uk

To order via any of these methods please quote the title(s) of the book(s) and your credit card number together with its expiry date.

For further information about our books and catalogue, please contact:

How To Books
Spring Hill House
Spring Hill Road
Begbroke
Oxford OX5 1RX

Visit our web site at

www.howtobooks.co.uk

Or you can contact us by email at info@howtobooks.co.uk